# Resurrecting Democracy

# Resurrecting Democracy

## A Citizen's Call for a Centrist Third Party

**Robert Levine**

THE
EDITING
COMPANY

*Westport, CT*

The Editing Company
252 Post Road East
Westport, CT 06880


*Book Design by Laura Case*


ISBN 978-0-9839156-0-7

*To my granddaughter, Isabel and her contemporaries,*

*who will bear the burden of previous generations' follies.*

# Contents

Acknowledgements
9

Preface
11

~ Chapter 1 ~
**Introduction: America's Dysfunctional Democracy and the
Reasons for a Centrist Third Party**
16

~ Chapter 2 ~
**Thoughts on Political Parties:
A Brief Recent History of American Political Parties**
65

~ Chapter 3 ~
**Creating a Permanent Third Party of the Center**
97

~ Chapter 4 ~
**America's Domestic Challenges
Origins and Current Status**
146

~ Chapter 5 ~
**America's Challenges**
**National Security and Foreign Policy**
207

~ Chapter 6 ~
**Laying the Foundation**
252

~ Chapter 7 ~
**Proposals For A Prospective Platform**
266

~ Chapter 8 ~
**Conclusion**
326

Index
333

*Three addenda are available through* www.robertlevinebooks.com. *They can be downloaded free of charge.*

Addendum I   *History of Political Corruption: The Early Republic Through 1992*

Addendum II   *History of Political Corruption: 1992 to 2011*

Addendum III   *History of America's Political Parties from the Founding of the Republic Through the Late 20th Century*

# Acknowledgments

I would like to thank my colleagues, Peter Cohn and Jan Mashman, for their ideas, criticism, and encouragement, which helped me complete *Resurrecting Democracy*. Leo Swergold, Peter Barth, and Mike Slosberg added their perceptive comments that also aided in shaping the book.

My son, Matt Levine, assisted with the early editing.

My wife, Anne, was my muse and the motivating force that kept me working, her thoughtful feedback and opinions essential in the development and completion of this project.

I would also like to thank Tish Fried and Patrick McCord of The Editing Company for their vision and ideas that ultimately brought *Resurrecting Democracy* to fruition.

—Robert A. Levine, June 20, 2011

# Preface

Americans are angry and confused. They feel impotent as the American dream rapidly sinks beneath an ocean of economic adversity that the federal government seems incapable of addressing. In a time of growing international and domestic challenges, the nation's political system is not working; gridlock is the order of the day. The legislative representatives elected from the two parties are prisoners of ideology, bound by the constraints of their belief systems and unwilling to compromise or seek pragmatic answers to unfolding crises. Instead, they offer temporary solutions for long-term problems or allow them to fester. Similarly, America's presidents, whether Democratic or Republican, have been unable to lead the country out of the wilderness, their visions also limited by ideology, hubris, or an inability to convince Congress of the need for bold measures. The main concerns of America's political parties appear to be how to expand their power and how to placate their bases, rather than how to improve society or assure a better life for future generations. For politicians, getting elected and reelected takes precedence over trying to fashion programs that will aid America and Americans in competing and surviving in a new world of globalization and advanced technology.

As a result of the government and political parties' failure to craft reasonable solutions to pressing problems, groups like the Tea Party movement have proposed simplistic answers, ignoring economic fundamentals and the possible negative consequences of their programs. In spite of this, they have captured the attention of many citizens who are disgusted with the mindset in Washington, inclined to repudiate all incumbents and willing to try anything new. Unfortunately, these converts have been swayed by sound bites and slogans, and are uninterested in delving deeper into the plans being advanced or to search for the flaws and inconsistencies that make them untenable. Unfortunately, the Tea Party's successes in the 2010 midterm elections make the possibility of significant compromises between the Republicans and Democrats in Congress even more difficult.

The culture of corruption that pervades the two parties has also contributed to undermining America's political processes, driven by the need for campaign funds and a desire for personal gain. Ethical considerations as a guide for behavior are ridiculed by most politicians, with inadequate oversight by legislative monitoring bodies to insure compliance with the rules. Lobbyists dispense money and perks like hors d'oeuvres at a Capitol Hill cocktail party to officeholders in return for access. In addition, a revolving door shuttles party stalwarts seamlessly between government jobs and into positions as lobbyists for special interests. Both elected and appointed officials know that high-paying careers await them in the private sector as soon as they are ready to switch gears and lobby their previous colleagues. At times of scandal Congressmen and senators acknowledge the need for ethical standards and stringent reforms, but bury or eviscerate related legislative measures as soon as the news articles slip from the front pages and ethics no longer seems to be a priority for the public.

With the bond of trust severed between the electorate and the elected, most Americans look upon politicians with contempt. Numerous polls confirm the low status of politicians. But there are still some citizens who believe that political reform is feasible within the confines of the present system; that the two parties can be changed for the better and made more responsive, even though repeated past attempts have met with failure and corruption is ever more widespread. Given the degree of internal rot and decay and the number of politicians wedded to the status quo, I am convinced that reforming the two parties is an impossible task unless an external force compels them to change. The force needed is a permanent third party of the center that can enter the game untainted and resolute. Vowing to remain clean, it will owe nothing to the special interests and see as its mandate a transformation in the "business as usual" mode of the politicians. This new party will be a party of moderates, a party of pragmatism, infused with positive energy in the American tradition. As this uncorrupted third party gains momentum and is willing to devise commonsense solutions to the nation's problems, the other parties will be forced to follow suit or eventually be abandoned by most citizens. (The amorphous storm of anger and distrust of government on the right that has coalesced into the Tea Party movement appears more interested in seizing control of the Republican Party than forming a new political entity. Though its future course is uncertain, it should not affect the need or support for a centrist party.)

Recent political contests have demonstrated the ability of candidates to raise huge sums of money over the Internet from small donors, showing that politicians no longer have to depend on lobbyists and special interests for financing. With social networking and viral Internet campaigns superseding other media models for enhanced communication, less money is necessary for savvy politicians to compete successfully for elected office. This means that a third political party of centrists could endure and flourish without sacrificing its soul to the special interests in order to obtain funding, as the current parties have done and continue to do.

To meet its objective of resurrecting democracy, this third party will have to persuade the youth of America to enlist in a crusade; to convince high school, college, and graduate students across the nation along with working men and women to commit to reforming a broken political system that holds their future in its hands. At present, young people even more than the general population have been turned off by politics. They have become apathetic and indifferent, inured to ethical transgressions and partisan conflict, believing that the system in place is immutable. But change can occur if enough people are outraged and become dedicated to reshaping American politics. It happened temporarily with President Obama's 2008 campaign before disillusionment set in again after the election. The passion of the Tea Party activists shows that people can be mobilized to engage in the political process. But independents and centrists are the ones who need to be participants now, with a collective will to generate the necessary changes.

In previous times, Americans were willing to sacrifice for the good of the nation and the generations that would follow. Sacrifice is again needed. America is in crisis and undergoing a steep decline. Its economy is battered with manufacturing jobs streaming abroad, its budget deficits and national debt climbing. The nation's infrastructure is old and crumbling while much of Europe and Asia enjoy modern highways and bridges, bullet trains connecting their main cities, gleaming new airports, and broadband connections to all sectors of their population. If America is to compete in this world and maintain its position at the top, its citizens will have to acknowledge the need for sacrifice and pain, will have to accept fewer benefits and services from the government and perhaps higher taxes. Americans will have to study harder and work longer, knowing that their struggles will allow democracy to flourish and that their children and grandchildren will reap the rewards.

I am not a political scientist, a political consultant, or an insider who has played any role in American politics, and have no special academic credentials. I am a concerned American citizen, a physician, who sees his country on the road to ruin because the two political parties who run the government have been unable to work together to produce the policies it needs to function properly. I was a history major in college and have been a political junkie ever since, following the twists and turns of American politics and the machinations of the dominant parties. I have written *Resurrecting Democracy* as an indictment of the two-party system and the two parties who collude to maintain their hold on power, reinforcing the need for a permanent third party of the center to institute reform. I am offering what I see as a prescription for the required changes in politics and government to heal and reinvigorate American democracy. In *Resurrecting Democracy*, I describe the ways to build a permanent centrist third party along with the various issues that must be addressed.

In America's formative years, professional politicians were not involved in the creation of its defining documents, the Declaration of

Independence and the Constitution, nor responsible for governing. These duties were managed admirably by public-spirited citizens: farmers, lawyers, and businessmen (and even some physicians), who wanted to participate in the noble experiment of democracy. Perhaps what America needs now are fewer career politicians and more ordinary citizens like our Founding Fathers to become engaged in the processes of government and democracy.

This book is called *Resurrecting Democracy,* although America's system of government is a republic and not a democracy. Democracy entails having the people vote to enable government action, while in a republic that power falls to a small number of agents. In the American system, the people do not legislate and directly make decisions about the running of the government, but instead elect representatives and executives to perform these tasks for them. However, it can also be described as a representative democracy, where every person's vote is supposed to be counted equally in choosing men and women who act on the behalf of their constituents, and whom citizens expect to make decisions that are beneficial to them. When lobbyists and special interests subvert this relationship and the people's desires are ignored, the system is failing.

(With many of the events I have noted occurring contemporaneously with my writing, I have used newspapers, magazines, and journals for some of my source material and references. This does not imply my agreement or disagreement with any position these publications may have taken on any particular issue.)

—*Robert A. Levine*

# CHAPTER 1

# Introduction
## America's Dysfunctional Democracy
## and the Reasons for a Centrist Third Party

People without vision perish.

—Proverbs 29:18

Society is produced by our wants, and government by
our wickedness; the former promotes our happiness
positively by uniting our affections, the latter negatively
by restraining our vices.

—Thomas Paine, *Common Sense*[1]

America needs a centrist third party. Its democracy has become
increasingly dysfunctional over the last half century with its two
political parties unable to address many of the nation's crucial issues. The country needs a permanent third party of moderates and
independents to make government more responsive, effective, and
efficient. Rabid partisanship and widespread corruption—intrinsic
characteristics of today's Democratic and Republican parties—have
paralyzed the democratic process. The recent Tea Party movement
is an indication of citizens' anger at the failure of the current political parties and the government to solve the nation's problems. But
the Tea Party's focus on returning to the past rather than moving
forward in a new and more complex world heightens partisanship
and cannot provide viable solutions to our problems.

Polls consistently show that the public has lost confidence in
the executive and legislative branches of the government, as well
as in the political parties responsible for shaping policy. An NBC/
Wall Street Journal poll taken in November 2010 after the election

found that President Obama's 49-percent approval rating was better than the ratings of the parties and their leaders. Only 14 percent felt very positive about the Democratic Party and 26 percent somewhat positive.[2] Similarly, only 11 percent (14 percent of the Tea Party) were very positive about the Republican Party and 23 percent (16 percent of the Tea Party) somewhat positive. The combined numbers for the leadership of both parties were dreadful. A total of 19 percent felt positive about the new Republican Speaker of House, John Boehner; 24 percent felt positive about the Democratic Minority Leader, Nancy Pelosi. A total of 14 percent felt positive about the Democratic Majority Leader of the Senate, Harry Reid; and 11 percent felt positive about the Minority Leader, Mitch McConnell. These numbers reveal how poorly Americans regard both Republicans and Democrats and their leaders. Polls have also shown that the majority of the nation's citizens would like to have a third party fielding candidates nationally to compete with the established parties.[3] But because those in power do not want a viable third party, it has not come to fruition.

Citizens are also very unhappy about the overall state of America, with another November 2010 poll revealing that only 28 percent of voters felt the nation was heading in the right direction, 47 percent saying that America's best days were behind her, and only 37 percent believing that her best days lay ahead.[4] Indeed, many economists and political scientists believe that America's problems have already reached crisis proportions. While Americans are concerned about unemployment, the housing market, outsourcing of jobs, immigration, and the ballooning deficit and national debt, the two parties can't agree on how to deal with these issues, jockeying instead for political advantage. Politicians boast about America's pre-eminent world position even as they ignore the fact that it requires the disgorgement of billions of dollars annually on war, military procurement, and reconstruction aid, a burden no other nation is willing even to consider. Meanwhile, the US must borrow money from abroad to keep Americans supplied with the necessities and luxuries of life, buying goods from other countries that its own workers no longer produce, while sinking deeper into an abyss of debt.

These quandaries are but several of many confronting America, a flailing giant enmeshed in a net woven of indecision, incompetence, corruption, and factionalism. Though the country depends on its political parties to govern and find solutions, the Republicans and Democrats have failed to overcome their ideological biases and ethical shortcomings to provide the ideas and leadership so desperately needed. The Founding Fathers understood that political parties would often have difficulty putting aside philosophical differences to forge mutual agreements on the basis of reason and compromise for the good of the nation. As Alexander Hamilton noted in *The Federalist Papers*:

> Were there not even inducements to moderation, nothing could be more ill-judged than that intolerant spirit which has at all times characterized political parties.[5]

James Madison also wrote of his trepidations:

> The latent causes of faction are thus sown in the nature of man; . . . A zeal for different opinions concerning religion, concerning government and many other points, . . . an attachment to different leaders ambitiously contending for pre-eminence and power; . . . render[s] them much more disposed to vex and oppress each other than to co-operate for their common good.[6]

And nowhere in the Constitution or *The Federalist Papers* does it suggest that America should have a two-party system, or that two parties are better than three or multiple parties.

While the Republicans and Democrats are problematic by themselves, the corrupting influence of the lobbyists and special interests in both Washington and the state capitals have made them worse, the parties becoming like crack addicts addicted to the money dispensed to keep them hooked. And just as many addicts won't go to rehab voluntarily, the Republicans and Democrats refuse to relinquish the money that keeps them in power, unwilling to face the voters while going cold turkey. The country needs a clean, centrist third party to keep the lobbyists and special interests at bay and to pressure the current parties to pass critical legislation that meets the long-term needs of the nation.

## Elections and the Voters

One measure of America's faltering political system is the level of cynicism of its citizens regarding the electoral process, evidenced by the low percentage of eligible voters taking part in elections. The presidential contests of 1996 and 2000 saw respective turnouts of 49 percent and 51 percent,[7] increasing to 60.1 percent in 2004 and 61.6 percent in 2008.[8] The figures are much worse in many individual states and in off-year elections when there are no presidential candidates on the ballot. The percentage of young people voting is even more discouraging.[9] In 2004, only 48 percent of those under 30 voted, rising to 52 percent in 2008.[10] (Overall participation in elections was at its peak at the end of the nineteenth century.[11])

Voters are discouraged, disillusioned, and angry, and have stopped going to the polls because they feel their votes are meaningless, with their choice of candidates limited and their voices unheard. In America's political parties, the public sees constant infighting and discord, ethical lapses, lack of transparency, and lying. Much of the electorate believes that candidates running for office will say anything and do anything in order to win, ignoring rules and ethics in the pursuit of victory. The common view is that once in power many lawmakers are on the take, benefiting personally or with campaign contributions in return for favors they've done for special interests. A February 2010 poll showed that 75 percent of the respondents disapproved of Congress and 80 percent believed that members of Congress favored special interests over their constituents.[12] These sentiments helped spawn the Tea Party movement in 2009, with its populist bent and opposition to political incumbents.

In addition, the electorate is aware that the results in many contests are virtually preordained. Prior to 2010, incumbency was a powerful bounty for officeholders, with a minuscule percentage of representatives and senators being defeated when they ran for reelection. Only seven incumbent candidates from the House of

Representatives lost in 2004; 394 were returned to office.[13] The Congressional incumbent reelection rate of 98 percent fell slightly to 94 percent in 2008,[14] with Obama's coattails bringing in some new Democrats. In many states, unfair legislative redistricting—gerrymandering—ensures congressional seats for one party, limiting the number of positions that are realistically competitive.[15] If an incumbent goes along with party leaders and plays the game with the special interests, the likelihood is overwhelming that he or she will be reelected (except when there is a major shift in sentiment, such as occurred in 2010). And once a congressman or woman is in office, it's a Herculean task to get him or her out, aside from death, retirement, an egregious gaffe, or jail. It's no wonder voters think their votes don't count. Citizens remember that the Civil War was fought to preserve a government "of the people, by the people, for the people," but many believe that the government is no longer working for the people. Instead, they are convinced it exists for the benefit of the politicians, the lobbyists, and the special interests—a non-erotic ménage à trois in bed together and inseparable.

## Political Corruption, Lobbyists, and the Special Interests

It is obvious to even casual observers that corruption is endemic in Washington as well as in statehouses and city halls. Contaminating both Republicans and Democrats, the degree of corruption is perhaps determined more by who holds power at the moment than by some inherent moral difference between the parties. The last decade alone saw the K Street Project, the Abramoff scandals, the defense contractors scandals, the PMA lobbying group scandal, as well as ethical and illegal activities by many individual Congressmen. While politicians should be like Caesar's wife, above suspicion, many of them are no better than streetwalkers, willing to take payment from any john that comes along, bestowing whatever favors are desired. Lobbyists and special interests have joined with these acquiescent politicians to subvert the premises of democracy—that each person's vote is significant and has equal weight with every other, and that elected representatives will serve the interests of their constituents and the country at large instead of trying to enhance their own personal power and wealth.

The Congressional Ethics Committee, the oversight body charged with reducing corruption and ethical lapses in Congress, has been woefully ineffective. In addition to a lack of support from both the Republican and Democratic leadership, there are questions of integrity in appointees to the committee themselves and the committee has frequently been deadlocked and unable to act. Though ethics reform was supposed to be a major objective of the Democratic leadership when they regained control of Congress in 2006, business as usual prevailed. In February 2010, the ethics committee cleared five Democratic and two Republican congressmen of ethical violations after they had taken campaign contributions from companies to which they had earmarked hundreds of millions of dollars, much of it in no-bid contracts.[16] The committee saw no improprieties or conflicts of interest in these actions. Charles Rangel, a Democratic congressman from New York who had been involved in multiple ethical lapses and tax violations, was allowed to keep his chairmanship of the House Ways and Means Committee until he stepped down under pressure from other Democrats in March 2010.[17] In November 2010, after being reelected by his district, he was censured by Congress but not expelled. To date, there have been no criminal proceedings against him.

Corrupt behavior on the Republican side includes that of Jack Abramoff, Congressmen Randy Cunningham, Bob Ney, Tom De-Lay, and a number of lesser lights, while the Democrats weigh in with Representatives William Jefferson, who stashed some of his bribery loot in his freezer,[18] Maxine Waters, and Rangel. Congressmen Dan Rostenkowski, James Traficant, Jim Wright, and many other Democrats also enjoyed extra paydays in the recent past when they were ascendant in Washington. In June 2010, twenty members of the Congressional Black Caucus, all Democrats, introduced a resolution to significantly limit the powers of the Office of Congressional Ethics (OCE) and prevent the public release of most of their investigative reports.[19] This new "independent body" had been examining questionable activities of members of the Black Caucus. So party is no guide to integrity. Even religion, worn proudly on their sleeves by some politicians, is no predictor of ethical behavior. If we accept the "cockroach theory," we expect that scores of other miscreants of both parties continue to exist hidden in the crevices while their less fortunate corrupt brethren have been exposed to the light of day.

In fact, there are very few "clean" politicians in Washington who refuse to break bread with lobbyists, or who decline contributions from special interest groups. And earmarks, those peculiar devices of Washington officeholders that benefit special interests, have metastasized at an alarming rate into Federal legislation, though perhaps less blatantly recently than in earlier years. Pork and earmarks are prerogatives of elected officials that border on being unethical, but are staunchly defended by many legislators. Pork is money appropriated specifically for pet projects of senators or members of Congress that may benefit their home districts or special interests they want to help. When inserted secretly or at the last moment into the plethora of paragraphs that constitute a Congressional bill, these appropriations become earmarks, though the 2007 ethics law decreed transparency. Usually of little value to the nation as a whole, these measures waste tens of billions of dollars of taxpayers' money. Although their party has been a major generator of earmarks, the Republican congressional leadership voted in with the 2010 elections vowed to eliminate them.

Even with the scope of political scandals, far-reaching reform to make legislators and their staffs more responsive to the electorate and less beholden to the special interests does not appear to be on the horizon. Though promised by the Democratic leadership in Congress in 2008, comprehensive steps such as lengthy restrictions on lobbying by former government officials and bundling of campaign contributions are still only promises. Before 2008, a Republican-controlled Congress proposed legislation to curb ethical violations; the House and Senate passed different versions, but no final bill was ever approved.[20] The attempt, however, did give politicians protective cover, allowing them to report to their constituents that they had backed lobbying reform to fight corruption.

Who are these lobbyists and special interests that undermine the democratic process and whose voices are heard above those of the electorate? Lobbyists, individuals who act as intermediaries for special interests or advocacy groups, attempt to influence legislation and executive actions or win government contracts. They are often former members of congress, senators, or staff members, high-level employees of government agencies or departments, or retired military personnel. Because of their previous positions, they have access to legislators who are writing laws and to members of the executive branch or top military officers who can make important decisions.

The special interests include a multitude of corporations seeking government contracts for products or services, government subsidies or special tax breaks, protection from foreign competitors through tariffs or import restrictions, or the waiving of environmental regulations. Business associations may have similar objectives for entire industries. Unions and labor groups are special interests that want to maintain or raise wages or want protection from low-wage workers abroad. Farmers may want subsidies for their crops or protection from imports. Cities, states and counties, foreign governments, social and religious advocacy groups, health organizations, environmental groups, the National Rifle Association and gun control groups, and countless others can act as special interest groups. All of these entities try to promote their own concerns and values over and above those of the general public. To do this they usually provide campaign contributions to officials who are friendly to their views and may be willing to mobilize voters to support them.

The drive for reelection requires raising huge sums of money, and members of Congress and senators feel indebted to those who contribute. Anyone or any group that provides significant aid gets access to the official, perhaps that official's willingness to craft legislation that benefits that person or group, and perhaps a willingness to block other legislation perceived as harmful. This *quid pro quo* makes legislators resistant to meaningful campaign finance reform, which along with lobbying reform could change the political structure now in place. Along with campaign help, many politicians and their staffers also accept personal blandishments from lobbyists and special interests, such as trips, dinners, and direct financial rewards (now supposedly prohibited), or the promise of plush jobs in the future. And the task of addressing the nation's real problems, making hard choices, and confronting divisive questions goes undone.

The amount of money that lobbyists and special interests need to gain access to an elected official depends on the office and how much the official needs to run a campaign, the costs escalating with each cycle. For some members of Congress, a contribution of a few thousand dollars may be sufficient to meet and talk with the donor. In the 2008 presidential campaign, all the candidates generated a total of nearly $1.7 billion, led by President Obama's $747 million and Senator McCain's $351 million.[21] (Obama refused to take public money, which would have restricted his fundraising. McCain was agreeable as his fundraising was lagging.) President Bush had fundraisers designated as Pioneers, who supplied $200,000, or Rangers, who came up with $100,000 for his presidential campaigns.[22] They delivered these amounts by bundling together funds from friends and associates to circumvent campaign financing laws that limited the amount of an individual's contribution to presidential candidates. Ken Lay, of Enron notoriety, was a major contributor to Bush and many indicted or convicted white-collar criminals give regularly to one or both parties. Total spending on the 2010 midterm elections reached $4 billion, according to the Center for Responsive Politics, compared to $2.8 billion four years earlier.[23]

The list of government officials who have subsequently become lobbyists is extensive. Many appear to have been rewarded for work performed while in office that benefited special interests, while others were hired for their potential clout in future dealings with government agencies. A prime example of the first scenario is former Republican Representative Billy Tauzin of Louisiana, who helped shepherd the Medicare prescription drug bill through Congress in 2003. He retired soon afterward and became president of the Pharmaceutical Research and Manufacturers of America

(PhRMA), the drug industry lobby, where he was able to command millions in salary and benefits.[24] An example of the second is conservative Republican John Ashcroft, who had been a senator from Missouri and attorney general for President Bush. Upon leaving the government, he started a lobbying firm in the fall of 2005, quickly establishing a stable of prominent clients.[25] Though Ashcroft had been head of the Justice Department only a short time earlier, his firm represented Oracle in its attempts to persuade the Justice Department that there were no antitrust implications in a billion-dollar acquisition it was pursuing. Needless to say, Oracle was successful in its quest and Ashcroft received $220,000 for his work.

The Center for Public Integrity reported in January 2006 that "more than 22,000 companies and organizations have employed 3,500 lobbying firms and more than 27,000 lobbyists since 1998,"[26] with 49 of the leading 50 firms neglecting to file required documents. Over 2200 former federal employees registered as lobbyists from 1998 to 2004, including 273 previous members of the White House staff and almost 250 members of Congress and heads of federal agencies. During this period, 50 percent of senators and 42 percent of congressmen who left office became lobbyists, 52 percent of departing Republicans and 33 percent Democrats.[27] Total spending by lobbyists reached $2.38 billion in 2005, according to the Center for Responsive Politics.[28] The yeoman's share went to Republicans, who received 84 percent of the money given by oil and gas interests and 75 percent from big tobacco. The pharmaceutical industry gave them 69 percent, insurance companies 66 percent, and defense contractors 61 percent. For the 2008 election campaign, however, Democratic candidates received more money from lobbyists than Republicans,[29] as contributors who wanted access believed the Democrats were more likely to win. In 2009, according to the Senate Office of Public Records, the top twenty industries alone spent $2.22 billion on lobbying[30] to convince public officials to acquiesce to the needs of the special interests, overriding their commitment to America's citizens. The 2010 midterm election has seen the lion's share of funding by special interests and lobbyists go to the Republicans. The amounts given also increased significantly, the result of the *Citizens United* decision by the Supreme Court earlier in 2010 that struck down the limitations on corporate spending for political campaigns.

While not all politicians are intimately tied to lobbyists and special interests, the vast majority are, and even the most righteous have to cooperate to some degree if they want to get reelected. Money is the mother's milk of politics and is necessary to finance election campaigns, unless the person running is inordinately wealthy and willing to fund it him- or herself. The national parties solicit funds to distribute to the members of their committees as well as to individual candidates. In addition to the Republican and Democratic National Committees, there are Republican and Democratic congressional campaign committees and senatorial campaign committees, raising and disbursing funds for candidates in each election. In the last several decades, members of the House and Senate have also taken to raising money for their colleagues through so-called leadership PACs (political action committees).[31] Some of these PACs have given large sums to struggling candidates, which of course obligates the recipient to the donor if he or she is elected. The PAC of Republican Majority Leader Dick Armey disbursed $879,892 to 122 of his Republican colleagues during the 1997–1998 election cycle, while Nancy Pelosi contributed over $600,000 to fellow Democrats two years later.[32]

In addition to the huge sums the two parties spent on the 2010 campaigns, special interests and affluent individuals with particular objectives provided advertising in support of candidates for various offices. The identities of these individuals remain secret. They provided the advertising funds through donations to so-called 501(c) groups operating as nonprofits, which are not required to disclose their sources of funding and whose primary purpose is not supposed to be political.[33] These organizations, primarily Republican in orientation, often tried to appear as if they were of grassroots origin, although they had been created by political operatives and financed by special interests working together in the shadows. With enormous amounts spent on targeted congressional and senatorial races, these 501(c) groups may have decided the composition of the new Congress while keeping their donors hidden from the electorate.

When the virus of corruption infects members of a group, it encourages corrupt behavior in others, with the belief they too can evade censure or penalties for their actions. Those involved in proscribed activities turn a blind eye to what their colleagues are doing, unwilling to investigate or punish possible unethical or illegal conduct. They are afraid that exposing a peer's disreputable deeds will cause the spotlight to be turned on their own corrupt endeavors. There is also a veneer of acceptability that covers the stain of unethical activities when there is a belief that others in a peer group are similarly engaged. Though it is understood that unethical behavior by one person in an organization can tar the entire body, it is ignored. Corruption has been present in American politics since the founding of the Republic but appears more prevalent than ever before.

In addition to corruption and ethical problems on a federal level, corruption infects state, municipal, and county governments, involving members of both political parties. A report in May 2006 noted that over 2000 investigations into public corruption were currently active by the FBI.[34] Over 1060 government officials at all levels were convicted of criminal acts in 2004 and 2005.

Readers interested in exploring political corruption in greater depth will find in the addenda on my website—www.robertlevinebooks.com—material that focuses on corruption in the federal government since the founding of the republic. But two scandals in particular show how extensive corruption is among high officeholders and how accountability is lacking. One was the House bank overdraft scandal in the late '80s and early '90s, in which hundreds of members of Congress issued 20,000 bad checks for $10.8 million without any penalties or fees.[35] Among those with overdrafts, none of whom were punished, were Dick Cheney, Newt Gingrich, and the Democratic House speaker at that time, Tom Foley. The other scandal was the savings and loan debacle in the late '80s, in which five senators, dubbed the Keating Five, among others, defended in a federal regulatory investigation a corrupt bank owner and real estate mogul, Charles Keating, who had made large contributions to fundraising groups for them.[36] The senators, including John McCain, were later rebuked by the Senate Ethics Committee for bad judgment, and Senator Alan Cranston of California was rebuked for breach of ethics, but they were never significantly disciplined.

## Campaign Promises

Campaign promises from both parties that are impossible to fulfill or that will be disregarded once the candidate is in office also spur citizen disenchantment with politics. Standard ploys are promises to cut taxes and increase services, as though money for the government can be pulled out of thin air. Some of the electorate realize the declarations are deceptive, but candidates from both parties use similar strategies, one pledging to do more than the other, with no realistic, straight-talking alternatives available. However, officeholders are sometimes actually able to both cut taxes and increase services by postponing payment of the debt incurred, moving it to the future when another legislative body will have to find a solution and another generation will have to pay. This has been the preferred way of doing business in Washington: running up a credit card bill that America's children and grandchildren will have to deal with later. In general, the Republicans are prone to increase the debt by cutting taxes and Democrats by heightened spending, but the result is the same, the nation drowning in an ocean of debt and raising the specter of catastrophic consequences.

Anxious to regain control of Congress in the 2010 midterm elections, Republican leaders announced "A Pledge to America" in September, crafted to convince the electorate that the party was fiscally responsible.[37] A reprise of Newt Gingrich's 1994 Contract With America, it vowed to continue the Bush tax cuts, reduce spending, and revive the economy while paring the budget deficit and national debt. However, it delineated no specific programs to show where curtailed spending of the required magnitude would originate, as the tax cuts would considerably increase the deficits. In February 2011, the Republican-controlled House did pass a bill cutting $60 billion from discretionary spending, knowing that it would be defeated in the Senate.[38] However, it did not pare Social Security, Medicare, or Medicaid, and made only minimal cuts in defense spending, the major areas fueling the national debt and budget deficits but sacrosanct to politicians. After the 2010 elections, when the bipartisan deficit commission appointed by President Obama suggested that the above areas be addressed along with raising some taxes as possible ways to reduce the deficit, both parties assailed the recommendations.[39]

## The Leadership Void

The lack of leadership by elected officials and politicians of both parties adds to the difficulty of enacting onerous but necessary legislation, adding to widespread misgivings about the nation's government. Legislators are unwilling to forge ahead of their constituents, or develop new ideas or new approaches to problems. Instead of explaining to the people back home why a certain bill is required even though it may cause pain, politicians watch polls that tell them how the voters will probably react. In other words, instead of trying to shape public opinion as leaders should do, they follow public opinion, unwilling to deal with the consequences of taking an unpopular stand. Neither the Democrats nor Republicans seem able or willing to tackle the hard issues, particularly when they involve increasing taxes, reducing benefits, or telling voters what they may not want to hear. Cutting open an abscess to drain it may cause immediate discomfort, but can ensure the long-term health of the patient. However, America's political leaders just keep ignoring vexatious dilemmas, shunting them off to the future, knowing that the longer they wait to confront these problems the more difficult it will be to find prudent answers. The legislation that does pass is often poorly constructed and does not necessarily have the desired effect, or has unexpected results or unpredicted costs hidden from the public. An example is the Medicare prescription drug bill of 2003, which is inordinately complex and confusing for the participants, will cost hundreds of billions of dollars more than originally projected, but is extremely profitable for the pharmaceutical companies. The health care reform bill passed in 2010 is also needlessly complex and does little to rein in escalating costs in spite of the promised savings. In addition, budgetary measures hailed by members of Congress and senators as cutting waste are loaded with earmarks and pork that elected representatives have inserted and are unwilling to cut.

The leaders of both parties in the House and Senate are usually individuals who know how to play the game and advance the party's agenda, but they are not necessarily bright, innovative people one would hope to see in those positions. They are well versed in the party's hymnals and able to carry the tunes well, but unlikely to create new melodies or develop new concepts to move the country forward. For the most part, they are ideologues rather than pragmatists and are ill suited to work out compromise solutions to problems that will win broad public acceptance. In fact, over the last few decades, combative party leaders have played a major role in the heightened partisanship in Congress that is now considered normal.[40] When the Democrats were in charge and Jim Wright was the speaker of the House in the 1980s, he did not reach out to the Republicans for help with legislation, but kept them in subservient, powerless positions. Subsequently, when the Republicans gained control of Congress in 1994 they retaliated in kind, perhaps even more aggressively, ignoring Democratic input on policy matters and legislation. Republican leaders like Newt Gingrich, Dick Armey, Tom DeLay, Roy Blount, and John Boehner kept their thumbs on the necks of the Democrats for over a decade, leading to greater hostility and bitterness on both sides of the aisle. Although they promised more bipartisanship, the Democrats, with Nancy Pelosi and Harry Reid as leaders, behaved similarly after returning to power in the midterm elections of 2006. In 2010, with the Republicans back in charge of the House, John Boehner as Speaker followed the same pattern. When Senate Republican leader Mitch McConnell was asked what his party's top goal would be in the new Congress, he declared that it was making sure that President Obama was not reelected in 2012.[41] This statement personifies the kind of leadership found in the Congress, where partisanship and the quest for power take precedence over the needs of the country.

In spite of Bill Clinton's emergence in the '90s, the era of Rockefeller Republicans and centrist Democrats appears to be long gone, with the more extreme elements of the parties in their leadership. A good example is Nancy Pelosi's reelection by House Democrats as their leader in November of 2010, after she presided over their lopsided losses in the midterm elections and polls showed that the vast majority of independents disapproved of her.[42] The parties enforce obedience to the party line in order to pass legislation, though the measures in question may contravene the personal beliefs of the legislators or be against their constituents' best interests. Senators and members of Congress know they must follow the party line to get maximal assistance in fundraising and to win appointments to important committees. It will help them as well to get their own bills passed in the future. Horse-trading has always been part of the legislative process, but never with the amount of coercion that goes on today.

Congressional and national party leaders also recruit candidates to run for elective offices when their party has no one to contest a position. While the leadership is principally interested in finding people capable of winning, they also favor individuals whose ideology is consonant with their own beliefs. They recruit candidates with offers of financial backing, logistical support, strategic guidance, and assistance from organizations connected to the party.[43] If these individuals are elected to the House or the Senate, they feel indebted to the leaders who selected them and are more likely to vote as the party dictates.

## Ideology and Partisanship

At present, it is clear that both political parties have been captured by ideologues to whom the word compromise is anathema and to whom bipartisanship in developing legislation is out of the question. As James Madison commented:

> It is a misfortune, inseparable from human affairs, that public measures are rarely investigated with that spirit of modera-

tion which is essential to a just estimate of their real tendency to advance or obstruct the public good.[44]

An article in *Political Science Quarterly* in 2005 noted:

... because lawmakers need the support of key constituents (partisans) to get reelected, they tend to avoid taking policy positions that might antagonize party activists, campaign contributors, and core supporters.[45]

Loyal opposition and reasonable disagreement over the issues are no longer acceptable as part of the democratic process in Washington. Each side is more focused on having its way and destroying the other than on finding a middle ground that may be beneficial for the country. During George Bush's recent terms in office, Republicans tarred legislators as "unpatriotic" or "soft on terrorism" for voting against measures that increased presidential power, and Democrats called legislators "right-wing extremists" for supporting the same measures. Opponents of health care reform or the financial stimulus package under Obama called supporters of that legislation "socialists." This pattern holds on issue after issue. There is little comity between members of the two parties, little socialization or strong friendships as occurred in the past.

Previously, members of Congress and senators were able to disagree and oppose government actions in an honorable fashion, and were respected by those in power. There were some centrists who tried to escape the iron vise of party discipline in order to find answers to the nation's problems. No longer. During the 1990s, a host of moderate leaders from both parties retired from the Senate because of the poisoned atmosphere of partisanship that made working there no longer rewarding.[46] In 2001, Senator James Jeffords of Vermont took the unusual step of disaffiliating himself from the Republican Party and changing to independent status[47] because he believed the party had become too extreme and did not reflect his ideals or those of his constituents. Republican Senator Arlen Specter of Pennsylvania switched to the Democrats in 2009 because he felt the Republican Party was hostile to his centrist views and he did not think he could win his state's primary against the hardliner running against him.[48] He subsequently lost in the Democratic primary.

The threat by Senate Republicans to abolish the filibuster in 2005 was another indication of how partisanship and extremism control the political agenda in Washington. The use of the filibuster in the Senate is a time-honored tradition that dates back to 1806.[49] Though its benefits can be debated, over the years it has forced the majority to consider the views of the minority, and has protected the country from some legislation and from nominees for various positions who were out of the mainstream. To advance narrow partisan goals (certain judicial nominees), the Republicans were willing to play bare-knuckle politics and overturn two hundred years of precedent, which would have led to even more hostility between the parties. Though the Republicans labeled the filibuster undemocratic in 2005, they had no compunctions about reversing their stand in 2010, using the filibuster or the threat of one to block legislation or nominees they opposed when the Democrats had a 59–41 advantage in the Senate. This example of the disregard for democratic practice further illustrates how partisanship in the halls of Congress rules the day, with a fervent minority able to obstruct the passage of measures the country needs.

In order to maintain the Constitution's checks and balances and to keep extremists in the executive or legislative branches at bay, Americans tend to vote for divided government in Washington. On Election Day they will often split the houses of Congress between the two parties, or vote to have the president and one or both houses of Congress belong to different parties. This can block radical actions from taking place, but it also curbs government efficiency and can heighten public contempt for elected officials if it seems that things are not getting done. From 1954 through 1994 the Democrats controlled the House of Representatives and usually the Senate, though a Republican was president more often than not. But having the presidency and both houses in the hands of the same party does not necessarily ensure that important bills will pass. Clinton could not do it with health care reform in the early years of his presidency and George W. Bush was unable to privatize Social Security with a Republican House and Senate. Similarly, Obama could not get the health care bill or immigration reform he actually wanted or all the financial stimulus money he thought necessary.

American's Founding Fathers believed in the value of public service as a duty to their fellow citizens, often neglecting their farms and businesses as a consequence. Imbued with optimism and good will, they were much more pragmatic and willing to compromise to benefit their new nation than the current lot of politicians who are driven by ideology and self-promotion. The Founders could also put personal animosity aside in dealing with opponents if they felt it was in the national interest. In fact, bipartisan support for important legislation was not uncommon until the last twenty or thirty years. Until then there was a stream of centrism and less ideological rigidity in both parties. The Democratic Party once contained a broad swath of political beliefs from segregationist Dixiecrats to near-socialists. Now Democratic ideology has narrowed, running from the far left to the center. Similarly, the Republicans, who like to consider themselves an inclusive party sheltering varying views under the so-called "big tent," presently have ideas that run from the far right to the center. But the parties are dominated by those elements in the extreme ends of their spectrums. In fact, conservative Republicans derogate moderates, calling them "RINOs"—"Republicans in name only."

## What the Current Parties Stand For

In America's system of government, ideology drives policy. There are certain core beliefs associated with each party that it tries to foster at every opportunity and that many party stalwarts consider non-negotiable. These "belief systems," or ideologies, of the two parties are in direct conflict, which does not allow for much accommodation. When one party is in power, legislation may reflect its precepts. When the other party ascends, legislation is shaped by their ideas, which may be the polar opposite of previous bills. Then it shifts back when the first party becomes dominant again.

Because of this, America's government is inefficient, with layers of laws piled one upon the other, a hodge-podge of ideas with different objectives. James Madison commented on mutable law in *The Federalist Papers*:

> It will be of little avail to the people that the laws are made by men of their own choice if the laws be so voluminous that they cannot be read, or so incoherent that they cannot be understood; if they be repealed or revised before they are promulgated, or undergo such incessant changes that no man, who knows what the law is today, can guess what it will be tomorrow.[50]

A simplistic but basically correct exposition of each party's core beliefs follows.

*Republican, or conservative, precepts*
- Government is bad
- Big government is particularly bad
- State and local governments are better than the federal government
- Government should not be used to solve problems
- Government should not interfere in people's lives
- Market solutions are the answers to most problems
- The private sector can always do better than government
- Less regulation is always better
- Taxes are bad
- Anything is permissible in the name of national security
- Against abortion
- Against gun control
- Anti-union

The recent prominence of the Tea Party activists and their expanding role within the Republican Party have placed the views of the Austrian School of Economists[51], with theorists such as Ludwig von Mises and Friedrich A. Hayek, at the forefront of GOP thinking. These men championed a classical, liberal, free-market approach to economics, defending free trade and property rights, and opposing taxes, regulations, and price controls. Indeed, as strong free-market advocates, they were against anything that might hinder enterprise.

In the past, and since Obama was elected, Republicans have favored a balanced budget and argued against deficit spending, though these were disregarded when Reagan and George W. Bush were in office. Some conservatives, however, have pushed the view that by cutting taxes and increasing the deficit, they could force a decrease in the size of the federal government, calling it "starving the beast." But this never happened. Under the Reagan and second Bush administrations federal spending, the size of the federal government, and the size of the national debt ballooned more than in any previous administration, including during World War II.

*Democratic, or liberal precepts*
- Big government can be good
- Many problems can be solved by government
- Government spending can be used to help people
- Taxes are not necessarily bad if the money is used properly
- The rich should bear a greater burden of taxes
- The problems of crime and poverty are mostly society's fault
- Individual responsibility and accountability should take into consideration upbringing and culture
- Civil liberties should not be forgotten when dealing with national security issues
- Pro-choice
- Pro-union

Notwithstanding their core beliefs, the two parties have violated these tenets when it has suited them. The Clinton administration pushed through welfare reform in the '90s forcing people to provide for themselves and assume more responsibility for their personal circumstances. Republicans have supported government interference in people's right to die, as in the Terry Schiavo case, and also have supported government meddling in women's lives over the abortion issue. Both of these stances are complex and the Republican positions are supported by their pro-life beliefs. They have also subverted states' rights in moving against the Oregon Death with Dignity law, which was supported by the citizens of Oregon, and in fighting against state laws that permit the use of medical marijuana. In addition, the right to privacy and unreasonable searches by the federal government has been overridden in allowing surveillance of the general population in the attempt to uncover terrorists. Whether these actions are right or wrong is open to question, but they show an inconsistency by the parties in adhering to what they call their core beliefs.

There are also special interests historically associated with each party that give them financial support and turn out voters for them at election time. For the Republicans, it is the religious right, big business, and the affluent segment of the population, while the Democrats depend on trial lawyers, labor unions, minorities, and academics for material assistance and campaign volunteers. Because of the need to keep their bases happy, legislation and executive action by the party in power favor their own supporters. Though a particular group may be allied with one party for many years, changes do occur. African Americans were indebted to the Republican Party for decades after Lincoln freed the slaves, but moved into the Democratic orbit by the mid-twentieth century because of the Democratic stance on civil rights. Conversely, southern whites shifted their allegiance from the Democrats to the Republicans in the latter part of the twentieth century over the civil rights issue.

James Bennet, the editor of *The Atlantic*, commented about the parties in the January 2011 issue:

> . . . since the 1960s, Democrats' defensiveness about government, driven partly by fealty to public-service employees unions, has turned them into the party of bureaucracy, rather than effective government, just as Republicans' fealty to incumbent interests has turned them into the party of Big Business rather than of free markets and innovation.[52]

## How the Primary System
## Encourages Extremism and Partisanship

The party primary system tends to push candidates to more extreme positions, adding to the disillusionment of the average voter. To start with, relatively few people participate in these ritualistic affairs. This allows dedicated groups of hardcore party members to hold sway, advancing the more ideologically pure candidates they support, a good example being the Republican senatorial primary in Delaware that picked Tea Party–backed Christine O'Donnell. Even though the majority of citizens label themselves centrist or moderate, the party primaries force them to choose between candidates in the general elections whose views are divergent from theirs. Instead of feeling passionate about the person they select, and agreeing with most of his or her ideas, they wind up picking the lesser of two evils, with lukewarm approval of that person's positions. By eliminating many centrist districts, gerrymandering has further resulted in more ideologues in Congress, generating greater adversarial relationships between the parties. True competition would make politicians hold opinions and promulgate policies that would attract the majority of their constituents. But if competition is limited to two parties, with beliefs skewed to the far ends, the electorate has insufficient choices, and the views of many citizens are not represented.

At times, candidates are willing to abandon their moderate beliefs to win an election, instead endorsing strongly partisan positions or catering to individuals who espouse extremism. This is another reason politicians are held in such low regard by the public. Senator John McCain is a good illustration. Just after the 9/11 terrorist attacks Rev. Jerry Falwell declared that they had been God's punishment for America's immorality and that the country had probably gotten what it deserved. He named abortionists, feminists, gays and lesbians, the ACLU, and all of those who had tried to secularize America, saying "You helped this happen." Senator McCain denounced Falwell along with Pat Robertson as "agents of intolerance." In April 2006,[53] however, McCain lauded Falwell and the

Christian right, suggesting that courses in intelligent design should be offered in the schools as an alternative to evolution. Since McCain was running for president, he needed the backing of the religious right in order to win the Republican primaries and said that his views had been misunderstood earlier. Then, in his attempt to be reelected as senator from Arizona in 2010, McCain renounced his previous stand on immigration, trying to attract anti-immigration voters in his state's primary. Another example is Governor Mitt Romney in his bids for the Republican presidential nomination in 2008 and 2012. He altered many of his positions on social issues and abandoned the health care reform he had pushed in his home state of Massachusetts, hoping he would have greater appeal to conservative primary voters.

Because they have been elected by larger population bases that have not been gerrymandered, senators in general tend to be slightly more centrist than their House colleagues, but because of the primary system may still not reflect the more moderate tenor of the states they represent. This is also true, although to a lesser degree, of presidential candidates. In times past party bosses chose the nominees and were more likely to select moderate, middle-of-the-road candidates who they believed could win the general elections, knowing that the public seemed to favor this type of contestant.

## Lack of Oversight

Public accountability is at the heart of a well-run and uncorrupted government. In recent decades, oversight of government activity through autonomous bodies or legislative committees has been lacking. During the first six years of the Bush administration both Congress and the president refused to authorize independent watchdogs to investigate problem areas, choosing to work within the structures that already existed. Since the same party controlled the legislative and executive branches, they could investigate themselves, making it unlikely that any major mistakes or breaches of the public trust would come to light. Though an independent commission that examined the failures that occurred on 9/11 made a number of corrective recommendations, that was not true of the response to Hurricane Katrina, the bungled attempt to corral Osama bin Laden at Tora Bora, the initiation and conduct of the Iraq War, or the waste of billions of dollars there. Those in leadership positions did not want to face scrutiny, fearing they might be embarrassed. The critical decisions made by Bush and Obama and their teams in regard to the financial crisis have not yet been subject to analysis by an independent panel to help provide guidance if similar situations arise in the future, although an independent panel has investigated the causes of the financial meltdown.

The Bush administration also chose to provide less oversight of industry and less protection for the public during its time in power. Throughout 2007, there was a rash of recalls of dangerous products from China, including toys, toothpaste, and drugs, and some made domestically, that had not been tested by the government before they were available for sale. The Consumer Products Safety Commission, whose staff and budget had been greatly reduced over the preceding ten years, had only one person to test all the new toys that came to market and was simply unable to examine all of these goods. Yet when legislation was proposed by Congress to increase the agency's staff, budget, and responsibilities to shore up consumer safety, the acting head of the commission, Nancy Nord, asked Congress to reject these measures, saying they would be unnecessarily burdensome.[54]

## The Arrogance of Power

Abuse of office and arrogance of power are common attributes of politicians and corporate executives, perhaps not surprising in view of the truism "power corrupts." The attitude and the resulting behavior by elected officials alienates citizens and drives them away from the political arena. When abuses occur, too often political parties fail to impose consequences on the perpetrators. Presidents, who hold the most powerful office in the world, may be particularly prone to see themselves as above the law, as with Nixon and

Watergate. Bill Clinton's affair with Monica Lewinsky in the White House may have stemmed from his belief that he could do what he wanted with no consequences. Senator Ted Kennedy's auto accident at Chappaquidick, Massachusetts, is another example of arrogance by a powerful person who faced no legal consequences for his conduct. He was driving after drinking and his passenger, Mary Jo Kopechne, drowned when he drove off a bridge. He did not report the accident to the authorities until the following morning, never had a test of his alcohol level, and tried to deny his culpability for the death. Vice President Cheney shot a man in February 2006 in an apparent hunting accident, yet did not call the police for several hours. The episode was not investigated until the following day, though Cheney admitted to imbibing alcohol while handling the weapon. Law enforcement agents did not require him to make a statement after the shooting and did not test his alcohol level. Arrogance of power may also explain the willingness of many politicians to disregard ethical considerations in their dealings with lobbyists and special interests, believing that they don't have to answer to their constituents. It may also be the reason for many of the sexual indiscretions that seem to afflict politicians.

During his time in office, President Bush demonstrated a disregard for tradition and the law, trying to increase the powers of the presidency with what some described as "creeping autocracy."[55] Using the threat of terrorism, Bush claimed surveillance and investigative powers that required no oversight, no consultation with Congress, and no judicial review. Though some officials at the Justice Department objected to the surveillance program on constitutional grounds, Attorney General John Ashcroft overruled them.[56] Using Article 2 of the Constitution, which delineates the function and powers of the president, Bush claimed that his expanded authority was inherent in his role as Commander in Chief.[57] While it was asserted that only suspicious individuals with terrorist ties were spied upon, some Republicans in Congress as well as Democrats were concerned about this domestic spying and eavesdropping,[58] as wiretapping and surveillance of American citizens without warrants under FISA (Foreign Intelligence Surveillance Act) were never approved by Congress or the judiciary. Eventually, Bush backed off and negotiated with Congress about how to handle this issue.

The administration also claimed that some of its other controversial actions were within the purview of the president under Article 2 of the Constitution, including imprisonment of enemy combatants at Guantanamo, rendition of suspected terrorists, military trials of enemy combatants, and the use of coercive interrogation techniques.[59] In July 2006, however, the Supreme Court established its control in these matters, saying that the use of military tribunals for terror suspects contravened both the law and the Geneva Conventions.[60],[61] When, after the Supreme Court decision, the president asked Congress for the same authority the Court had denied,[62],[63] prominent members of his own party opposed him, including Senators John McCain, Lindsey Graham, and John Warner, the Chairman of the Armed Services Committee. In response, the president declared that those rejecting his recommendations were putting America at risk and "hindering the fight on terrorism."[64] Subsequently, a compromise between the senators and the president was worked out.

A conservative legal scholar, Jack Goldsmith, who headed the Justice Department's Office of Legal Counsel (OLC) from October 2003 until resigning in June 2004, wrote a scathing indictment of the Bush administration's efforts to expand the powers of the presidency, whether or not these actions had a legal basis. In his book, *The Terror Presidency*, Goldsmith asserts that Bush, Cheney, Gonzales, and their aides ignored the international agreements of the Geneva Conventions, the Constitution, and congressional mandates in such matters as torture of prisoners, detention of enemy combatants, and domestic surveillance.[65]

Bush also claimed nearly unlimited power to conduct the war in Iraq, requesting that Congress unquestioningly fund everything he asked for in that regard. He ignored the fact that the Constitution grants Congress the power of the purse specifically to check the president's authority to conduct war, and can restrict his actions by cutting appropriations. Though he berated Congressional Democrats for trying to micromanage the war, they did not have to acquiesce to his demands.

Another interesting maneuver by President Bush were his statements when he signed enacted legislation, presenting his conception of the new laws and how he intended to execute them. If accepted by the other branches of government, these "signing statements" would greatly increase presidential power and could subvert Congress's intentions in passing legislation. A bipartisan panel of the American Bar Association reviewing the use of signing statements stated that "President Bush was flouting the Constitution and undermining the rule of law by claiming the power to disregard selected provisions of bills that he signed."[66] The panel felt that this broad assertion of executive power in these signing statements was "contrary to the rule of law and our constitutional system of separation of powers."

Though President Obama decried President Bush's use of executive power and signing statements when he was on the campaign trail in 2007 and 2008, he has acted in the same manner.[67] He has used signing statements to protect what he has seen as the executive domain against Congressional intrusion, particularly in foreign affairs, just as the Bush–Cheney White House did. While his use of signing statements and claims of executive fiat have not been as extensive as the previous administration's, those who viewed Obama as an idealist who would be willing to curtail executive power have been sorely disappointed.

## Attack Politics (The Politics of Personal Destruction)

The increasingly vicious tenor of political contests at all levels as refined by political gurus such as Lee Atwater and Karl Rove in the last few decades has turned off much of the electorate. Though negative campaigning has been a fact of life since the birth of the Republic, the new media have magnified its virulence and reach. Candidates are not content to focus on the issues and their opponents' platforms, but instead direct personal attacks at those running against them, questioning their motives and character. Newspapers, mailings, radio, television, and the Internet are all used for these "attack ads." There are also "whispering campaigns" over the phone in which volunteers working on behalf of one candidate impart false information about his or her opponent, which is later disavowed. In one attack ad despicable claims were made against Democrat Max Cleland of Georgia in the 2002 senate race. Senator Cleland, a Viet Nam veteran and a triple amputee as a result of war injuries, was accused by his Republican adversary and the national party of being unpatriotic and soft on terrorism because he had questioned some of President Bush's initiatives. These charges were repeated innumerable times until enough voters believed what was being said, despite the fact that Senator Cleland's injuries spoke eloquently to his patriotism; he lost the election. An article in *Political Science Quarterly* subsequently noted: "According to a 1999 Institute for Global Ethics study, 80% of voters believe that attack campaigning is unethical, undermines democracy, lowers voter turnout, and produces less ethical officials."[68] Yet it continues because politicians are convinced that it works. If a charge is repeated often enough and loudly enough, many voters can be persuaded that it is true, as they do not seek independent sources for verification.

Many of these attack ads do not come directly from candidates but from special interest groups that support them, or from party-affiliated groups that seek to evade campaign finance laws. Among the many aggressive entities in the 2004, 2006, and 2008 elections were the 527 committees, not overseen by any regulatory body, that raised money supposedly in support of particular issues but actively pushed attack ads. Also active in the 2010 midterm elections were 501(c) organizations whose donors are secret.[69] The candidates or parties who benefit may later chastise these groups or disavow them for their offensive narratives, but that occurs after the damage has been done. It is often difficult for victims of the attacks to respond effectively to the innuendos and allegations, and the public perception of the beleaguered candidates suffers. The Swift Boat Veterans ads against John Kerry employed this technique in the 2004 presidential campaign, while Moveon.org ran ads against President Bush.

In the 2008 presidential election, attacks against Obama labeled him a socialist and a Muslim, using as apparent proof the fact that some acquaintances were left-leaning or Muslims. There was also an emphasis in these diatribes on Obama's middle name, Hussein, to reinforce his Muslim heritage. To this day the so-called "birthers" insist that Obama is an illegal president since he supposedly was not born in the US, notwithstanding his Hawaiian birth certificate, which they claim was forged. Attacks against McCain focused on rumors that he had had an extramarital affair with a female lobbyist based in Washington, in spite of denials by both of them.

Office-seekers use so-called "push polls" and "robo-calls," phone calls in which voters are asked questions that seem to relate impartially to a political race but in fact simultaneously impart negative information, often untrue, about the opposing candidate.

Politics have become so dirty that smear campaigns and personal attacks occur not only in the heat of elections but are also used by parties and connected organizations to tar opponents who disagree with them on policy, even when this is done in good faith.

## Political Consultants

The use of consultants and pollsters by politicians has also contributed to popular cynicism and dissatisfaction with the political process. These hired guns have taken spontaneity away from public discourse, scripting responses for candidates after analyzing the effect of their words on focus groups or through polling. As Joe Klein, a columnist for *Time* magazine, noted in his book, *Politics Lost*, television made politicians into performers and with "every last word or handshake a potentially career-threatening experience, they sought creative help to navigate the waters. And so the pollster–consultant industrial complex was born."[70]

Most consultants are innately cautious and afraid their patrons will say things before reaction to their words can be gauged. But in trying to have their candidates deliver messages that will appeal to the most voters and alienate the fewest, they manage to craft pronouncements that are instant pabulum, often devoid of real meaning. They also choose special venues for their candidates to spout their wisdom and may pick audiences who they know will respond positively. Unfortunately, the performances do not end when politicians are elected. The glare of the media requires permanent campaign mode for officeholders, with polling before policy decisions and focus groups before speeches. The president's itinerary for the various policy statements he makes is purposeful: perhaps some words about health care before a group of seniors at an assisted living residence, or before workers at a manufacturing plant to push a bill about American products, or on an aircraft carrier before a naval audience to speak about military strength.

## Religion and Politics

Because of their importance to the Republican Party in mobilizing voters, the views of organized zealots are heard and acted upon and thus gain inordinate power. Over the last two decades, conservative religious groups have been outspoken in pressuring Republicans to be more resolute about issues of importance to them. They threatened to sit out the 2006 election unless the party showed more resistance to same-sex marriage, obscenity, and abortion.[71] In response, Congress debated an amendment sponsored by conservative Republicans to ban same-sex marriage. President Bush also vetoed a bill supporting embryonic stem cell research that had passed both houses of Congress by a wide margin, with polls showing a majority of Americans in favor.[72]

In his book, *American Theocracy,* Kevin Phillips expounded on how religious elements gained control of the Republican Party, and how their beliefs drive the nation's policy. He noted in 2006 "the last two presidential elections mark the transformation of the GOP into the first religious party in US history."[73] Phillips is convinced that evangelicals' literal interpretation of the Bible has had a detrimental impact on the teaching and acceptance of modern knowledge and science in America.

The Republican coalition's clash with science has seeded a half-dozen controversies. These include Bible-based disbelief in Darwinian theories of evolution, dismissal of global warming, disagreement with geological explanations of fossil-fuel depletion, religious rejection of global population planning, derogation of women's rights, opposition to stem-cell research, and so on.[74]

Whether or not Phillips's suppositions are entirely valid, there is little question of the prevailing influence of conservative Christians on the Republican Party and their effect on government actions. It has been estimated that 42 percent of Republicans are white evangelical Protestants versus 26 percent of the general population.[75]

## Pandering

Pandering to their base or particular interest groups is another common practice of the two parties that offends the centrist electorate and delays action on crucial issues. A prominent example of pandering and political posturing was the struggle over Terri Schiavo. Under a Republican initiative, the federal government inserted itself into the debate on life support of this unfortunate brain-damaged woman in Florida. After a prolonged period in a persistent vegetative state, Schiavo's feeding tube was withdrawn at the request of her husband, in accordance with her wishes. The feeding tube was removed on March 18, 2005, during a Congressional recess. Senator Bill Frist, the majority leader and a cardiac surgeon, made statements after seeing a videotape that Schiavo was "clearly responsive" though neurologists who had examined her had testified to her persistent vegetative state. On Saturday, March 19, the Senate and House of Representatives were called back into emergency session by the Republican leadership to enact legislation siding with Schiavo's parents against removal of the feeding tube. Congress passed the bill, meaningless from a legal standpoint, the following day, and President Bush flew back to Washington from his ranch in Crawford, Texas to sign it early on Monday morning, March 21.[76] All of this was a huge waste of time and money, but the effort was hailed by Christian conservatives, winning significant political points. Subsequently, a temporary restraining order to stay the removal of the feeding tube requested by her parents was denied at multiple levels of the court system, all the way to the Supreme Court. Terri Schiavo died on March 31. It is instructive to remember how difficult it is to get any legislation approved in Washington, with the House and Senate passing separate bills after much debate, then a committee to reconcile the two bills, then the votes again. Important legislation may sit there for months, or sometimes never get passed, yet this bill covering a single person was debated, passed, and signed in two days.

Pandering to the electorate as a whole is another strategy, offering citizens band-aids to cover major wounds in an attempt to assuage them over inflammatory issues. Sometimes this can backfire. When Americans were livid about gasoline prices that spiked to over $3 a gallon in April and May of 2006, the Republicans, led by Senator Frist, recommended a $100 rebate to taxpayers to help them pay for gas. The Democrats suggested a reduction of the gasoline tax for sixty days to temporarily lower prices. Both of these proposals were quickly withdrawn under scathing criticism from private citizens and the media. They were short-term solutions that did not address the underlying problem, meant simply to placate voters and make it seem as if action was being taken. Formulating and passing a comprehensive energy policy was never advanced.

## Incompetence and Ineffectiveness

The limited choices of candidates for various offices can sometimes saddle citizens with ineffectual or incompetent officeholders, with major consequences for a district or the country. Jimmy Carter was considered an ineffectual president by many observers, in spite of the fact that he was intelligent and a "nice guy." Yet he was unable to end the Iran hostage crisis, tame galloping inflation, or control skyrocketing oil prices. Herbert Hoover was another intelligent man who seemed to have all the right qualities for president, but was ineffectual when faced with the overwhelming problems of the Great Depression. Historians have described other presidents and many senators and congressmen as ineffectual or incompetent.

President Bush is one of those labeled incompetent in his handling of several vital matters. Some of his difficulties can be traced to his advisers and his choices for cabinet and sub-cabinet posts. Of course, he was responsible for the people he appointed and in many instances kept them in place even after their inadequacies were obvious to others. The most blatant blots on his presidency were the misreading and slanting of the intelligence on Iraq, the conduct of the Iraq war, and the response to Hurricane Katrina. Whether or not one agrees with the rationale for the war, and even though the initial battles and capture of Baghdad went fairly smoothly, the aftermath was totally bungled until the surge in 2007. Other major blunders: the reluctance to initially commit enough troops in Afghanistan and the disaffection of US allies because of American arrogance and policies.

Also under President Bush, the Minerals Management Service (MMS) of the Department of the Interior, which handles oil leases, extraction, and collecting royalties, was known to have a history of corruption and to be in bed with the oil industry. Members of the service received sexual favors, drugs, and gifts from the industry to "go easy" in inspections and in enforcing regulations. Although the Obama administration and the Secretary of the Interior, Ken Salazar, were aware of this background when they took office, they did little to reform the agency until the oil rig debacle in the Gulf of Mexico in April 2010.[77] Their inertia in overhauling the MMS may have played a role in the blowout, since it became apparent afterward that BP had bypassed stringent safety measures prior to the explosion.[78] Not only did the Obama administration fail to rehabilitate the MMS, but the congressional committees responsible for oversight were also lax. According to the Center for Responsive Politics, committee members were recipients of outsized campaign contributions from the oil industry.[79] This may have made them reluctant to pursue the relationship between the MMS and the industry it was supposed to supervise.

In addition to MMS's failure to prevent the oil rig blowout, the Obama administration's response to the environmental calamity in the Gulf was inadequate. The government itself did not have the equipment or expertise to cap the leaking well a mile below the water, but it could have done a better job mobilizing people for the cleanup and trying to keep the oil from reaching land. Their reaction and decision making with the numerous government agencies involved was described as "slow, conflicted, and confused."[80] The administration's public relations effort in dealing with this unanticipated event was also inept. The final chapter in this episode will not be written until the government extracts the costs for all the damage from BP and makes sure that the people whose lives have been affected are sufficiently compensated.

## Cronyism

The rescue, relief efforts, and rebuilding after Hurricane Katrina demonstrate how the combinations of incompetence and cronyism can lead to disastrous outcomes. President Bush's appointment of a politically connected individual, Michael Brown, to run the Federal Emergency Management Agency (FEMA) along with other unqualified officials was a disaster waiting to happen, and Katrina provided the proper elements.[81] Before heading FEMA Brown had been chief of an Arabian horse association, with no expertise in disaster relief or running a large agency. In truth, the entire chain of command through Brown, Michael Chertoff as Secretary of Homeland Security, and President Bush must share responsibility for the inefficient, inadequate, and sometimes callous response to the storm, the breaching of the levees, and the destruction of a major American city. Afterward, everyone involved pointed to other officials as responsible for the fiasco and minimized their own contributions.[82]

Alberto Gonzales's role within the Bush administration is another illustration of how cronyism in concert with incompetence and arrogance can lead to problems. Gonzales had worked for Bush when Bush was governor of Texas and followed him to Washington, where Bush appointed him counsel to the president. As counsel, he advised the president that various initiatives were legal, including the secret surveillance of Americans without approval of the FISA court (in violation of the law), in addition to the incarceration, torture, and harsh interrogation of suspected terrorists. Gonzales argued that presidential powers allowed Bush to take these actions without judicial or congressional approval, though the Supreme Court subsequently disagreed.

In spite of Gonzales's questionable performance as presidential counsel, Bush appointed him Attorney General after John Ashcroft stepped down. Gonzales's tenure at the Department of Justice was disastrous, with disgruntled personnel, low morale, and the dismissal of a group of federal prosecutors for political reasons. Prior to their firings, the regional federal attorneys who were removed had received good ratings from their superiors at the Department, but apparently had not been partisan enough for Gonzales. Either they had not indicted Democratic officeholders before the 2006 elections, as requested by other Republicans, or they had pursued Republican corruption too vigorously.

Several of Gonzales's staff members admitted before Congressional committees that the firings had been political in nature, saying that Gonzales had been in the loop and was aware of the actions, contradicting his statements.[83] In an appearance before the House Judiciary Committee a former deputy attorney general, James Comey, described the federal attorneys who had been dismissed as "highly competent prosecutors."[84] In his own testimony, Gonzales insisted that the firings had been merited, yet said he was uncertain why the attorneys had been ousted. When asked pointed questions about the actions he was unable to recall any of the specifics. Other discrepancies in his testimony revolved around the warrantless domestic surveillance program, with the director of the FBI making statements that conflicted with what Gonzales had said.[85] Afterward, Bush reaffirmed his confidence in Gonzales, in spite of calls for Gonzales's resignation not only by Democrats across the board but many Republicans as well. Finally, after months of resistance, Gonzales stepped down at the end of August 2007, receiving further praise from President Bush.

Appointment of cronies and politically connected individuals without experience or qualifications to government agencies is common in most administrations, but was particularly blatant under Bush. No-bid contracts went to friends and firms with political links for the cleanup and rebuilding after Katrina,[86] for Iraq, and various other situations. Relationships and ideological *bona fides* appear to have been more valuable in obtaining jobs than professionalism, experience, knowledge, and administrative skills. The Bush administration also saw fit to appoint people to environmentally sensitive posts who were formerly lobbyists or advocates for business or mining interests, in direct conflict with the agencies they had to supervise. Some of them rolled back regulations on clean air and water, or reduced restrictions on pollutants, toxic chemicals, carbon dioxide, and sulfur emissions, benefiting corporate interests. President Obama's inner circle also contains long-time friends and associates, but professionals from outside his group are important parts of his team. In addition, he appears more open to receiving conflicting information on the issues before making decisions. The cronies he has chosen so far do not appear to be incompetent, though that can be assessed more fully after his term in office is over.

## Lack of Transparency

The lack of transparency in important deliberations that affect citizen's lives has fueled public dissatisfaction and anger. All three branches of the government are guilty of working behind closed doors, but the executive branch and its agencies are particularly prone to function in this fashion in both Democratic and Republican administrations. Though it may be easier to debate policy in this manner, it does antagonize segments of the population and lead to conspiracy theories. Of course, on national security issues, it is a given that secrecy may be required.

Vice President Dick Cheney's development of an energy policy in 2001 generated intense controversy when he purportedly used advisers from the energy industry without significant input from consumers and conservationists. The deliberations were secret and then protected afterward by invocation of executive privilege when press and public sought information under the Freedom of Information Act. This emphasis on secrecy was characteristic of the Bush White House, which formulated policy, then limited the release of information to the public. Bruce Montgomery, who has written extensively about this problem, observed in an article in *Political Science Quarterly*:

The Bush–Cheney White House moved with more alacrity than had perhaps any administration since World War II to orchestrate an even greater concentration of executive power in the White House and to expand the mantle of secrecy surrounding executive branch actions. . . . The Bush administration's instinct has been to disclose as little as possible and search for opportunities with which to reverse legislative oversight.[87]

Career civil servants who gave data to Congress or the news media that the Bush White House wanted to conceal were chastised and threatened with severe punishment or loss of jobs. When Congress was debating the Medicare drug bill, Bush officials provided projections of how much these benefits would cost. The estimates given were purposely low to try to convince conservative Republicans to support the bill. When an actuary from Medicare released the true projections, which were hundreds of billions of dollars more, his superior threatened him with firing for releasing unauthorized information. Other whistle-blowers were disciplined, as well as scientists who did not adhere to the party line. In the Bush administration, "politics often trumped science,"[88] with a need for all members of the team to stay on message.

Though President Obama promised on the campaign trail and after he was elected that transparency would be a hallmark of his administration, his record on this issue has been mixed. The *Columbia Journalism Review* rated some of the Obama initiatives regarding transparency in January 2010[89] with grades from A-minus to F. Regarding a number of these policies, Obama hewed closely to the stands taken by the Bush administration. In addition, the negotiations over health care reform were done out of the public eye, conflicting with Obama's promise to make all the transactions and bargaining available on C-SPAN so that the reform process would be out in the open.[90] Also contrary to Obama's pledges about transparency were his behind-the-scene attempts to manipulate the primary process to get preferred senatorial candidates on the ballot in Pennsylvania and Colorado in 2010, secretly offering jobs to the insurgent challengers.[91]

Transparency has also been missing from various congressional deliberations and actions, with earmarks inserted into bills favoring special interests and agreements on legislation often hammered out behind closed doors. One of the more questionable maneuvers is the "Senate hold" that allows any senator to block legislation or nominations anonymously for an indefinite period, unless overruled by a 60-vote majority.[92] This allows senators to delay or kill bills or prevent nominations in secret, without having to justify the action to colleagues or the public, and can be done for reasons of partisanship or simple payback. The secret Senate hold is a tradition that dates back to the 1950s and gives inordinate power to individual senators to obstruct the process of government.

## Politics and the Media

Elements in the media have reinforced the ideological divide between the two parties and made it more difficult for them to compromise. In the past, newspapers and magazines often took partisan positions and were supportive of a specific party, as is true today. But with radio and television reaching a much greater audience, news programs and political shows have become an effective means of propagating ideology. People expect the news to be reported in an unbiased way, and if it is slanted, or if pushes a covert agenda, it undermines the democratic process. Rupert Murdoch's Fox News under Roger Ailes has a motto of "Fair and Balanced," but there is little question that it firmly embraces conservative Republican views. It is also hard to separate what is really news on this network and what is opinion, with commentators like Glenn Beck, Bill O'Reilly, and Sean Hannity constantly spewing venom about Obama and the Democrats. Fox's hiring of Sarah Palin and Mike Huckabee as pundits also says something about its orientation. On the other hand, MSNBC, with commentators like Rachael Maddow and Chris Matthews, tilts considerably to the left. NBC itself, ABC, and CNN appear to be fairly neutral from a political standpoint, while CBS appears to be to the left of center, although this assessment of neutrality is not universally accepted. The *New York Times* and *Washington Post* generally espouse liberal positions, while the *Wall Street Journal* is staunchly conservative in its editorials.

Talk radio shows are mostly forums for diehard conservatives, though a few exist with a liberal outlook. The huge listener base and combative attitude of talk radio hosts make politicians reluctant to cross them or moderate positions on any issue. Rumor and innuendo are often presented as fact and used to attack whomever the host disagrees with. There is no oversight of these programs and no one to rebut the assertions made, which are protected as free speech. Figures like Rush Limbaugh, Martin Savidge, and others with attentive audiences repeatedly mock Obama, the Democrats, and liberal positions, unwilling to consider that anything they are doing might be beneficial for the country. Coming from the far right, the words "compromise" and "pragmatism" are not in the talk radio hosts' lexicons, though "socialist," "communist," and "fascist" certainly are. The questions about Obama not being born in America and being Muslim have also been promulgated on these shows.

Political comedy shows on television tend to have more of a liberal slant, though they skewer politicians on both sides of the aisle. Liberal bloggers are more prevalent on the Internet than conservatives, with little restraint on either side over their commentaries. More and more, younger people have been relying on the Internet for news and information, increasing its political importance. Unfortunately, much of what is disseminated is not vetted and it is not clear to most readers what is fact and what is opinion.

With hard-core partisans of both parties in Congress consistently energized and their positions supported by ideological opinion-makers in the media, it becomes nearly impossible for Republicans and Democrats to come together and find ways to advance the country's interests. With almost religious undertones, both sides believe their worldviews are right and those of the opposition border on evil. How do you make agreements with the devil or his surrogates?

# The Financial Meltdown

The recent recession and the nation's subsequent economic plight provide additional confirmation of the inability of the two political parties to craft solutions to America's pressing problems. Though Wall Street's speculative excesses and the mortgage debacle may have directly caused the financial meltdown, proper oversight by government agencies and regulatory legislation by Congress could have prevented the collapse from occurring. In fact, many analysts believe that congressional actions, such as the repeal of the Glass-Steagall Act in 1999 at the urging of financial industry lobbyists, were to a large degree responsible for the economic tsunami and its aftermath. Deregulation by Congress and oversight bodies allowed banks and financial firms to take excessive risks in search of profits, requiring the American taxpayer to rescue them when the market imploded. The constraints of moral hazard were essentially eliminated. There was socialization of risks and losses by these firms—bailouts by the government if things went wrong, along with privatization of profits—gains accruing to executives and stockholders while risks were assumed by the government. The structure of compensation for financial company executives also favored risk-taking, with short-term profits leading to large bonuses and long-term risks disregarded.

Both Republicans and Democrats were complicit in allowing the financial industry to run amuck, the politicians harvesting huge sums from these companies and their executives to fund election campaigns and PACs while ignoring the potential damage to the American economy. After the collapse, the anger at Wall Street reached epic proportions, provoking a crescendo of calls for reform. However, the Dodd-Franks bill that was finally passed by Congress left many of Wall Street's egregious practices unchanged, though it did address some issues like risky derivatives trading, proprietary trading by the banks, and unfair consumer practices.

There is little question that in addition to excessive risks, blatant fraudulent activities played a significant role in the meltdown, particularly in the origination of mortgages, their securitization and sale, and their ratings. Yet aside from some civil fines, none of the major figures who benefited from these operations have gone to jail. Instead, they have walked away with tens or hundreds of millions of dollars. And they continue their contributions to the politicians to keep the Justice Department from their doors and their tax burdens lowered.

When looking at the aftermath of the financial crisis in 2011, it is evident that Wall Street is virtually back to normal, with outsized salaries and big bonuses as the usual way of doing business. But Main Street continues to struggle, with unemployment near double digits, retirement accounts depleted, young people's careers on hold, and the economy just limping along. Yet the two political parties can't seem to find ways to right the floundering economic ship, with each accusing the other of nefarious behavior and an unwillingness to act for the good of the country. Scoring political points is more important to them than negotiating solutions. (There is further discussion of the economy in Chapter 4, America's Domestic Challenges.)

## The Need for a Third Party

The two-party structure of American democracy is not a child of the Constitution that must be honored. It is clear that the political system of two adversarial parties that has evolved since the nation's birth is not working. Though some identify big government as responsible for the nation's problems, it is not actually the size of government but the current political parties that make governing impossible. Evidence for this is reinforced by the continuing inability of these parties to pass critical legislation such as realistic health care reform, Social Security overhaul, immigration reform, an energy policy, comprehensive ethics measures, the reining in of the national debt, and on and on. Since the present system is ineffectual, change must occur if America is to remain strong and vibrant and able to deal with the many challenges it faces. A permanent third party of the center, open-minded and pragmatic, not in thrall to the lobbyists or special interests, could spearhead the passage of the necessary reform measures, revitalizing the nation to compete effectively in the world of the twenty-first century.

An article in the *Atlantic Monthly* in March 2006 proclaimed:

> Republicans and Democrats are at rough parity, each commanding about a third of the country, each captive of a partisan base that is well to the electorate's right or left. Neither party can govern except in coalition with independent voters, most of them moderates and many of them dismayed.[93]

As noted, recent polls have shown dissatisfaction with both Republicans and Democrats, as well as with Congress and the executive branches of government. Though independents and moderates are unhappy with America's political system, they do not see a viable alternative to the two parties. The political scientist Lisa Jane Disch queried why, in a country that is passionate about free markets, do voters accept that two political choices provide them with "the ultimate in political freedom . . . they would surely protest as consumers?"[94] Why should citizens have just two options, forcing them to choose candidates from parties that don't represent them? Whether the Tea Party remains a faction within the Republican Party, gains control of it, or eventually forms an actual working political party makes no difference, as it provides no additional non-ideological choice for voters.

The constant ethical transgressions by politicians that are disregarded by America's parties are of comparable importance to the ideological divide between them. Aside from a few mavericks, both Republicans and Democrats are cut from the same corrupt cloth, unwilling to embrace true campaign finance reform or do what is necessary to constrain the lobbyists and special interests. They laugh at the idea that politicians should be held to high ethical standards, serve the people who voted for them, and consider the needs of the country. Even if sweeping legislation is enacted to assuage the public, the two parties will find ways to evade the laws they have written, for in their hearts they do not care about reform. They are interested only in winning elections and holding onto power. The vast majority of America's citizens regard political parties as so sullied that it is impossible now for the parties to shed their aura of corruption no matter what steps they take. To paraphrase what Ronald Reagan once said about government, the parties are the problem, not the solution.

Clean, competent government in America will not emerge while the established parties have unchallenged power. The best chance for transformation of the system lies with a new and permanent third party whose members are devoted to ethical change, who believe that uncoupling the politicians from the lobbyists and special interests is necessary to rescue the nation. This party must be centrist and pragmatic and not shackled to the philosophy of the right or left, a party willing to examine solutions to America's problems through an unbiased lens. Common sense will be its guiding principle. This party will aggressively try to attract young people, convincing them to participate in the nitty-gritty of politics, that their votes will count, and that they can make a difference. This party can set the standard for ethics and honesty in government.

Past generations were willing to sacrifice to ensure a more secure future for their children and grandchildren. Today's politicians don't ask citizens to make any sacrifices for the future; politicians are afraid to tell them the truth about the nation's problems not only because they don't trust their constituents to deal with adversity and make the right choices but also are afraid that their constituents might vote them out, and so sugarcoat everything for them. America needs new kinds of leaders who will be open and straightforward with the public, willing to treat citizens as partners in the governing process. Unfortunately, the political system has discouraged idealistic, ethical people from participating, leaving the field open to men and women who are egocentric and power-hungry.

An in-depth study in July 2007 of political independents conducted by the *Washington Post*, Harvard University, and the Henry J. Kaiser Family Foundation showed that independents are the fastest-growing segment of American voters.[95] Thirty to forty percent of adults described themselves in this category. Sixty percent noted that the two-party system was not addressing the issues of greatest importance to them. Seventy-seven percent declared they would "seriously consider an independent presidential candidate"[96] in the 2008 election if one ran.

Given Americans' disenchantment with the established parties, the time is ripe for the birth of a third party with broad, moderate appeal, providing a realistic option to dispirited citizens. This party's message of purity and transparency will resonate with American voters and will gain momentum as people understand that clean, responsive government is actually feasible. With the use of the Internet, social networks, and modern communications technology, word can spread quickly of this new entity dedicated to the transformation of American politics. An army of advocates can be recruited. With the proper Internet campaign, money can be raised to support this party without depending on lobbyists and special interests. Commitment, participation, and sacrifice will be necessary for those who want to change the system, but it can be done. The planets are in alignment and a third political party of the center can be successful in resurrecting American democracy.

## References

[1] Thomas Paine, *Common Sense*, Penguin Classics, New York, NY, 1986.

[2] NBC–Wall Street Journal Poll, November 11–15, 2010, http://onlineWSJ.com/public/resources/documents/WSJpoll111710.pdf.

[3] John F. Bibby and L. Sandy Maisel, "Two Parties or More?" Westview Press, Boulder, CO, 2nd ed., 2003, 57.

[4] Rasmussen Reports, November 19 and 24, 2010, www.rasmussenreports.com/public_conetnt/politics/mood_of_America/america_s_best_days.

[5] Alexander Hamilton, *The Federalist Papers*, No. 1, New American Library, New York, NY, 1961 (originally published in 1787–1788), 34.

[6] James Madison, *The Federalist Papers*, No. 10, New American Library, New York, NY, 1961, 79.

[7] Marjorie Randon Hershey, *Party Politics in America*, PearsonLongman, New York, NY, 2005, 137.

[8] "2008 Voter Turnout," FactCheck.org, January 8, 2009, www.factcheck.org/2009/01/2008-voter-turnout/

[9] Hershey, 148.

[10] Factcheck.org.

[11] Hershey, 137.

[12] Factcheck.org.

[13] Demetrios James Caraley, "Complications of American Democracy: Elections Are Not Enough," *Political Science Quarterly*, Vol. 120, No. 3, 2005, 400.

[14] "Re-election Rates Over the Years," OpenSecrets.org, Center for Responsive Politics, www.opensecrets.org/bigpicture/re-elect.php, downloaded June 4, 2010.

[15] Thomas Friedman, "Thou Shalt Not Destroy the Center," Op-Ed, *New York Times*, November 11, 2005.

[16] "Statement of the OCE Regarding Evidence Collected in OCE's PMA Investigation," May 27, 2010, http://oce.house.gov/

[17] Michael Mcauliff, "Scandal-plagued Rep. Charles Rangel struggles in latest fund-raising period," NYDailyNews.com, April 15, 2010, www.nydailynews.com/news/politics/2010/04/16/2010-4-16_cash_woes_for_Rangel.html.

[18] Associated Press, "Ex-Congressmen gets 13 years in freezer cash case," USAToday.com, November 13, 2009, USAToday.com/news/nation/2009-11-13-jefferson-bribe-sentence_n.htm.

[19] Eric Lipton, "20 in Black Caucus Ask For Curbs on Ethics Office," *New York Times*, June 2, 2010, A17.

[20] "Prospects for Ethics Reform in the 110th Congress," Source Watch, July 12, 2007, www.sourcewatch.org/index.php?title=Prospects_for_Ethics_Reform_in_the_110th_Congress.

[21] "Presidential Campaign Finance," 2008, Federal Election Commission, www.fec.gov/disclosureSearch/mapApp. downloaded June 4, 2010.

[22] Thomas B. Edsall, Sara Cohen, and James V. Grimaldi, "Pioneers Fill War Chest, Then Capitalize," *Washington Post,* May 16, 2004, A01.

[23] Eduardo Porter, "The Cost of a Vote Goes Up," *New York Times*, Week in Review, November 7, 2010, 7.

[24] Paul Krugman, "The K Street Prescription," *New York Times*, OpEd, January 20, 2006, A17.

[25] "John Ashcroft," http://en.wikipedia.org/wiki/John_Ashcroft, downloaded May 20, 2010.

[26] Elizabeth Brown, "Lobbying FAQ: What is Permissible? Out of Bounds? Punishable?" The Center for Public Integrity, January 18, 2006, http://publicintegrity.org/lobby/report.aspx?aid=775.

[27] Aron Pilhofer, "Revolving Doors Spin Open Once Again," *New York Times*, November 12, 2006.

[28] Hubert B. Herring, "Lobbying Scandals? They Can't Slow This Juggernaut," *New York Times*, August 6, 2006, Business, 2.

[29] "Campaign contributions of selected industries," OpenSecrets.org, Center for Responsive Politics, www.opensecrets.org/pres08/select.asp?Ind=B12, downloaded June 3, 2010.

[30] "Lobbying Spending Database," OpenSecrets.org, Center for Responsive Politics, April 25, 2010, www.opensecrets.org/lobby/top.php?showYear=2009&indexType=i.

[31] Larry J. Sabato and Bruce Larson, *The Party's Just Begun*, Longman Press, New York, NY, 2002, 85.

[32] Ibid.

[33] Michael Luo and Stephanie Strom, "Donor Names Remain Secret as Rules Shift," *New York Times*, September 20, 2010, A1.

[34] David Johnston, "FBI's Focus on Public Corruption Includes 2000 Investigations," *New York Times*, May 11, 2006, A32.

[35] George Childs Kohn, "House Overdraft Scandal," *The New Encyclopedia of American Scandal, Facts on File*, New York, 2001, 189.

[36] Ibid., "Charles Keating," 217.

[37] David M. Herszenhorn, "Republicans Offer Their Agenda for Midterm Elections," *New York Times*, September 23, 2010, A17.

[38] Catherine Dodge and Brian Faier, "House Republicans Aim to Cut Funds for EPA, Energy," Bloomberg Businessweek, February 10, 2011, http://www.businessweek.com/news/2011-02-10/house-republicans-aim-to-cut-funds-for-epa-energy.html.

[39] David Leonhardt, "O.K., You Fix The Budget," *New York Times*, Week In Review, November 14, 2010, 1.

[40] Sabato and Larson, 48.

[41] Michael A. Memoli, "Mitch McConnell's remarks on 2012 draw White House ire," *Los Angeles Times*, October 27, 2010 http://articles.latimes.com/print/2010/oct27/news/las-pn-obama-mcconell-20101027.

[42] Charles Babington, "Anxious, feuding House Democrats keep Nancy Pelosi as their leader despite big election losses," chicagotribune.com, Associated Press, November 17, 2010. www.chicgotribune.com/news/politics/sns-ap-us-democrats-disarray,0,1313579.story.

[43] Sabato and Larson, 78.

[44] James Madison, *The Federalist Papers*, No. 37, New American Library, New York, NY, 1961, 224.

[45] Peter Trubowitz and Nicole Mellow, "Going Bipartisan: Politics by Other Means," *Political Science Quarterly*, Vol. 120, No. 3, 2005, 435.

[46] Bibby and Maisel, 122.

[47] Bibby and Maisel, 39.

[48] Chris Cilizza, "Specter To Switch Parties," The Fix, Washingtonpost.com, April 28, 2009, http://voices.washingtonpost.com/the_fix/senate/Specter-to-swicth-parties.html.

[49] Caraley, 399.

[50] James Madison, *The Federalist Papers*, No. 62, New American Library, New York, NY, 1961, 381.

[51] Ludwig von Mises Institute, "What is Austrian Economics?" http://mises.org/etexts/austrian.asp.

[52] James Bennet, "Not Angry Enough," Editor's Note, *The Atlantic*, January/February 2011, 10.

[53] Adam Nagourney, "McCain Emphasizing His Conservative Bona Fides," *New York Times*, April 9, 2006, 33.

[54] Stephen Labaton, "Safety Chief Is Opposing More Money," *New York Times*, October 30, 2007, C1.

[55] Stuart Taylor, Jr, "The Man Who Would Be King," *The Atlantic*, April 2006, 25.

[56] Scott Shane, "Behind Power, One Principle as Bush Pushes Prerogatives," *New York Times*, December 17, 2005, A1.

[57] Ibid.

58 Sheryl Gay Stolberg, "Republican Speaks Up, Leading Others to Challenge Wiretaps," *New York Times*, February 11, 2006, A1.

59 Shane.

60 Adam Liptak, "The Court Enters the War, Loudly," *New York Times*, July 2, 2006, Week in Review, 1.

61 David E. Sanger, "Congress and Courts Try to Restore Balance," *New York Times*, July 14, 2006, A15.

62 Editorial, *New York Times*, September 15, 2006, A24.

63 Kate Zernike, "Lawyers and G.O.P. Chiefs Resist Tribunal Plan," *New York Times*, September 8, 2006, A1.

64 Jim Ruttenberg and Sheryl Gay Stolberg, "Bush Says G.O.P. Rebels Are Putting Nation At Risk," *New York Times*, September 16, 2006, A12.

65 Jack Goldsmith, *The Terror Presidency*, W.W. Norton and Company, New York, NY, 2007.

66 Robert Pear, "Legal Group Faults Bush for Ignoring Parts of Bills," *New York Times*, July 24, 2006, A12.

67 Rob Warmowski, "President Obama's Clear Abuse Of Power Cited By...President Obama," The Huffington Post, June 27, 2009, www.huffingtonpost.com/rob-warmowski/president-obamas-clear-ab_b_221836.html.

68 Quoted by Darrell M. West, L. Sandy Maisel, and Brett M. Clinton, in "The Impact of Campaign Reform on Political Discourse," *Political Science Quarterly*, Vol. 120, No. 4, 2005–2006, 637.

69 "The Secret Election," editorial, *New York Times,* Week in Review, September 18, 2010, 8.

70 Joe Klein, *Politics Lost: How American Democracy Was Trivialized By People Who Think You're Stupid,* Doubleday, 2006; excerpt in *Time* magazine, April 17, 2006, 64.

71 David D. Kirkpatrick, "Conservative Christians Criticize Republicans," *New York Times*, May 15, 2006, A1.

72 Sheryl Gay Stolberg, "First Bush Veto Maintains Limits on Stem Cell Research," *New York Times*, July 20, 2006, A1.

73 Kevin Phillips, *American Theocracy*, Viking Press, New York, NY, 2006, vii.

74 Ibid., xiv.

75 Daniel Yankelovich, "Poll Positions," *Foreign Affairs*, September/October 2005, 8.

76 George J. Annas, "Culture of Life Politics at the Bedside—The Case of Terri Schiavo," *Legal Issues in Medicine, New England Journal of Medicine*, 2005, 352;16:1710.

77 John M. Broder and Michael Luo, "Reforms Slow to Arrive at Drilling Agency," *New York Times*, May 30, 2010, www.nytimes.com/2010/05/31/us/politics/31drill.html?sq=mineral management serv...

78 Ian Urbina, "In Gulf, It Was Unclear Who Was in Charge of Oil Rig," *New York Times*, June 6, 2010, A1.

79 Broder and Luo.

80 Urbina.

81 "Cronies at the Till," editorial, *New York Times*, September 27, 2005, A24.

[82] Adam Nagourney and Anne E. Kornblut," White House Enacts a Plan to Ease Political Damage," *New York Times*, September 5, 2005, A14.

[83] David Johnston and Eric Lipton, "Ex-Aide Rejects Gonzales Stand Over Dismissals," *New York Times*, March 30, 2007, A1.

[84] David Johnston, "Ex-Justice Dept. Official Defends Ousted U.S. Attorneys," *New York Times*, May 4, 2007, A18.

[85] David Johnston and Scott Shane, "F.B.I. Chief Gives Account at Odds With Gonzales's," *New York Times*, July 27, 2007, A1.

[86] Philip Shenon and Anne E. Kornblut, "Democrats Say Relief Effort Needs Independent Inquiry," *New York Times,* September 21, 2005, A15.

[87] Bruce P. Montgomery, "Congressional Oversight: Vice President Richard B. Cheney's Executive Branch Triumph," *Political Science Quarterly*, Vol. 120, No. 4, 2005–2006, 616–617.

[88] Ibid.

[89] Clint Hendler, "Report Card, Obama's Marks at Transparency U," *Columbia Journalism Review*, January 5, 2010, www.cjr.org/transparency/report_card.php?page=all&print=true.

[90] Chip Reid, "Obama Reneges on Health Care Transparency," CBS News, Washington, January 6, 2010, www.cbsnews.com/stories/2010/01/06/eveningnewa/main6064298.shtml.

[91] Peter Baker, "White House Role in Primaries Spurs Sharp Debate," *New York Times*, June 4, 2010, A13.

[92] Carl Hulse, "Senate May End An Era of Cloakroom Anonymity," *New York Times*, August 2, 2007, A13.

[93] Jonathan Rauch, "Demolition Man," *The Atlantic*, March 2006, 29.

[94] Lisa Jane Disch, *The Tyranny of the Two Party System*, Columbia University Press, New York, NY, 2002, 7.

[95] Dan Balz and Jon Cohen, "A Political Force With Many Philosophies," Washingtonpost.com, July 1, 2007, A01.

[96] Ibid.

CHAPTER 2

# Thoughts on Political Parties
## A Brief Recent History of America's Parties

It is a misfortune incident to republican government,
though in a less degree than to other governments,
that those who administer it may forget their obligations
to their constituents
and prove unfaithful to their important trust.
—James Madison, *The Federalist Papers*[1]

America's Founding Fathers were men of the enlightenment, men of reason who were willing to compromise to midwife the birth of a new nation. In writing the Constitution, the document that gave coherence to that nation, they were able to bridge great differences between North and South, urban and rural, and differences in vision about what America should become. There is no mention of political parties in the Constitution and as Jethro Lieberman notes in *The Evolving Constitution*, the "two-party system . . . came about largely independent of the law."[2] America's early leaders did not view political parties in a positive light and were not sure what role they would play in the new government. In fact, some of them were quite hostile to the concept of parties, which they saw in a somewhat naïve way as causing conflict and dissension rather than merely reflecting the differences already present among men. George Washington in his Farewell Address noted, "Let me warn you in the most solemn manner against the baneful effects of the spirit of party."[3] Yet the organization of people coalescing around particular ideas and supporting like-minded candidates for elective office suggests the usefulness of political parties in a democracy in avoiding chaos. Indeed, soon after the first federal government was in place, with

Washington as president and Congress assembled, nascent parties were appearing. By the presidential election of 1796, there were two dominant parties locked in combat, and many of those individuals who had spoken out against political parties had played a major role in their formation.

## The Need For Political Parties

In every modern democracy, political parties are a fact of life and it would be impractical for governments to operate without them. Parties serve an administrative function, grouping individuals with similar beliefs to elect candidates for local, regional, and national offices who will promote their ideas. They also provide individuals the opportunity to run for office with an organization to back them, or to nominate others whom they support. The larger a society is, the more important parties become, since sheer numbers make it impossible for solitary voices to be heard. In a party, people can pro-pound their views at a local level and if there are enough adherents, the message filters through to a regional and perhaps a national level. If elected to power, the party can legislate those beliefs into law or act upon them in the executive sector of the government. Primaries run by the parties also allow the sorting out of candidates with similar beliefs so that one person will be chosen to carry the party's banner in the general election and the vote for that belief will not be divided. Parties are also agents of stability, channeling anger at perceived wrongs in a constructive fashion, allowing people to work within the system to bring about change. Where parties are banned or powerless, conflict and rebellion are more likely to occur as frustration in the population grows.

Some political scientists describe political parties as consist-ing of three formal parts. These consist of the party in the electorate in which affiliated voters and low-level activists reside; the party in government consisting of the party's elected officials; and the party as organization in which the party workers and volunteers raise money, educate and propagandize voters, develop policy proposals, and map strategy.[4] Through education and propaganda parties try to convince the general public about the validity of their beliefs so they will vote for the party's candidates. Party organizations also mobilize voters and get them to the polls. Because of their commitment, people are willing to register as party members to vote in the primaries, and that loyalty may grow over the years. People identify with their party and its positions, even on issues that don't directly affect them, and activists are willing to work and contribute money to get their candidates elected.

All legislative bodies are structured along party lines. Lawmakers of each party try to choose leaders who concur with their views and in turn receive appointments to legislative committees that increase their power. If an elected official is defeated for office or decides not to run, he or she may be given a position in the executive branch of government by other party officeholders or within the structure of the party itself. Party members may also be appointed to the judiciary or obtain patronage jobs within the legislative or executive sectors. Positions outside of government may also be available to them because of their party affiliation.

Notwithstanding the necessity of parties and the positive role they play, there are also unwelcome aspects inherent in them, as our Founding Fathers realized. Parties can institutionalize divisiveness that already exists and enhance discord within government, legislative bodies, and throughout entire nations. They promote ideologies that their members can rally around, which also bind them within philosophical straitjackets, compelling them to adopt narrower worldviews and be less open to competing ideas. Parties are almost secular religions for their adherents, with a code of beliefs, many of which must be accepted on faith, as well as a rationale for action and a coterie of priests and bishops.

## The Origins of the Two-Party System in America

Though America's mother country, Great Britain, had two parties during Colonial times, there was nothing that preordained a two-party system as the preferable mode for political engagement in the new nation. However, two parties developed rather quickly as American citizens gravitated to two opposing views of the federal government. The Federalists, who eventually morphed into the Republicans, believed that a powerful federal government was required to run the country with the individual states subservient to it. Alexander Hamilton and John Adams were its leading proponents, and George Washington was thought to favor this vision, though he never formally supported the party. Its main constituents were in the urban centers of the Northeast and the commercial interests, particularly merchants and manufacturers. The Republicans, later to become the Democrats, thought that the United States should have a weaker federal government, with greater power residing in the component states. Thomas Jefferson and James Madison were the intellectual forces behind this party, which got much of its backing from rural, agrarian interests, and was strongest in the South.

In considering the evolution of America's political parties, it should be remembered that the framers of the Constitution were not enamored with the idea of absolute democracy, where all the people had a say in how the country was run and voted for all officeholders. They viewed this as akin to mob rule that would only result in problems for this new nation. Instead, the states restricted the early franchise to property owners whose qualifications were delineated by their legislatures, which were given the power by the Constitution to decide on "The Times, Places and Manner of holding Elections for Senators and Representatives."[5] The senators from each state, however, were to be chosen by the state legislators themselves, and the president by electors from each state, equal to the number of senators and representatives together.

During the early part of the nineteenth century, ownership of property was dropped as a stipulation for voting in most states and suffrage was extended to all free men. In 1870, the Fifteenth Amendment guaranteed the right to vote to all men regardless of race or color. It was not until the Seventeenth Amendment to the Constitution was ratified in 1913 that senators were elected directly by the people (men). Universal suffrage giving women the vote did not occur until the Nineteenth Amendment was ratified in 1920. The president of course is still chosen by the Electoral College rather than the popular vote, leading to presidents who have gained office without the support of a majority or even a plurality of the voters. The structure of the Electoral College with its winner-take-all mechanism in each state has favored the two-party system, as smaller parties would have trouble winning the presidential vote in any individual state, making compiling a national majority almost impossible.[6] Third parties have appeared and disappeared with some regularity throughout American history, however, from the Know-Nothings to the Greenback Party to the Progressive Party. These entities often focused on a single issue and at times were able to elect a number of candidates to the Senate and House of Representatives.

## Political Parties in the '90s

One of the most impressive third-party forays in American history occurred in 1992 when Ross Perot, a Texas billionaire who had made his money in Electronic Data Systems, challenged George Bush and Bill Clinton for the presidency. He announced his candidacy on the CNN television program, *Larry King Live*, in February and volunteer supporters subsequently accumulated sufficient signatures to get him on the ballot in every state.[7] With a folksy, down-to-earth style and enough money to finance his campaign, he used infomercials with charts and graphs as well as regular advertising and television interviews to make points about the sorry state of the country, telling the electorate that the United States was in "deep voodoo."[8] Focusing on profligate spending by the federal government, the huge budget deficit, and the national debt, he forged ahead of Bush and Clinton in the opinion polls in June, after the primaries were over and before the party conventions. In time, however, questions about his personality and authoritarian tendencies made voters wonder whether he had the temperament to be president and his percentages in the polls began to drop.

Without warning, Perot withdrew his candidacy in mid-July, then re-entered the fray six weeks later, having lost vital time when he could have made his case to the electorate. The explanation for his withdrawal had elements of conspiracy theories and paranoia, and his campaign never regained the traction it once had. Naming his organization United We Stand America, Perot presented some interesting ideas on reducing the budget deficit, including a hike in the gasoline tax.[9] He also struck a populist chord against globalization and the loss of American jobs with his opposition to NAFTA (North American Free Trade Agreement), telling voters to "listen for the 'giant sucking sound' of American jobs heading south to Mexico should NAFTA be ratified."[10] Without a party organization to back him, Perot was nevertheless the choice on 18.9 percent of the ballots, garnering nearly 20 million votes on Election Day. This was the best showing for a candidate outside the major parties since Teddy Roosevelt on the Bull Moose ticket in 1912.[11]

Though Perot may not have been the most appealing candidate, there were a number of reasons that he generated so much support—among them the country's growing dissatisfaction with the way the federal government was being run and its unhappiness with the two major parties and their candidates. Perot's ability to finance his campaign independently kept his name and ideas constantly in front of the electorate. As Rosenstone, Behr, and Lazarus note in *Third Parties in America*, "What distinguishes Perot from his predecessors, foremost, and what explains much of his phenomenal showing in 1992, is money, and plenty of it."[12] The almost $73 million that Perot spent on his campaign allowed him to organize in every state and bought him television and radio time on the air. Additionally, he was able to attract significant support because he was allowed to participate in all of the presidential debates, being judged by the Commission on Presidential Debates to be a viable candidate. This revealed him to be at least comparable in seriousness to the major party nominees, and willing to take a stand against globalization and the loss of American jobs.

After 1992, Perot maintained the structure of United We Stand America, with chapters in every state, and continued to speak out against NAFTA and on the need to rein in the burgeoning national debt. In 1995, he organized the Reform Party as an alternative to the Republicans and Democrats, securing its nomination for president in 1996. In this attempt he did not tap his personal wealth.

Instead he received $29 million to fund his campaign from the federal government, due him on the basis of his performance in the previous election,[13] and accepted contributions from other people. Although he used the same approach to campaigning as he had in 1992, he was unable to produce the same enthusiasm and support. With his poll numbers in the mid-single digits, the Commission on Presidential Debates excluded Perot from this forum, believing that his chances of winning were extremely unlikely. On Election Day, he managed only 8.4 percent of the vote, a far cry from his earlier showing.[14] This meant, however, that the Reform Party could expect $12.6 million in federal funds for the 2000 election and a place on every state ballot.

Unfortunately, instead of building on the support acquired in the 1996 election, the Reform Party declined into insignificance. It was unable to erect a structure on local, congressional district, and statewide levels to offer credible candidates for the various elective offices, although Jesse Ventura did win the governorship of Minnesota on the Reform ticket in 1998. Part of the problem was the lack of a coherent vision that would attract a base of voters, with wide ideological differences among the party's supporters that led to divisiveness and infighting. Pat Buchanan, a conservative Republican who sought the Reform Party's presidential nomination in 2000, held views on social issues opposed by many party members. Another candidate, John Hagelin, was a previous Natural Law Party candidate with some ideas that were out of the mainstream. Conflict between supporters of the two candidates led to a split of the Reform convention into two separate assemblies that advanced both nominees, each of whom asserted he was the real candidate of the party and should get the federal funds. The Election Commission gave the nod to Buchanan, who subsequently fell ill and was unable to mount a decent campaign.[15] Ventura left the Reform Party over Buchanan's nomination and Ross Perot threw his support to George W. Bush. Buchanan won a mere 0.42 percent of the popular vote on Election Day, signaling an end to the Reform Party as a force in American politics. The opportunity to establish a permanent third party had foundered on personalities and the absence of shared beliefs.

Using the mantra "It's the economy, stupid," Bill Clinton burst onto the scene in 1992, defeating the incumbent George H. W. Bush and Ross Perot for the presidency. With little national exposure as governor of Arkansas, Clinton was able to establish himself as a centrist Democrat with an appeal to independents. In his campaign, Clinton hammered away at the problems of the economy and the need for change, along with the importance of increasing productivity and investing in education and infrastructure. He was able to unite all the factions of the Democratic Party behind him while the Republicans were fractured and unenthusiastic about their candidate. On Election Day, Clinton won 42.9 percent of the popular vote versus 37.4 percent for Bush, easily capturing the Electoral College.[16] In addition the Clinton coattails brought control of both houses of Congress to the Democrats.

Clinton presided over a major expansion of the American economy, with a booming stock market and tax revenues that produced large budget surpluses, raising the expectation that the national debt could be reduced and possibly eliminated. His stewardship of the economy was probably the reason Clinton was able to get reelected in 1996, despite scandals that shrouded his years in the White House and his administration's abject failure on health care reform. The problematic Whitewater investment dogged him during and after his first election, with the suicide of Vince Foster, one of Hillary Clinton's confidants and a deputy White House Counsel, complicating the issue. A special counsel was appointed to investigate the matter in 1994. There were also several previous sexual liaisons, or attempted liaisons, that came back to haunt Clinton, most notably with Paula Corbin Jones, who sued him for sexual harassment in 1994.

The midterm election of 1994 brought the Republicans back into control of Congress, riding in on Newt Gingrich's Contract With America, the first time in forty years that both houses of Congress had GOP majorities.[17] The Whitewater investigation lingered after Clinton was reelected in 1996, his dalliance with Monica Lewinsky and subsequent impeachment proceedings making it difficult for him to focus on running the government. The African embassy bombings by Al Qaeda in 1998 provoked an American retaliatory cruise missile attack on training camps in Afghanistan and on a pharmaceutical firm in the Sudan, but did not seriously disrupt the terrorist group's activities.

## The New Millennium

The 2000 election was a triumph of the take-no-prisoners approach to campaigning by the Republicans George W. Bush and his guru Karl Rove. The first victim of the Bush strategy was John McCain, who mounted the only other credible effort to capture the Republican presidential nomination. After winning in New Hampshire, McCain was unable to deflect Bush's blistering attacks in South Carolina, with whispered stories of marital infidelity by McCain, assertions that he was antireligious, that he had fathered an interracial child, and that he was not a true conservative. Following his victory in South Carolina, Bush's bond with the social conservatives, who dominated most of the Republican primaries, helped him secure the nomination. With the support of the party apparatus, Al Gore easily beat his only challenger, Bill Bradley, to become the Democratic candidate.

During the general election campaign, Bush attacked the Clinton administration over the American undertaking in Somalia, declaring in the second debate, "I don't think our troops ought to be used for what's called nation building,"[18] an interesting comment from a man who involved America in a similar but much more extensive venture in Iraq. With the scandals in the Clinton White House in the forefront, Bush also pledged to bring moral integrity back to Washington. And Bush's stand against abortion, against activist judges, and for faith-based initiatives helped to mobilize his conservative base, as did his desire to strengthen American's military and cut taxes. While campaigning, Gore distanced himself from Clinton and his disreputable behavior, focusing on the country's prosperity and economic issues, promising to improve the lot of the poor and middle classes.

When the votes were counted after the polls closed on election night, the outcome was unclear. Bush had 246 Electoral College votes and Gore 255, with 270 needed for victory. Florida, with its 25 electoral votes the key to the election, was too close to call definitely. Though Bush led in Florida in the initial count by about 1000 votes, a month of court challenges and recounts was necessary before he was declared victorious by the thinnest of margins. When the recounts were halted, Bush was ahead by 537 votes in Florida, 0.009 percent of the state's ballots.[19] But the legal maneuvering by both sides over the disputed counts continued. With a strongly partisan Republican, Katherine Harris, supervising the voting and recounts, and Bush's brother Jeb as governor, questions were raised about the fairness of the process. On December 12, after the Florida House of Representatives voted on a party-line basis to certify the state's electors for Bush, the Supreme Court ruled 5 to 4 in his favor. This ended any further review of the voting with Bush still ahead, but with the true will of Florida's electorate unknown. Gore lost the presidency even though he had polled over 500,000 more votes nationally than Bush. Bush received 271 Electoral College votes, one more than necessary for victory.

This election marked the fourth time in United States history that a candidate had won the presidency while losing the nationwide popular vote,[20] the previous instance having taken place in 1888. There is little question that irregularities occurred in the voting in Florida, but whether Gore or Bush would have ultimately won the recount probably would have depended on the method used to vet the ballots. Sadly, the decision-making process that characterized this election was politicized and will forever remain tainted, tarnishing America's democratic credentials and the way it chooses its highest officials. The final results of the 2000 presidential election gave 48.4 percent of the vote for Gore, 47.9 percent for Bush, 2.7 percent for Nader and 0.4 percent for Buchanan: in raw numbers, 51,003,926 versus 50,460,110 versus 2,883,105 versus 449,225.

The Republican Party maintained control of both houses of Congress throughout Bush's first term, allowing a number of his initiatives to come to fruition. Some observers believed there had been a permanent realignment of voting patterns that would lead to continued Republican dominance in the future, while others thought it was just a temporary blip on a long-term graph. Certainly when the economy was the major concern of the electorate, it tended to favor the Democrats, but when social issues drove people to the polls, the Republicans had an advantage. The religious right was a trump card in their pocket, with the once solidly Democratic South now dependably in the Republican camp. Worries about terrorism that gnawed away at Americans after 9/11 seemed to add another weight on the Republican side of the scale. The way the Iraq War was managed, however, along with Hurricane Katrina, intelligence problems, and the Republican legacy of corruption, made the return of the Democrats to power almost inevitable.

An outside challenge for the presidency was mounted in 2000 and 2004 by Ralph Nader and the Green Party. Originally trained as a lawyer, Nader had a long history as a political activist, corporate watchdog, and environmentalist, and was particularly known for his early work on automobile safety and consumer rights. Many of the studies conducted by Nader and the young activists who joined him—Nader's Raiders—and Public Citizen, a national, nonprofit consumer advocacy organization that he created in 1971, resulted in important changes in federal laws and agencies that improved consumer safety and the environment.[21] A number of nongovernmental organizations inspired by Nader helped protect the public from government insensitivity and alliances with special interests, as well as from corporate neglect and malfeasance.[22] During the campaign, Nader focused on environmental issues and took an anti-free-trade stance, attracting considerable exposure in the media. As usual, he was pugnacious and outspoken, saying whatever was on his mind and letting the chips fall wherever they might.

Much of Nader's backing in 2000 appeared to come from individuals who would have otherwise supported the Democratic ticket, draining votes from Al Gore. The consensus of opinion from most analysts is that Gore would have won those states that he lost by narrow margins, including Florida, Tennessee, and New Hampshire, if Nader had not been running, and would have fashioned an Electoral College victory.[23] However, Nader refused to withdraw his candidacy in spite of being urged to do so by a number of liberal figures. He had been antagonistic to the Democratic Party for some time, feeling that because of their sellout to corporate interests they were worse than the Republicans, who had always been allied with big business. In 1990, he commented that "the Democratic Party had become so bankrupt, it didn't matter if it wins any elections."[24] He reiterated these feelings during the 2000 campaign and promoted Green Party hopefuls in state contests against even the most liberal Democrats.

Nader declared that "while Gore was perhaps marginally preferable to Bush, the differences between the two were not great enough to merit support of Gore."[25] Because they hoped Nader would siphon off some of the votes that might have gone to Gore, Republican groups paid for advertising extolling Nader in several states. Democrats pushed the dictum that "A vote for Nader is a vote for Bush." Yet with all the hype surrounding the Nader candidacy, he garnered only 2.7 percent of the popular vote, falling short of the 5 percent he wanted to obtain federal funding for the Green Party in the 2004 election.[26] In Florida, Nader collected 97,488 votes, far exceeding the 537 votes that were the margin of Bush's victory.[27] Nader may not have won the 2000 presidential election, but it appears that he played a decisive role in Bush's Electoral College triumph.

President Bush ran for reelection in 2004 against John Kerry, helped by a tailwind from the 9/11 disaster and the fight against terrorism for which the public gave him high marks. What the public did not fully understand at this point because of Republican spin, administration misrepresentations, and half-truths was that Saddam Hussein did not have any weapons of mass destruction or any connection to Al Qaeda. In addition, they did not realize that the invasion and occupation of Iraq may have reduced American security rather than enhancing it, by encouraging the growth of radical Islam and the recruitment of new jihadists. (This was shown in a declassified National Intelligence Estimate in September of 2006.[28]) Kerry did not use the issues of Iraq and terrorism to his advantage, and there was a public perception of him as vacillating and indecisive.

Though there was no significant opposition to the renomination of George W. Bush and Dick Cheney on the Republican ticket, Kerry had a number of formidable challengers blocking his path to the Democratic nomination. Early in the race, Governor Howard Dean of Vermont was out in front with his own brand of populism, generating strong poll numbers, appealing to young supporters known as Deaniacs, and using the Internet for successful fundraising. Neither Senator Joe Lieberman, Gore's vice presidential nominee in 2000, nor General Wesley Clark was able to build a base of support. At the Iowa caucuses in January, John Kerry and John Edwards emerged in front, with Dean far behind in third place and Richard Gephardt even further in the rear. Immediately after the caucuses, Dean gave an emotional speech that was poorly received, producing a negative reaction among many party stalwarts. At the end of January, Kerry took the New Hampshire primary and soon after, Edwards triumphed in South Carolina. However, Kerry won every state primary except Vermont on Super Tuesday in March, essentially ending the race,[29] and chose John Edwards as his running mate.

During the campaign, Bush emphasized his role as a wartime president, willing to make the hard decisions and do whatever was necessary to protect the country. The "victory" in Afghanistan, removing the Taliban from power, had been accomplished with a minimum of troops and few casualties, but Iraq was a different story. On May 1, 2003, less than two months after the invasion of Iraq, George Bush landed a jet on an aircraft carrier in a great photo op, making his "Mission Accomplished" speech. A CNN–USA Today Gallop poll soon afterward had Bush's approval ratings at 66 percent.[30] Unfortunately the war in Iraq persisted with deadly consequences, and after Bush's performance and Rumsfeld and Cheney's optimistic slants on the war, Kerry could have gone after Bush like a bulldog. But Kerry's comments never got much traction with the public because they were not hard-hitting or pointed enough. He did speak about the escape of Bin Laden and Zawahiri at Tora Bora, and the poor planning for the aftermath of the Iraqi war, saying that he would be more competent than Bush on military matters, but his words did not appear to resonate with the electorate.

Through considered comments and clever advertising, Bush and his campaign team were able to paint Kerry as a "flip-flopper" who took contradictory positions on issues at different times. To a certain degree, this portrait of Kerry captured the public's imagination and he had to fight, with questionable success, to peel off that label and show that he was a strong leader. In addition, the 527 committee of Swift Boat Veterans who were allied with Bush hammered away at Kerry's status as a war hero who had saved a comrade's life under fire, had won Purple Hearts, and had displayed leadership in combat situations. Kerry's failure to respond immediately to the lies and innuendos about his service record cost him dearly in votes and credibility, further feeding the perception that he was ineffective. He also never attacked Bush in kind about Bush's avoidance of duty in Viet Nam and his absences from the Air National Guard unit he was assigned to, issues Bush had previously deflected. Kerry did score points with the electorate on domestic considerations such as the economy and health care, outsourcing, and the loss of jobs, and was able to make some inroads over the war in Iraq. But he had allowed his opponent to define who he was and ultimately was unable to escape that characterization.

Though Bush easily won the popular vote, the Electoral College winner was uncertain until the day after the election, with Ohio holding the balance of power. When Ohio was shown to be in the Bush column, Kerry conceded. Bush garnered a total of 286 electoral votes to 251 for Kerry,[31] achieving 50.7 percent of the popular vote versus 48.3 percent for Kerry and 0.4 percent for Nader. The vote totals were 62,040,610 versus 59,028,111 versus 463,653. Bush spent $367,228,801 on the campaign, or $5.92 for every vote he obtained. Kerry spent $326,236,288, or $5.52 for every vote; Nader spent $4,556,037, or $9.85 for every vote.[32] The funding required to run a presidential campaign had simply become staggering, necessitating a constant effort to raise money, along with the potential favors and conflicts of interest this entailed. In the 2004 election, the Republicans also added to their majorities in both the Senate and the House.

Ralph Nader ran for president again in 2004 as an independent rather than as the Green Party candidate. Meeting privately with John Kerry in May, Nader refused to withdraw from the race. Groups associated with the Democratic Party were subsequently organized to try and convince potential Nader supporters not to vote for him, using TV commercials as well as other methods. Toward the end of June, Nader proclaimed that he was willing to accept the endorsement of the Green Party for his candidacy, but would not pursue the party's nomination. At their convention shortly afterwards, the party chose David Cobb as their candidate instead of Nader.[33] This eliminated his ability to use the party label to get on the ballots in a number of states. His 405,623 votes did not influence the election in any way.[34]

## The Midterm Election of 2006

There were significant issues separating the two parties in the 2006 midterm election, but aside from Iraq, substance was generally lacking in campaign advertising and debates between the candidates. The focus was on slogans and sound bites repeated endlessly. Continuing a trend that had begun in the 1980s, the election was marked by negative characterizations and dirty tricks, with personnel in both parties expecting over 90 percent of broadcast advertising to be of the attack variety.[35] These ads, on radio, TV, and through mailers, were filled with deliberate distortions, inaccuracies, and outright lies injected into local races by the national campaign committees of the two parties and independent 527 groups.[36] The chairman of the National Republican Congressional Committee, Congressman Thomas Reynolds, admitted that his investigators had been digging for dirt on possible Democratic challengers for well over a year, even before the actual candidates were chosen. Their findings, including statements said or written by these individuals as college students or decades earlier or comments by ex-wives or past business associates, were aggressively shaped into messages designed to tarnish the Democratic candidates.

In this election cycle, the Republicans once more had an advantage in fundraising, allowing them to spend more on advertising. They focused on the war on terrorism and national security issues, which they again felt were their strong suits, trying to depict the Democrats as being weak and not fully understanding the potential threat to the country. In a Republican fundraising event President Bush described the Democrats in regard to Iraq and terrorism: "The party of FDR and the party of Harry Truman has become the party of cut and run."[37] Republican candidates also incessantly stressed that the Democrats would raise taxes. In some states, the GOP pushed social issues as well, highlighting their opposition to same-sex marriage, which they felt would mobilize their base.

The Democrats pounded away at the Republicans over the war in Iraq, which they depicted as unnecessary and poorly managed, trying to link all the Republican candidates to the increasingly unpopular President Bush, while most Republicans were distancing themselves from him. They also emphasized ethical problems, the need to raise the minimum wage, and improve the health care system. In states where they felt it would have resonance, they spoke of moving forward with stem cell research to find cures for different diseases. As usual, a measured rational dialogue about the issues between the parties did not occur. Instead, it was the customary name-calling and attacks by the candidates on both sides.

Though middle-class feelings of economic insecurity and the specter of congressional corruption helped propel the Democrats to victory in the election, there was little question afterward that the war in Iraq and President Bush's poor standing with the electorate were the determining factors in many congressional and senate races. While the administration spoke of progress being made in Iraq, the news seemed to get worse each week prior to the election, giving more credibility to Democratic questions about the war. However, after the Democrats took control of both houses of Congress, there was still no consensus on an exit strategy for Iraq. Of other concerns confronting the new Democratic congress, only raising the minimum wage was easily enacted. With a broad spectrum of views among the Democratic forces in Congress, issues like free-trade agreements, health care reform, and taxes did not result in significant legislation. Ethics reform, though stated as a

Democratic objective, did not produce a comprehensive measure that some advocates had hoped for.

It should be emphasized that the Democratic victory in the 2006 election was not because most citizens had confidence in them, with positive feelings that they could turn America around. Instead it was because of the increasingly negative perception many Americans had of the Republicans, stemming from the poor job they had done running the country while they had been in charge. Both parties continued to have low public approval ratings and people chose the Democrats mainly as the lesser of two evils. In addition to the Republican losses across the board, another casualty of the 2006 midterm election was Secretary of Defense Donald Rumsfeld, who "resigned" after consultations with President Bush immediately following Election Day.[38] Rumsfeld had become a lightning rod for all the discontent with the Iraq War and with the situation deteriorating daily, Bush decided that Rumsfeld had become too much of a liability. Bush's new choice for the job, Robert Gates, was a former head of the CIA and thought to be less dogmatic and more pragmatic than his predecessor.

In January 2007, a few months after the election, President Bush announced the deployment of additional military personnel to Iraq to try to control the insurgency and stabilize the country. It was hoped that this policy initiative involving 30,000 combat troops and known as the "surge" would also help the Iraqi Army tamp down sectarian violence and increase security. Despite Congressional opposition and polls that showed the American public's resistance, the new plan under the leadership of General David Petraeus was generally successful. Many of the Sunni resistance fighters joined the so-called Awakening Councils, abandoning Al Qaeda and the insurgency, and fought on the side of the Americans. After his election as president in 2008, Obama persevered with this strategy, even though he had initially been against the troop buildup. With violence decreasing, he was able to start withdrawing combat units in 2010, leaving 50,000 troops behind to train the Iraqi forces. The departure of the American soldiers essentially removed Iraq from the political debate.

Both before and after the 2006 midterm election, some observers believed a transformation was under way in the previously Republican western states, with a swing toward the Democrats.[39] After the election, Montana, Colorado, Arizona, and New Mexico all had Democratic governors, with more Democratic congressmen and senators. Some of the change had occurred because of new people moving into the region from California and the East Coast and because of an increase in Hispanics. The shift was also due to a rise in populist sentiment, with antipathy to big business and corporate control of people's lives. Environmentalism and libertarianism were in the mix as well. Many of the new Democrats in this area were conservative on social issues, particularly against gun control, and some were pro-life, but they all contributed to the Democratic resurgence., Many of them, however, were also ripe for the Tea Party when the economy collapsed and Wall Street was bailed out a few years later.

## The Election of 2008 and the Obama Years

The 2008 campaign for president started shortly after the election of 2006 with potential candidates making forays into the early primary states of Iowa and New Hampshire, as well as other trips around the country to gauge and stimulate enthusiasm. The main players in the Democratic race were Barack Obama, Hillary Clinton, and John Edwards, with the Republicans John McCain, Rudolph Giuliani, Mitt Romney, Fred Thompson and Mike Huckabee battling it out.

Though Clinton was the initial favorite among Democrats, Obama's ability to mobilize young people and minorities, his prodigious fundraising ability over the Internet, and the power of his oratory made a fight for the nomination a near certainty. When Obama won the Iowa caucuses in the beginning of January 2008, it became evident that his appeal extended to the predominantly white rural Midwestern states and that Clinton's presumed place at the head of the Democratic ticket was in jeopardy. Running strongly in New Hampshire and Nevada in January, Obama won South Carolina, and by the end of the month John Edwards dropped out of the race.

(Rumors about an extramarital affair of Edwards and a campaign worker did not gain traction until mid-2008.) In multiple primaries on February 5, Super Tuesday, Clinton and Obama were fairly even. Obama sprinted ahead by winning the ten remaining February contests. In March, Clinton battled back by taking Ohio, Rhode Island, and Texas, but Obama acquired more delegates in Texas by winning the caucuses in that state. By June, with multiple super delegates choosing to endorse him, Obama had nailed down the nomination as the first African-American candidate. Though there was considerable Democratic support for Hillary Clinton to be on the ticket as the vice-presidential nominee, Obama picked Senator Joe Biden as his running mate.

Polls in 2006 and 2007 had Rudolph Giuliani as the early leader to head the Republican slate. As more of the Republican base came to learn about Giuliani's moderate positions on social issues, his candidacy lost its luster. Giuliani dropped out early in the primary races and backed McCain, who was the big winner on Super Tuesday in February of 2008. Romney withdrew shortly afterward, also throwing his support to McCain. By March, McCain had amassed enough delegates to secure the Republican nomination and in a major surprise he selected Sarah Palin, the governor of Alaska, to be his vice-presidential partner. Though this energized his conservative Republican base, it left much of the country wondering about her qualifications to be president should the need arise.

The battle between Obama and McCain for the presidency was dirty and expensive, with attack ads emanating from both sides, and Obama's American citizenship and religion frequently challenged. Though the wars in Iraq and Afghanistan were significant issues, the overriding concern of the electorate was the economy and which candidate would do a better job of getting it back on track. Both candidates highlighted the need for transforming the culture in Washington, each claiming to be a stronger agent of change. Given the immense disparity in fundraising between McCain and Obama, it was not shocking when the latter elected to reject public financing for his campaign, though he had previously agreed to accept it. Opting out allowed him to have a major advantage in spending, since McCain was constrained by his acceptance of federal assistance. Obama raised $778 million for the 2008 presidential campaign, McCain over $380 million.[40] Hillary Clinton raised $245 million. As one of their tactics, Obama and the Democrats campaigned against Bush, linking McCain and other Republicans to the unpopular president. Obama also made good use of the Internet and social networking to obtain the support of young voters. On Election Day, Obama easily beat McCain, 53 percent to 45.7 percent, with 365 electoral votes to 173. Only the Deep South and some of the western states backed McCain.

When Obama was inaugurated in January 2009, he had Democratic majorities in both houses of Congress, which should have helped in governing. The Republicans, however, were in lockstep against any measure he favored and the Democrats did not have the sixty votes necessary in the Senate to overcome possible filibusters. In addition, conservative Democrats often did not support legislation their more liberal colleagues proposed. With the recession and unemployment the top concerns of the electorate, Congress passed a federal stimulus package of over $700 billion, the result of compromise by the president to garner enough support. Though the Obama administration heralded its passage and declared that unemployment would be reduced to eight percent in two years, many analysts believed the amount of the stimulus was inadequate to lift the economy and make a serious dent in unemployment. Most economists did believe that the stimulus along with the bank bailout under Bush and the actions of the Federal Reserve prevented an economic collapse that might have mirrored the Depression of the '30s. But the administration was ineffective in communicating this message to America's citizens, who were already chafing at the increase in federal expenditures and the expanding debt level.

The soaring cost of health care and the numbers of uninsured made health care reform a priority for the Democrats, but the way legislation was developed in the Congress and the bill's final structure became a public relations disaster for Obama and the Democrats and a bonanza for the Republicans. Though the Congressional Budget Office asserted that the measure would save money over the years and reduce the budget deficit, a majority of citizens believed that it would raise costs and lower the quality of care, and so were opposed to what its detractors labeled "Obamacare." The fact that the bill also made health insurance coverage mandatory enraged libertarians who along with many other Americans were hostile to any expansion of the federal government's powers. And in reality, the law was complex, difficult to understand, and did not produce the kind of unequivocal savings that were needed to take a significant bite out of the budget deficits and national debt. On the other hand, no comprehensive plans were put forth by the Republicans to tackle the deficiencies in the health care system. But perhaps even more galling to many Americans than the health care plan was the fact that Obama and the Democrats had focused on health care rather than the economy and unemployment during a deep recession that was causing great pain for citizens of every occupation and social class.

The attempt to address global warming and formulate an energy policy also ran into strong resistance from Republicans and some conservative Democrats. While the House passed a cap-and-trade bill to try to advance the debate over carbon emissions, the Senate never considered similar legislation, and the measure was left to die. While the House effort may have been seriously flawed, there were again no counterproposals from the Republicans to try to craft a compromise measure. Many Republicans were not convinced of the reality of global warming and remain unconvinced. In fact, the Republicans, who were opposed to every major piece of Democratic legislation, never offered their own programs to deal with the nation's problems, sticking to the general mantra of no new taxes and cutting government spending. Prior to the 2010 midterm elections, the two parties could not even reach an agreement on whether to extend President Bush's tax cuts for the middle class, with the Republicans insisting that the most affluent segment of the population continue to be included in the tax cut. That this would further increase the budget deficits and national debt did not seem to deter them, as they saw their unified stance against what they viewed as Democratic overreach as their ticket to resurgence in the midterm elections. Cooperation by the parties for the good of the country was not as important as getting elected and attaining or retaining power.

The Republican strategy paid off on Election Day 2010 when in an historic reversal they achieved a majority in the House and took back five Senate seats, making it even more difficult for the Democrats to pass meaningful legislation. Of course, it was just as difficult for the Republicans, with their numbers, to enact any laws, making governmental gridlock or near gridlock a greater possibility.

The Republicans had won the election because they were well prepared and had remained on message. They emphasized their desire to lower taxes, cut spending, and reduce the deficit, giving no specifics of how they were going to get all of this done. Repealing health care reform was also high on their agenda, with no hint of what would replace it. The election campaign was the most expensive ever, around $4 billion, with opaque organizations and secret contributors used to promote candidates, overwhelmingly Republican, and attack their opponents, overwhelmingly Democratic, turning the tide in many close contests.

The Tea Party also played a major role in the election. This amorphous group supported many Republicans and elected some of their own members who had triumphed in the state party primaries against regular organizational candidates deemed not conservative enough. Senator Bob Bennett of Utah was the first one eliminated in an April convention, with lawyer Mike Lee winning the primary and then the general election. Marco Rubio, with Tea Party backing, forced Governor Charlie Crist to bolt the Republican primary in Florida, with the latter running as an independent and losing to Rubio in the general election. Rand Paul in Kentucky defeated the organization candidate supported by the Senate Minority Leader Mitch McConnell, then beat his Democratic opponent on Election Day. Though the Tea Party generated great enthusiasm and participation among the Republican base, there were negative aspects to its agenda and image that caused problems for some of the primary winners it had backed. In addition, some of its candidates came across as bizarre or extreme, with pronouncements that cost them significant votes. For instance, in the Republican primary for the Senate in Delaware, Tea Party adherent Christine O'Donnell eliminated Representative Mike Castle, a moderate who was expected to easily win the Senate seat against his Democratic opponent, Chris Coons. Instead, Coons handily beat O'Donnell in the general election, because of O'Donnell's apparent previous dabbling in witchcraft, evidence of financial irresponsibility, and misreading of the Constitution. In Nevada, virtually any Republican might have beaten Democratic Senate Majority Leader Harry Reid, who was quite unpopular in his home state. But Tea Partier Sharon Angle was so strange and unpredictable in her race for the senate that Reid was reelected. Angle made a number of misstatements, avoided questions from the press, and spoke of "Second Amendment remedies" if Congress didn't change. Similarly in Colorado, Democratic incumbent Michael Bennet retained his senate seat against the Tea Party favorite Ken Buck, whose statements were disturbing to portions of the electorate. And the same pattern held in a number of races for the House, where the Tea Party was a positive force in some contests and a negative one in others.

After the election, there was still the matter of legislation that the lame duck session of Congress needed to pass. This included raising the national debt level, establishing an operating budget for the country, and an extension in some form of the Bush tax cuts. Though Congress continued these cuts for two years, Republicans insisted that the wealthiest Americans be part of the package, further increasing the budget deficit. Obama and the Democrats did, however, get an extension of unemployment insurance and some tax benefits for small businesses.

Since the new Congress was seated in January 2011 with a strong Republican majority in the House and the Democrats with a narrow majority in the Senate, there has been difficulty getting important legislation passed. The Republicans were adamant about cutting $60 billion in discretionary spending out of the budget, while the Democrats were reluctant to approve that magnitude of reduction, afraid that it would stunt the economic recovery.[41] There has also been no appreciation by the budget cutters of the need to fund education, infrastructure, and basic research, which are necessary for future American prosperity and cannot be financed by the private sector. Neither party has so far (as of July 2011) been willing to go after the unfunded liabilities of Medicare and Social Security where the real problem of government debt resides, afraid of the reaction that might elicit from the electorate.

The states are also aggressively pursuing reductions in spending in attempts to balance their budgets. Some of this has come at the expense of public service workers, who have enjoyed benefits disproportionate to those of private workers. The public service unions have agreed to givebacks in benefits to cut the deficits, but the Republican leadership in some states has not been satisfied. They have been trying to end the unions' rights to collective bargaining and make other structural changes to weaken the unions, who generally support Democratic candidates.[42] To underscore the political motivation behind these moves, Republican Governor Scott Walker of Wisconsin has not included the police and firemen's unions in the bill to end collective bargaining, two groups that gave him support in the recent election.[43],[44]

During 2009 and 2010, combined state sales, income, and corporate taxes dropped more than 10 percent.[45] In addition to the decrease in revenue stemming from the economic downturn, temporary gimmicks previously used to avoid tax increases or spending cuts along with inadequate funding of public service employee pension plans have resulted in the states' financial problems. Many of these pension plans now have shortfalls of tens of billions of dollars. The budgetary difficulties are not only on a federal and state level, but also involve many municipal and county governments. Unfortunately, the states' and municipalities' budget cuts and layoffs of workers will heighten unemployment and prolong the nation's economic pain. While state and municipal officials could not have predicted the recession and the drop in revenue, their unwillingness to adequately address financial imbalances in the past created many of the current problems. Neither the Republicans nor the Democrats have been willing to make the hard choices necessary and talk to their constituents about the need for higher taxes and reduced benefits in order to insure the financial stability of the states and cities. This is further proof of the inability of the current political parties to govern responsibly. Decisions are made only in the face of emergencies, and even then ways are sought to delay the inevitable, solving the immediate problems with trickery and artifice.

## The Structure and Operation of the Two Parties

Over the last forty or so years, the Republican and Democratic Parties have grown into professional organizations similar to corporate entities, with permanent, trained staffers to assist candidates, members, and elected officials.[46] The parties also have a plethora of specialized fundraisers, researchers, media coordinators, campaign planners, and so forth. They have spawned committees with hundreds of employees that focus on electing their candidates to the House and Senate. A formidable get-out-the-vote operation has also been important to both organizations. While Ralph Nader said that the two parties were basically the same, and indeed they do operate similarly, there are still profound differences between them in terms of ideology, with the more extreme elements in both parties setting their agendas.

Edward Glaeser and Bryce Adam Ward note: "Political parties have had an increasing tendency to divide on cultural and religious issues rather than economic differences."[47] This was so also in the nineteenth century when anti-Catholic sentiment characterized the Republican Party, but for most of the twentieth century economic issues were a stronger determinant of voting practices. The decline of labor unions may be related to the rise of cultural and religious politics trumping economics;[48] church attendance has been a better predictor of voting patterns than income. Now, however, with the recent recession and unemployment, the bank bailouts, and the mortgage mess, economic concerns are again at the forefront, giving rise to populist sentiment and the growth of the Tea Party. Though much of Republican Party funding comes from affluent individuals and large corporations, there is some discontent among business interests about the Republican stress on social issues, particularly where it may interfere with new technology such as stem cell development, or where it may affect education, as with the uproar over intelligent design. Furthermore, not all the Republican evangelicals, with a streak of populism just below the surface, are happy about the emphasis on tax-cutting measures that benefit mainly the affluent.[49] The grand coalition of the GOP may not be as stable as the tentmakers would have Americans believe, though distaste for Democratic policy may help to keep it aloft.

As shown previously, the Democratic coalition is also constructed of disparate parts that periodically come unglued over various issues. The party includes liberals, Blue Dog conservative Democrats, the black caucus, Hispanics, gay activists, and others. It may be that the main force holding it all together is its opposition, and occasionally overt hostility, to the Republicans and their programs.

Since the electorate in the smaller, rural states tends to vote Republican, the party has a structural advantage over the Democrats and inherently more power as expressed in the Constitution. This is seen in the pattern of the "red and blue states" on the electoral map. There are two senators from each state, meaning that Wyoming with 600,000 people has the same representation and power in the Senate as California with a population over 30,000,000. Democrats polled 2.4 million more votes than Republicans in the three Senate elections prior to 2005, yet the Republicans won eleven more seats. And the 55 Republican senators in the 2004 Congress represented 131 million Americans versus 161 million for the 44 Democrats.[50] The Electoral College, which chooses the president, is also tilted toward the smaller states, which is why George Bush was chosen as president in 2000 though he polled a half million fewer popular votes than Al Gore. Through aggressive gerrymandering in many states, the Republicans have also shaped Congressional districts that strongly favor them and are more likely to send their party members to Washington. Twelve new Republican-leaning districts were created between 2000 and 2004,[51] making it more difficult to vanquish their incumbents in the House. And their 2010 election victories at state levels will give the Republicans more power to fashion Congressional districts to maximize their advantage, with Republicans completely controlling 26 state legislatures, Democrats 17, and 5 having split control.[52]

Since the presidency and Senate recently have more often been in Republican hands, they have also chosen more of the judicial nominees, and now conservative Republicans dominate the federal judiciary as well. Obviously, this can play a role in determining the outcome of elections. Thus, in addition to the financial impediments the Democrats must overcome, there are also structural barriers that hinder them. For the Republicans to be thrown out of power in Washington as happened in 2006 and 2008, they have to be doing an exceedingly poor job and stoking people's anger. Of course, the Democratic victories were fleeting, with many incumbents unable to hold onto their seats in the wave that swept them out of office in 2010, when their approval ratings were disastrous. It may simply be that when things go wrong, such as the Iraq war in 2006, or the economy in 2010, the party in charge is the one blamed by the electorate, whether or not its officeholders have been at fault.

## Obstacles to the Development of a Third Party

The difficulty third-party candidates have in obtaining ballot access in many states is the result of collusion between Republicans and Democrats working to keep the political status quo. Various state laws insist on petitions and large numbers of valid signatures as a prerequisite to getting on the ballot. And unless a certain number of votes are attained in an election, the process must be repeated for the following contest. This is done purposely to stifle the growth of these fledgling parties. The hurdles differ from state to state, with some less restrictive than others. The regulations seem unrelated to whether the state is controlled by Republicans or Democrats, as in general the two parties will do whatever they can to subvert third party candidates. As an example, Indiana once required minor political parties to poll 0.5 percent of the votes in order to automatically qualify for the ballot in the next statewide election.[53] When the Libertarian Party attained that goal in 1982, the state legislature raised the requirement to 2 percent.

A "duopoly of power" further helps to curb third parties[54]—in the current system the second party has a privileged position, that of a monopoly on opposition. If the voters are unhappy with office-holders, they can kick them out by voting for other candidates, but their choice is limited to candidates from the second party. The only way they can vent their dissatisfaction is with this one other party, or by not voting. The single party plurality system in each district, with winner taking all, is another significant obstacle for third parties.

Media coverage of politics reinforces the two-party system as well, as every twist and turn of their primaries is reported and analyzed, providing a huge amount of unfunded publicity. This is also true in the general election. The two parties are the power brokers in the American system of government and they expect the media to disseminate the words and detail the actions of their important players. With Congress and the Federal Communications Commission having a regulatory role in terms of the media, perhaps there is an implied threat if coverage of the parties is unsatisfactory. The media also hamper the fundraising of third parties by labeling their candidates' efforts futile, tilting at windmills, and so forth, instead of focusing on substantive issues. Since people rarely want to waste their money or back a loser, financial support for third party candidates never approaches a competitive level.

Notwithstanding the barriers they must contend with, third parties continue to arise, with some of them making reasonable showings and having influence on the overall outcome of elections. The book *Third Parties in America* noted in 1996:

> Minor parties have managed to capture over 5 percent of the popular vote in a third of the presidential elections since 1840; they have won over 10 percent of the vote in one out of five contests. Because of third-party strength, 14 of the last 36 presidents have entered the White House without a popular vote majority. Through the years, third parties have

controlled enough votes in the right states to have theoretically changed one-third of the Electoral College results.[55]

Over one hundred lesser parties have participated in American elections since 1840, running the gamut in motivation, ideology, personalities, and financial strength.[56] This points to the reservoir of discontent with the two parties that control the political system.

## Third-Party Successes in Non-Presidential Contests

Throughout American history there have been successful bids for office by third parties on a state or local level. During the nineteenth century, there were often senators and congressmen who were independent or belonged to minor parties or, with frequent changing of alliances, joined and rejoined different parties. In the first half of the twentieth century as well, there were some senators and congressmen affiliated with third parties. Over the last half century, however, this has occurred less frequently, though there has been some shifting membership between the two major parties. Currently, the senator from Vermont, Bernie Sanders, is an independent who served a number of terms in the House and as a senator caucuses with the Democrats. Joe Lieberman from Connecticut is also an independent who caucuses with the Democrats. Though an incumbent Democratic senator, Lieberman lost the Democratic primary in 2006, but went on to win as an independent to return to the senate. However, Lieberman did nothing to build a party structure or organization that would survive his candidacy and play a role in future political campaigns.

There have also been third-party governors, other statewide-elected officers, and mayors of large cities over the last two centuries. Lowell Weicker and Walter Hickel were elected governors of Connecticut and Alaska respectively in 1990 on Independent tickets, Jesse Ventura as a Reform candidate in Minnesota in 1998, and Angus King as an independent in Maine in 1994 and reelected in 1998.[57] Ventura's success in Minnesota may have been related to the state's liberal statutes regarding ballot access, registration, and campaign financing. He also had the advantage of being considered

a major party candidate (Reform Party) with the ability to participate in public forums.[58] But none of these successful gubernatorial
candidates built permanent state-level parties that could endure to
permanently influence the political process.

## A New Third Party

The original parties that arose shortly after the founding of the republic in the eighteenth century morphed over more than two hundred years into the Republican and Democratic parties. In recent
years, these entities have been unable to deal with the demanding
tasks of governing, trapped in a web of corruption, self-interest, and
partisanship. Since it is unlikely that they can extract themselves
and operate in a competent fashion, a third party is needed to institute effective, practical governance. While there are structural,
historical, and emotional barriers to the success of a third party,
dedication and hard work by committed adherents can overcome
these barriers. Previous third parties have failed because they were
driven by individual personalities or single issues and did not construct long-term constituencies and activist bases. Public attitudes
toward the current parties and cynicism about the nation's government, however, indicate that this is a propitious moment for the formation of a new third party, with the potential for it to reform and
revitalize American politics.

> A spirit of faction, which is apt to mingle its poison in the
> deliberations of all bodies of men, will often hurry the
> persons of whom they are composed into improprieties
> and excesses for which they would blush in a private ca-
> pacity.
> —Alexander Hamilton, *The Federalist Papers*[59]

# References

[1] James Madison, *The Federalist Papers*, No. 62, New American Library, New York, NY, 1961 (originally published in 1787–1788), 378.

[2] Jethro K. Lieberman, *The Evolving Constitution*, Random House, New York, NY, 1992, 385.

[3] Marjorie Randon Hershey, *Party Politics in America*, Longman Classics in Political Science, 11th ed., PearsonLongman, New York, NY, 2003, 5.

[4] John H. Aldrich, *Why Parties?* University of Chicago Press, Chicago, IL, 1995, 10.

[5] The Constitution of the United States of America, Article 1, Section 4.

[6] Lieberman, 385.

[7] en.wikipedia.org/wiki/Ross_Perot.

[8] John F. Bibby and L. Sandy Maisel, *Two Parties or More?* Westview Press, Boulder, CO, 2nd ed., 2003, 41.

[9] en.wikipedia.org/wiki/Ross_Perot.

[10] Ibid.

[11] Steven J. Rosenstone, Roy L. Behr, Edward H. Lazarus, *Third Parties in America*, 2nd ed., 1996, Princeton University Press, Princeton, NJ, 231.

[12] Ibid., 232.

[13] Bibby and Maisel, 42.

[14] Ibid., 42.

[15] Ibid., 63.

[16] en.wikipedia.org/wiki/U.S._presidential_election_1992#Democratic_Party_nomination.

[17] Hershey, 303.

[18] en.wikipedia.org/wiki/U.S._presidential_election_2000.

[19] Ibid.

[20] Ibid.

[21] en.wikipedia.org/wiki/Ralph_Nader.

[22] Eric Foner and John Garraty, eds., "Ralph Nader," in *The Reader's Companion to American History*, Houghton Mifflin, Boston, MA, 1991, 768.

[23] Bibby and Maisel, 46.

[24] en.wkikpedia.org/wiki/Ralph_Nader.

[25] Ibid.

[26] Bibby and Maisel, 46.

[27] en.wikipedia.org/wiki/Ralph_Nader

[28] David Sanger, "Study Doesn't Share Bush's Optimism on Terror Fight," *New York Times*, September 27, 2006, A16.

[29] en.wikipedia.org/wiki/U.S._presidential_election_2004

[30] Ibid.

[31] Ibid.

[32] Ibid.

[33] en.wikipedia.org/wiki/Ralph_Nader.

[34] Ibid.

[35] Adam Nagourney, "Theme of Campaign Ads: Don't Be Nice," *New York Times*, September 27, 2006, A1.

[36] John Broder, "As Election Nears, Groups Plan Negative Ads," *New York Times*, October 11, 2006, A27.

[37] Jim Rutenberg, "Bush Attacks Democrats Over Iraq and Terror," *New York Times*, September 29, 2006.

[38] Sheryl Gay Stolberg and Jim Rutenberg, "Rumsfeld Resigns; Bush Vows To 'Find Common Ground,' " *New York Times*, November 9, 2006, A1.

[39] Ryan Sager, "Purple Mountains," *The Atlantic*, July/August 2006, 37.

[40] Federal Election Commission, Campaign Finance Reports and Data, Summary Reports Search Results 2007–2008 Cycle, http://query.nictusa.com/cgi-bin/cancomsrs/?_08+00+PR.

[41] Bob Willis and Danielle Ivory, "Republicans Aren't Seeking Shutdown, Budget Chairman Ryan Says," Bloomberg, February 21, 2011, http://www.bloomberg.com/news/2011-02-21/republican-lawmakers-say-house-majority-isn-t-seeking-government-shutdown.html.

[42] Steven Greenhouse, "Strained States Turning to Laws to Curb Labor Unions," *New York Times*, January 3, 2011, A1.

[43] Nicholas Riccardi and Abigail Sewell, "Controversial collective-bargaining measure clears Wisconsin Assembly," *Los Angeles Times*, February 25, 2011, http://articles.latimes.com/2011/feb/25/nation/la-na-midwest-union-20110225.

[44] MSNBC.com staff and AP, "Wis. governor refuses to budge on budget bill," msnbc.com, 2/22/2011, www.msnbc.msn.com/cleanprint/CleanPrintProxy.aspx?1298836740301.

[45] Editorial, "The Looming Crisis in the States," *New York Times*, December 25, 2010, Week in Review, 13.

[46] Aldrich, 256–260.

[47] Edward L. Glaeser and Bryce Adam Ward, "Myths and Realities of American Political Geography," Harvard Institute of Economic Research, Discussion Paper, No. 2100, January 2006, available at SSRN:http://ssrn.com/abstract=874977, 4.

[48] Ibid.

[49] Chuck Todd and Marc Ambinder, "The Six-Year Itch," *The Atlantic*, March 2006, 42–43.

[50] Jacob S. Hacker and Paul Pierson, "The Center No Longer Holds," *New York Times,* November 20, 2005, Magazine, 32.

[51] Ibid.

[52] Dan Balz, "The GOP takeover in the states," *The Washington Post*, November, 13, 2010, www.washingtonpost.com/wp-dyn/content/article/2010/11/13/AR2010111302389_...

[53] Hershey, 37.

[54] Lisa Jane Disch, *The Tyranny of the Two Party System*, Columbia University Press, New York, NY, 2002, 9.

[55] Rosenstone, Behr, Lazarus, 4.

[56] Ibid., 215.

[57] Bibby and Maisel, 52.

[58] Disch, 1–2.

[59] Alexander Hamilton, *The Federalist Papers*, No. 15, New American Library, New York, NY, 1961, 111.

# CHAPTER 3

# Creating A Permanent Third Party of the Center

> It must be realized that there is nothing more difficult to plan, more uncertain of success, or more dangerous to manage than the establishment of a new order of government; for he who introduces it makes enemies of all those who derived advantage from the old order.
> —Niccolò Machiavelli, *The Prince* [1]

The time has come for a seismic shake-up of America's political system. As we have seen, the nation's political parties are corrupt and self-serving, tethered to the lobbyists, special interests, and their own partisan bases, and unable to govern productively. To bring about change, America needs a permanent third party of the center to recalibrate the political equation and start the country on the road to reform. The political scientists Gordon Black and Benjamin Black note: "The only force capable of fundamentally altering the political environment [in America] is a political party, but not a party whose candidates depend on PAC financing."[2] They further observe that no matter what well-intentioned reform proposals are offered, they will not come to fruition, because there is no "political force with both the motivation and power to institute the reforms that are needed."[3]

The idea of a permanent third party for America is not new; the reasons that argue for its creation have existed for many decades. Indeed, there have been a number of unsuccessful attempts at gestation, all resulting in failure. Currently, disillusionment with the government and dismay about the ability of the established political parties to fix matters remain at a high level. The growth of the

Tea Party is a reflection of these feelings. Unless the nation is able to accomplish a meaningful revision in the way it is governed, the United States is destined to decline. To effect the required metamorphosis, the nation needs a permanent third party that values moderation and pragmatism. Though revolutionary changes in political systems and mass social movements are usually initiated by the left or the right, this revolution will arise from the center, a protest against America's two entrenched parties. John Avlon in his book, *Independent Nation: How Centrists Can Change American Politics,* remarked,

Centrism frees voters from the false dichotomies that dominate American politics by offering them a third choice between the rigid extremes of the left and right, a commonsense path that acknowledges the inevitability of change while never straying far from fundamental American values or founding principles. . . . Centrism is the most effective means for achieving the classic mission of politics: the peaceful reconciliation of competing interests. Extremists and ideological purists on either side of the political aisle condemn compromise. But inflexibility either creates deadlock or dooms a cause to irrelevance.[4]

In polling during the 2006 midterm elections, 47 percent of voters labeled themselves as moderates,[5] with the percentages even higher in other surveys. Independents and nonaffiliated voters are a fast-growing segment of the electorate and 77 percent of independents stated in a survey in 2007 that they would regard a third party candidate for president favorably.[6] As the political analysts Ted Halstead and Michael Lind noted:

It is this moderate majority of Americans—composed of self-identified independents, along with significant numbers of centrist Republicans and Democrats—who feel most alienated by today's increasingly dogmatic two-party system. Although their numbers in the electorate far outweigh those of the special interest groups on the right and left, the latter nevertheless continue to wield more political power as a result of the archaic design of our electoral process, which in effect limits political choices to an option between two extremes.[7]

Mobilizing the moderates through a new party will transform the political dynamic in America. In 1992, *Newsweek* columnist Joe Klein labeled the legions of Ross Perot supporters as the "radical middle."[8]

The task will not be simple or straightforward as the political deck is stacked against any new entry. With state and federal laws barring the path of any upstart that might challenge their control, the current parties hold a duopoly of power and will not relinquish their dominance easily. Aside from the legal obstacles, there are also emotional impediments in America's citizenry that must be overcome to allow a new third party to gain traction. Steven Rosenstone, Roy Behr, and Edward Lazarus observe in their book, *Third Parties in America*:

> It is an extraordinary act for Americans to vote for a third party candidate. Loyalty to the two-party system is a central feature of their political being. To vote for a third party, citizens must repudiate much of which they have learned and grown to accept as appropriate political behavior.[9]

This was written over twenty years ago. Since then circumstances have changed significantly. Though every inch of ground gained by an additional player will have to be earned in combat, a new permanent third party of the center can be viable, with the opportunity to realize its goals and win both local and national elections. There are new tools and transformative technologies available for an interloper to level the playing field with the two established behemoths, even though the lobbyists and special interests are constantly refilling the deep pockets of the two major parties. And over the last few decades, many of the hindrances that blocked the path to ballot access for third-party candidates have become less formidable,[10] which could make the process somewhat easier. The past organizing efforts of Perot and Nader supporters to get on state ballots across the country attest to the fact that it can be done.

The main asset this new entity will have in its favor is the dissatisfaction of Americans with the current political climate. Some of this discontent is apparent in the number of citizens who have voted for third-party candidates in presidential, senatorial, and gubernatorial elections since 1990—more a rejection of the Republicans and Democrats than a belief in the programs put forth.[11] However, as the political analyst Micah Sifry has asserted:

> The victories of a few independent candidates are certainly suggestive of the potential for efforts outside the two-party box. But they are not the same thing as creating a durable third party. A political party, defined as an ongoing, self-conscious organization of individual voters and officeholders with a common identity and ideas that seeks to win and exercise power, is a rare thing. Building one—even at the local level where most of the real work of politics happens—takes endurance and social solidarity.[12]

John Bibby and Sandy Maisel note:

> Political parties have a formal organizational structure and formal procedures; they contend for a variety of offices; they develop and present platforms that state their views on the issues of the day; they persist for a period of time and win the allegiance of followers because of their candidates, their issue positions, their records of achievement.[13]

There is a vast body of citizens in America who do not participate in the political process or vote in elections because they feel their voices will not be heard. Some of these men and women can form the base of a new party, along with independents and centrist Republicans and Democrats who hold their noses when they go to the polls, casting their ballots because they feel it is their obligation as citizens. These people might flock to a political organization that pledges to run incorruptible candidates and would try to end the ideological bickering that has precluded action on so much necessary legislation. To be successful in this insurrection, the new party must persuade Americans that it is a real alternative to the Republicans and Democrats, will have staying power, and will not fold after one election cycle. It must be able to convince average citizens that it is worthwhile for them to cast their ballots for an untested political upstart who has a vision for a new way of governing. If it is able to gain credibility among the electorate, it will make centrist politicians who are on the fence more willing to commit themselves to this intriguing new player.

Whatever happens in the first few elections it contests, this new party must work and build for the future, trying to bring about permanent political restructuring. Though several years may be required for the party to achieve its goals, its adherents must have perseverance and the will to see it through. Lisa Jane Disch, a political scientist, has reminded us that the two-party dominance of politics was not written in stone by our Founding Fathers.

An effect of rules, habits and beliefs that have been with us since the turn of the twentieth century, the two-party system is an entrenched hierarchy that affords established parties a political embargo against challenger candidates. Whereas the dominant parties legislated this arrangement into being, it is the voters who shoulder the blame for this dysfunction.[14]

It must also be the voters who extricate America from this morass by supporting a new third party of the center.

Some Americans may feel that having three or even four political parties works better in a parliamentary system of government, where the prime minister acts as the executive rather than the president. However, there is no reason why Washington shouldn't be able to function effectively with House members and Senators from more than two parties, perhaps requiring a coalition and even shifting alliances to govern.

## Differentiating a New Third Party

The questions will be asked by many citizens—how will this party be different from the Republicans and Democrats and why should I vote for its candidates or support it financially? How well this party is able to distinguish itself from the others during its initial stages may determine whether or not it is ultimately successful. It will be characterized by:

- Integrity and ethical conduct
- A pragmatic approach to problems
- Competent governance
- Transparency

Though the current political parties claim to be guided by these principles, recent history shows that those claims camouflage the true situation. During the new party's gestation and when it first begins its operations, it will suffer from a lack of recognition. This is actually good. The organization will be starting from scratch and will not be burdened with partisanship and old enmities, nor will it be infested with a long-standing culture of corruption. Its slate will be completely clean, and with no history to live down or apologize for, the party will be able to write its own narrative and demand accountability from its members.

### *Integrity*

The new party will be built on a bedrock of integrity and trustworthiness. From its inception, the organization will have a strict code of conduct that its members agree to abide by and that the leadership enforces, unlike the Republicans and Democrats, who often ignore ethical lapses. Legislating ethical reform does not work when legislators are constantly seeking ways to subvert the laws they have enacted and when they value the veneer of respectability more than actually ethical conduct. Self-policing and transparency are better ways to encourage integrity, particularly if there is a threat of onerous penalties from the party for deviant behavior. Just as a culture of corruption in an organization can spawn more corruption, a culture of integrity is likely to foster ethical conduct.

To demonstrate its commitment to attack corruption, this fledgling party will create a written Oath of Ethical Conduct. In this document, members will pledge to work toward a different system of financing political campaigns. Though the party will be actively trying to generate campaign funds, as we'll discuss later, its candidates will agree not to take payments from any groups or individuals personally, but will direct all donations toward designated party administrative entities. Party members will also eschew political action committees and will never use political funds for personal gain. They will promise as well not to accept meals, trips, vacations, fact-finding junkets, or tickets to any events from individuals or organizations that have an interest in current or future legislation or executive actions. Lobbyists will not be permitted to do research for party members, write speeches for them, or help them draft legislation. Any party member who is elected to office, appointed to an executive position, or serves on the staff of an elected or appointed official will agree to refrain from seeking or accepting a job as a lobbyist or working for a special interest group for five years after he or she leaves office or ceases employment as a legislative or executive staffer. Elected officials from this new party will be free to meet with lobbyists or representatives of special interests as they would with any constituent, but the discussions will be open and they will not accept any favors or funds.

To enforce the Oath of Ethical Conduct, party members who run for office or receive staff or executive positions in the government will sign the document and confirm that they understand its intent. The Oath will also contain an agreement for signatories to forfeit a monetary sum to the party if their pledges are not honored. The amount of the penalty can be set by a party ethics board prior to the signing, along with the details of the contract, but should be severe enough to dissuade members from abrogating the agreement. If members do not comply with their contracts and do not pay the penalties, they can be sued by the party. To be certain there is no deception, members will be required to list their assets with the party when holding an office or government post. Every two years, this will be updated as a further guarantee of financial rectitude. This information can be used as corroborative evidence in a suit if the ethics board feels that a member has broken his or her pledge. The Oath of Ethical Conduct and the willingness of party members to place their assets on the line if they breach the code should prove to the public that this new party is serious about wiping out corruption and conflicts of interest. In addition to the enforcement provisions, the existence of the contract itself will reinforce the party's image for probity. The use of the Oath may seem draconian to some observers, but only robust measures will remove the stain of ethical laxness that most citizens associate with politicians.

There are some questions about whether the Oath, with its penalty for damages, will be legally enforceable if there is a breach of contract as it may be difficult to demonstrate an injury to the new party that can be defined in monetary terms. The threat of a suit and a court case, however, may be enough to prevent abrogation of the contract. We will leave it to attorneys to craft the document in ways that will strengthen compliance.

## *Pragmatism*

Pragmatism will also be a central tenet of the new party. The organization will not be wedded to any ideology regarding the role of government or economic precepts, rejecting the dogma of both the right and the left. Answers to problems will be sought and policy generated by ideas that are felt to be practical, guided by common sense rather than by the perceived wisdom of ideologues. There will be no one-size-fits-all solutions. Instead, the party will pick and choose from a smorgasbord of ideas to devise programs appropriate for particular problems. In both domestic and foreign policy, no approach will be off the table because of preconceived notions; any idea will be open for consideration. Historical positions will not be cause to reject a premise, with reevaluation and modification of past concepts perfectly acceptable. Negotiation and compromise will not be considered as a retreat from strongly held beliefs, but as a way of getting things done. Innovative and novel plans of action will not be given short shrift, but will be carefully assessed for potential benefits. None of this means a repudiation of the nation's history and past programs. Instead, the party will try to build upon what has come before to move America forward in a constructive fashion.

In this vein of pragmatism, given the numerous challenges the nation faces, contentious social issues will be de-emphasized and placed on the back burner until solutions are found for the problems that threaten America's national security, economic prowess, and world stature. Federal government bodies have expended too much time and effort trying to find answers that will assuage individuals and groups with irreconcilable stances on matters like same-sex marriage and abortion, while vital concerns have been left in abeyance. Elected officials need to focus on the national debt and budget deficits, unemployment and the mortgage mess, improving economic competitiveness, lowering the enormous trade deficits, reforming education, and protecting the nation from international terrorism. Although many believe social issues are also of critical importance, a pragmatic approach cannot possibly bridge the gap because the chasm between the two sides on these questions is so vast. It is sensible to put them aside for the time being. Individual states rather than the federal government can still address these issues.

## Competence

Competence in governance will be another cornerstone of the new party, with a mandate to make government work effectively and efficiently. This contrasts with the present system where ideological *bona fides* and connections often determine government appointments, rather than expertise, knowledge, and administrative ability. Though civil service jobs are no longer allotted by patronage as they were in the nineteenth century, it is also true that there are no comprehensive tests for policy-making or top administrative posts. We have seen how disastrous it can be when inexperienced or incompetent cronies are given crucial jobs because of party allegiance, friendships with the right people, or affiliation with particular organizations. Before appointments to high-level positions are made by officials of the new party, a panel of independent experts will be asked for advice on those who are being considered, making it more likely that qualified personnel will be selected.

Though many federal departments have inspector general's offices to evaluate employees' work and the policies they generate, very often the evaluations are superficial and do not lead to consequences for individuals for unsatisfactory work. The new party's independent panels of experts will evaluate top executive and congressional appointees of party members periodically to be certain they are functioning capably, making suggestions if necessary to help them improve their job performance. If the staff members continue to perform poorly, the panel can recommend censure or dismissal. It is important that an appointee not be allowed to compound mistakes previously made. These panels, however, will play no day-to-day role in the running of the government.

Lower-level government employees who are not political appointees must also be held accountable for their performance with established parameters for bureaucratic operations in all areas. Though the civil service unions may object, merit pay should be instituted and promotions based on ability and effort rather than seniority. Making the huge federal bureaucracy function efficiently and responsively to citizens' needs will not be easy, but it can and must be done to help restore the public's belief in its government.

Although elected officials answer to their constituents for their performances when new elections are held, most citizens do not have specific metrics to assess how well their representatives have done their job. The new party's panels will provide a general outline of the work of legislators and elected executives, including votes on important bills, measures sponsored, attendance records, work on committees and sub-committees, funds taken from lobbyists and special interests, and so forth. These analyses will be presented to voters in a simplified format and will include data on officeholders from all parties, with only factual information offered. These evaluations will be available to any interested person online and will also be mailed to every household. The objectivity of the information given will reinforce the public's perception of the new party as dedicated to competent officeholders and good government.

Party legislators who are given leadership posts or committee chairmanships in the House or Senate will receive feedback from their peers regarding their job performance. Those who are felt to be ineffective in their positions will be voted out by the party caucus.

## Transparency

Transparency in party operations and government activities, aside from sensitive economic data, intelligence, and national security, will be another mantra of the new party. Unlike the Democratic and Republican parties, there will be no hidden information and concealed deals. Business will be conducted in the open with the belief that the public has a right to know how its government works and what its elected representatives and officeholders are doing. This will lead to greater confidence in the government and the new party, diminishing cynicism about the nation's political system and instilling a greater willingness to vote and participate in civic affairs. Though 95 percent of what occurs in government's various processes and actions should be available to the public, politicians have been afraid to allow public scrutiny. There are a number of reasons for this.

In the legislative arena, though Congressional debates are usually covered by cable television, the cameras focus on the speakers, since full scanning of the floor to see what other members are doing is not permitted. At times, speakers may be addressing their comments to empty or near-empty chambers, merely to get them into the record. There are also closed sessions that no one views and closed committee meetings where bills may be hammered out in private. Politicians want the current mechanisms to remain in place to shield them from embarrassment, since they often say things they may later regret, behave foolishly, betray ignorance about certain subjects, or even fail to attend sessions. Aside from injudicious remarks and unintelligent statements, their silence may also indict them if they do not participate in debating the issues. Falling asleep during discussions, for example, is bound to play poorly with their constituents. In addition, trading votes on legislative measures or approving pork or bills for special interests, which can occur in closed sessions, will not endear them to the folks back home. When in the glare of the public spotlight, politicians know they will have to conduct themselves differently, be on their best behavior, and be prepared and knowledgeable about matters that arise. Transparency and public scrutiny will provide another layer of oversight to keep politicians in line and make them attend to the country's business.

Agencies and departments in the executive branch of the government should also open their deliberations about policy to the public. It may not be necessary to have television cameras grinding away in every small corner of the government where policy is being formulated, but certainly the transcripts of all discussions, with records of any decisions and actions taken, should be public information. The only exceptions to this would be national security and intelligence issues and financial discussions of sensitive matters, such as those by the Treasury Department, the Federal Reserve Board, or the SEC, where transparency might have unintended consequences.

These descriptions of methods to guarantee the integrity and competence of party officials are suggestions and can be revamped according to practical considerations or legal questions.

## Naming the New Party

When this new party is created, its founders will select a name, but for convenience in the current context, we will use the name, "Civic Alliance Party" (CAP). Interestingly, almost all the names one would associate with an American political party, i.e., Liberty, Freedom, Reform, and so on, have either been used in the past or are currently being used. There is no evidence of a Civic Alliance Party, though it is possible some small, local group may have employed the title previously.

One of the definitions for "civic" in the dictionary is "of citizenship."[15] Alliance is defined as "any union or connection of interests between persons, families, states, or corporations."[16] Thus, the Civic Alliance is a union of citizens working together for clean, competent government. The hope is that the party's principles and objectives will entice the disparate elements within the nation's society to participate in this movement to revitalize America. The more people who join, the stronger the party will be.

The abbreviation for the Civic Alliance Party, CAP, gives the party a symbol it can adopt, a baseball cap, like the Democratic donkey and the Republican elephant. Although a small part of a new party's presentation, caps have historical connections in the United States. During the revolution Americans used so-called "Liberty caps," soft conical forms, often held aloft on a pole,[17] to symbolize freedom. The French also used caps to represent freedom during their revolution. The caps supporting the new party symbolize freedom too—a liberation of the nation from the old political order.

## Creating the Civic Alliance Party

In the two-party system that currently governs America, it is worth noting how close and competitive the two entities have been over the years on a national level.[18] The power of each one ebbs and flows during a period of time and in different geographical regions, but overall the margins of victory have been quite small. This is not to say that some states and districts are not overwhelmingly for one party or another. The minimal separation between the two parties in total votes is an indication that a well-organized and well-financed third party could compete and conceivably hold the balance of power between the other two, leading to significant political change. As mentioned previously, the core constituents of this new party would be disaffected centrists and moderates of the current political parties, along with independents who are wary of the ideological constraints of the Republicans and Democrats. There are many Americans fitting these categories who might jump at the opportunity to support a new party, particularly one that stresses the integrity and flexibility of its candidates. All religious and racial groups and members of different economic classes would be welcome in this organization.

To be a truly national party, play a major role in American politics, and be a real and permanent force for change, the Civic Alliance Party would have to develop a structure that encompassed all levels of government. In other words, the party could not be Washington-centric, but would need a strong foundation on the state, municipal, and ward levels, with members who were politically active whether they were in or out of government. While national figures would be in the limelight, giving the party its cachet and helping to recruit members, the party would have to have workers involved in the nitty-gritty of daily politics to be effective and vital on a long-term basis. The party would have to have a presence in all regions of the country, whether or not the people in an area were initially receptive to the Civic Alliance's objectives. In 2006, there was a conflict in the Democratic Party over whether to devote resources to developing an infrastructure in the red states they were unlikely to win, or to allocate funds and effort only to states where the Democrats were competitive.[19] Their strategy of working the red states as well as the blue proved to be a good decision, particularly in some western states where the Republicans had been dominant. As we have seen, third parties in the past that were organized around one person's outsized personality or a particular issue vanished from the scene after one or several election cycles and did not influence the course of the American ship of state.

With party members active in a particular community, it will be easier to convince their friends and neighbors to join, swelling the party's membership and voting power. In addition to reinforcing the party's strength, people involved at a lower level will provide training and the development of cadres, members who will run for local, municipal, and state offices and assist in organization. Those who emerge later on the national stage will have solid on-the-job training. Just as a good professional team needs a strong bench to be successful, the party will have strong candidates better able to function competently and efficiently in more difficult and complex positions. Along with congressmen and senators, the party will need mayors, city councilmen, and representatives on the local zoning boards and boards of education, both to further their own political educations and to promote the party's ideals. If the new party cannot recruit members to join and participate politically, the Civic Alliance will be doomed to wither just like its one-issue forebears.

It will be vital for Civic Alliance members to monitor and get elected to the state legislatures, since these chambers control the redistricting process. How the states draw the lines of their election districts determines the outcome of future congressional elections and the direction of the federal government. This kind of change will take time. One Alliance goal will be to have the legislatures in every state transfer responsibility for redistricting to independent bodies to minimize political bias and gerrymandering. Even if the Civic Alliance does not have a majority in a state legislature, a small block of votes could hold the balance of power between the other two parties. This lever can then be used to ensure that the process of redistricting is conducted fairly.

~~~

There are three ways to create a new party, each of which has its pros and cons. They are not mutually exclusive and the different methods can be used in combination. The descriptive terms used for each method are top-down creation, bottom-up creation, and fragmentation of the current parties.

## Top-Down Creation

This method can be initiated with a national figure or figures committed to the formation of a new, centrist, permanent third party and willing to assume the burden, along with those he or she recruits, of midwifing the birth of this organization and helping it through its growing pains. A strong and skillful leader can bolster the chances for success of any organization, including political parties, and is particularly relevant when the enterprise is in its infancy. One or several powerful leaders founding the Civic Alliance Party, with a distinct vision of how he, she, or they want it to develop, and with specific objectives all of which can be easily and cogently articulated, can be crucial in launching the organization off to a fast start. This scenario could help attract members and aid in soliciting funds. In addition, if one of the founders is a potential presidential candidate who is charismatic and credible, it would enhance this fledgling party's status with the media and the public. *Third Parties in America* observed:

> The relative success of a third party depends in part on who heads its ticket: support is highest when a prestigious or nationally prestigious politician runs. . . . [however] . . . most prestigious and nationally prestigious third-party candidates of the twentieth century have been self-starters. The candidate recruited the movement, not the other way around.[20]

The founding figure or figures of the Civic Alliance must of course subscribe to the ideals and principles of the party, be willing to change the system of campaign financing to reduce the power of the lobbyists and special interests, and subscribe to a non-ideological, pragmatic approach to the country's problems. Though having a national figure who wants to run for president on the Alliance ticket would be helpful for the party early on, this person must be dedicated to the development of the party. It would be harmful if the nominee was merely using the party as a vehicle for his or her own advancement, to be abandoned after the next election. Potential Civic Alliance candidates for president and vice president could come from outside politics or from either the Republican or Democratic parties. The latter would be men and women willing to leave their established political homes because they were unhappy with the corruption and partisanship and looking for a new way to serve the country. In the first election that the party contests, it might have one candidate from each party running for president and vice president, or an outsider and someone who had defected from a political party, or even two individuals who came from outside of politics. Any officeholder or politician would be able to join the Alliance, even if previously tainted by lobbyists, as long as he or she was willing to work to change the old way of doing political business and sign the Oath of Ethical Conduct. There would have to be a total commitment to clean government and a vow to avoid future ethical missteps.

Since funding is vital to a party's prospects, it would be helpful if some of the early supporters were extremely wealthy and willing to apply significant capital to financing the Civic Alliance, increasing the probability that the party would remain viable and become a permanent player in the political process. Finding a stream of income for the Civic Alliance in the initial stages will be extremely important, whether the money comes from a few affluent individuals or many smaller contributors. Ultimately, to be sustainable, the party will need a broad base of long-term financial support. An early infusion of funds would permit the party to hire professionals and administrative personnel to supplement volunteers in a number of roles. These would include the planning and implementing of advertising campaigns, dealing with the media, recruiting members and potential candidates for multiple offices, and helping to shape coherent policy. The development of a hierarchical administrative structure for the party will be important to eliminate chaos, confusion, and duplication of tasks. In spite of their devotion to a cause, a horizontal grouping of individuals without direction cannot be nearly as productive as a defined structure and people with assigned functions.

## Bottom-Up Creation

Creating a political party from the bottom up without a national figure around whom members can coalesce might require more time and effort, but it can be done and be successful. The bottom-up, grassroots formation of a new centrist party would be a citizen's movement and would have great appeal to those Americans who feel disenfranchised, similar to the appeal of the Tea Party movement on the right. The party could start with small "discussion groups" on college campuses, and in cities, suburbs, and small towns with individuals who are fed up with the current political system and want change. These would be people dedicated to liberating America from the lobbyists and special interests and from government officials linked to these predators, as well as from the ideologues of the left and right. Citizens in these discussion groups could organize further into political committees and put forth candidates to run for office at district, municipal, and state levels. These local committees would also form a national network with the same goals and code of conduct for all their members, creating hierarchical as well as horizontal linkages, evolving into a party. The Internet and social networks would be the key mechanisms for communication among these geographically separated groups, allowing them to integrate and adopt the common ideals and objectives characteristic of a party.

As the party develops, candidates who believe in its tenets would be recruited from all walks of life. Professional politicians and members of other parties would again be encouraged to join, even with previous ethical transgressions, as long as they had done nothing illegal and were willing to renounce their past actions and sign the Oath of Ethical Conduct. Ideologues would not be welcome even if they were proponents of clean government.

Forming the party after a presidential election and contesting only local and state elections initially might give the party time to grow competitively as a national player. If a presidential contest was in the offing, however, it would be helpful to recruit a national figure to run on the Civic Alliance ticket as a presidential candidate, to keep the party in the public eye and aid its other candidates running for office. Even better would be to have several national figures vying for the party's presidential nomination, as this would capture the interest of the media and the public. Fundraising would again be critical and several options for this will be described further on. With a structure in place, committed party members and candidates carrying the party's banner in elections for every level of office, and a message that resonates with America's citizens, it would only be a matter of time before the Civic Alliance Party cracked the duopoly of the Republicans and Democrats in the political arena.

## Fragmentation of Current Parties

It is also possible that the Civic Alliance Party could be formed through fragmentation of the current parties. Elected officeholders and other politicians on both sides could defect from their established habitats and come together to create this new entity. A number of moderate Republicans and Democrats might consider leaving their parties if they believed a third party offered credible options. While at times a Republican will defect to the Democratic Party and vice versa, for most party members affiliation with the opposition is not a reasonable alternative. Senator Jim Jeffords, a New England centrist, left the Republican Party in 2001 because he disagreed with its partisan stances, but became an independent rather than join the Democratic Party, even though he usually voted with the Democrats. Republican Senator Arlen Specter of Pennsylvania joined the Democrats in 2009 because he believed he was too moderate to win his state's primary.

Most party members continue their associations even if they are dissatisfied with party policy or ideology because they don't want to be perceived as disloyal or branded a turncoat. They also don't see any benefits in independence and won't join a party that has always been considered "the enemy." The Civic Alliance could provide a new home for those who are discontented. In fact, Republicans and Democrats who can no longer stand to be a part of the old corrupt order could join with other like-minded colleagues to generate this new party. They would agree to abide by the Oath of Ethical Conduct and work to free themselves from special-interest money in the future. Moderate Republicans in particular are no longer at home in their party, which is controlled by conservative ideologues, and would find their values a good fit with the Civic Alliance. We will discuss this further in another section of this chapter.

In reality, a combination of the three methods of creating this new party — top-down creation, bottom-up creation, and fragmentation of the current parties—will probably be used. Fragmentation of the Republicans and Democrats will occur with all methods. Converts from the established parties will have come to the realization that their allegiance to the nation is greater than to their old party. They will have understood the depth of America's problems and will have concluded that a transformation of the political system is necessary to find solutions. In addition, they will have rejected the accepted wisdom that third parties cannot win national elections and will be willing to work to build this new entity. It may mean they are forgoing power in the short run, but they know the current system is failing and are forging the Civic Alliance to change America's course.

## Use of the Internet and Social Networks

Both Democrats and Republicans are learning how to use to greatest advantage the emerging, growing giants of communication, the Internet and social networks. The use of Internet-based social media can be politically transformative for any nation, as the revolutions in the Middle East show. Entities like Facebook and Twitter can play an enormous role in helping to create and sustain a new party. In fact, without them it is unlikely a third party could succeed. Their availability, ease of use, and their power to spread ideas and bring people together to change the political landscape is increasingly acknowledged.[21],[22] They are particularly important because of their central place in the lives of America's youth, who generally eschew involvement in politics. Ken Mehlman, the former Republican national chairman, has said, "The effect of the Internet on politics will be every bit as transformational as television was."[23] From an organizational standpoint, they are wonderful facilitators, allowing structures to be created in weeks or months that would otherwise take years to develop. Networking and finding like-minded people who believe in the objectives of the Civic Alliance could assist in the recruitment of new members to join the organization and serve in various functions. Party members around the country would be able to connect, share their experiences, and debate the issues. They could disseminate ideas virally, encouraging virtually immediate participation and mobilization when necessary.

The current political parties are devoting tremendous resources to these tools. To date, the Democrats have been more successful than the Republicans, both for fundraising and generating support for candidates, with the "blogosphere" crammed with liberal bloggers.[24] Liberal netroots activists undoubtedly played a role in the Democrats' 2006 victory, but there are bloggers from both parties, the majority of whom tend to have partisan axes to grind. The Obama campaign succeeded in 2008 at least partially because of its use of the Internet and social networks. There are also news sources like Politico and political gossip sites like the Drudge Report that may have an influence on the way a portion of Americans think and vote. Not infrequently, information from these sites finds its way to the mainstream media, enhancing its effect. Yet most of the reports circulated on the Internet are not vetted and can be speculative or wrong, sometimes with malicious intent. However, young people over the last several years pay less attention to the Internet, having become addicted to social networking.

People using social networks to rally around the Civic Alliance would be participating in the birth of a new entity. They would be in on the ground floor of a burgeoning mass movement with the excitement that would generate. The passion of the Alliance's adherents would be multiplied by other believers dedicated to achieving the same goals. Party members could vote online about policy initiatives, planks in the platforms, and establishing priorities, aiding the leadership in their decisions. More important, local, statewide, and national party primaries could be easily organized and conducted online, allowing greater involvement of the membership in choosing candidates. In the past, vice-presidential nominees have been selected by the presidential candidates and rubber-stamped by party members at the conventions. Online primary elections for the Civic Alliance nominees for both president and vice president would generate more interest in the electoral process and more support for the candidates in the general election.

Internet primaries could be structured in various ways. The most interest and credibility might come from an elimination system run over a period of weeks or months, those candidates with the fewest votes in each segment dropping out. Individuals running in these online primaries would use the Internet to present their programs to party members and give speeches to this audience, with the campaign continuing sequentially until someone attained a majority of the votes. Debates among candidates could be shown online as well. The entire political process would become more democratic in this Civic Alliance model, with members truly connected to the party and sharing in the action. Primary campaigns would also be significantly less expensive if they were conducted mainly over the Internet, with less need for travel and advertising. Anyone interested could monitor and participate in party activities online in real time. And if rallies were held or speeches given by party officials or candidates outside of cyberspace, social networks could be used to encourage party members to attend, ensuring a large and receptive audience.

The Internet and social networks would also be vital in generating funds for the new party, using various techniques to find those individuals sympathetic to the cause who might be willing to provide financial support. As Howard Dean demonstrated in the 2004 Democratic primary campaign for president, considerable sums of money can be harvested online. All the 2008 presidential candidates followed this model, most successfully Barack Obama and Hillary Clinton, who raised hundreds of millions over the Internet from small contributors.[25,26] Even more impressive perhaps was the ability of the then little-known Republican candidate with libertarian views, Ron Paul, to accumulate cash through the Internet, enabling him to sustain his campaign.[27] In the third quarter of 2007, he raised $5 million, and more than $6.84 million in the first five weeks of the fourth quarter. In a single day, November 5, a concerted effort signed up over 21,000 donors and collected over $4 million. The Civic Alliance would try to tap both large and small donors, soliciting from party adherents as well independents who believed in the party's objectives. It is likely that enough money could be collected online and through individual donations outside of cyberspace that funding from lobbyists and special interests would be unnecessary.

Internet blogs and advertising would be used extensively to garner support for the new party's candidates and goals. Though it is the younger portion of the nation's population that currently pays most attention to these blogs, their readership may grow over time and their opinions and ideas may become more important. The

Civic Alliance would have to make its presence felt in this area as an alternative to the dueling blogs of conservatives and liberals.

The social networking site, MySpace, opened the "Impact Channel" focusing on politics in March 2007, highlighting the 2008 presidential race.[28] This made it easier for the 60 million users of MySpace each month, overwhelmingly young and uninterested in politics, to identify with candidates by viewing their personal MySpace pages. Users were able to see the candidates' personal videos and photos, read their blogs, and link to other sites where specific ideas were discussed. As of 2010 Facebook was the preferred social network, with Twitter and MySpace following. YouTube was also important. Candidates hope that users of these social platforms will add them to their friends list and that their friends will follow suit, spreading the candidates' messages virally and reaching potential voters who would otherwise stay on the sidelines. They can also use Twitter to keep party members and the general electorate abreast of their activities in real time. Mechanisms will be in place as well to aid candidates in soliciting campaign contributions and to help voters register. In addition, on Election Day, the social networks will help to get out the vote of party members and those sympathetic to the party's objectives.

## Unity08

Instituting an online campaign to try to generate a bipartisan presidential ticket in 2008, a group of politicians and political consultants along with a number of nonprofessionals formed an organization called "Unity08."[29] Among its founders were Democrats Hamilton Jordan (Jimmy Carter's former chief of staff) and Gerald Rafshoon, Republican Doug Bailey, and the former governor of Maine, independent Angus King. They stated that this initiative "is a reaction to a system that has 'polarized and alienated the American people' through partisanship and interest-group politics."[30] Unity08's website listed three goals:

- Elect a truly bipartisan Unity ticket to the White House in 2008

- Make history and nominate the next president and vice president through the first-ever online, virtual convention
- Demand a focus on crucial issues by creating a New American Agenda[31]

Information posted online declared that the group did not want to start a third party, but wanted to make Republicans and Democrats more responsive, open, and attentive to the critical problems facing America.[32] They envisioned members joining Unity08 online and participating in a virtual convention to choose the nominees. Unfortunately, their marketing of the concept was deficient, the effort fading into insignificance before the election. But prior to starting their organization, a national poll initiated by Unity08 found that 82 percent of respondents believed that politics were too polarized to permit the country's problems to be solved.[33] Of those polled, 75 percent were also unhappy about having to choose only Republicans or Democrats when voting and wanted more choices to be available. However, Unity08's unwillingness to build a party from the ground up, with the grunt work necessary to fashion an organization, limited the group's ability to affect the political system.

~~~

The Internet and social networks will certainly play an increasingly important role in politics and the democratic process as new options as yet unknown are discovered and used. However, while these online networks offer the siren song of participatory democracy, citizens must be careful, for though the idea is seductive, dangers abound. The tyranny of the majority and demagogic appeal become real considerations, with the potential to ride roughshod over minority and individual rights. Hate groups and rogue organizations love the Internet for the opportunities it provides them to spread their messages and recruit new adherents. With information rapidly disseminated and exchanged over the Internet, lies and misinformation may be able to convince people to vote or take actions they might not have done upon further reflection, or when contrary data was available. Politicians may also become more immediately responsive to public opinion because of the Internet, driven by the inference of the moment and a desire to please the voters.

Mistakes or gaffes of various kinds by politicians or their campaign teams will also travel widely over the Internet, with video clips seen by vast numbers of people.[34] Past actions and contradictory statements may come back to haunt candidates as well. Because of this, politicians may become even more cautious about what they say or how they behave, not wanting to damage their images and their campaigns. (With aspirants for office parsing every word they utter, there is also the possibility that the intolerably lengthy campaigns become unbearably boring.) It will be important for candidates to react quickly to any real or perceived blunders and get their message out to limit the negative effects of these lapses and show the public decisive leadership qualities.

## Fundraising

While the Internet will be a potent tool for gathering funds for the Civic Alliance, other mechanisms will have to be employed as well, particularly in the early stages of the party's development. Though one of the Civic Alliance's objectives will be the elimination of campaign financing from lobbyists and special interests, corporations and wealthy individuals may have to be approached for money initially if the new party is to have adequate resources to lock horns with its established competitors. However, to ensure separation between donors and politicians, Civic Alliance campaign committees will be created as quasi-independent bodies. Campaign contributions will be given to these committees, rather than directly to party members running for office. Candidates will subsequently receive funds from the campaign committees instead of from the donors. Elected officials and those running for office will not be told who provided the money for their campaigns so that no favors can be granted in return. Donors can still designate those whom they want to receive the funds and the money will be disbursed appropriately, but the recipient will remain in the dark as to the source. This way there will be no questions about conflict of interest or decisions being influenced by campaign contributions. The aim will be that enough affluent citizens see the value of the Civic Alliance's goals and be willing to provide financial support to the party even if it does not benefit them personally. These will be people concerned about America's future and able to look beyond their own self-interest. Though this is not the optimal way to raise funds, the Civic Alliance has to be practical and understand that it can transform the accepted way of doing things only by attaining power, which can happen only with adequate funding.

Eventually, the other political parties will probably follow the Civic Alliance's lead or face the voters' wrath. Cynics will question whether this fundraising arrangement will work, since political contributions currently and in the past have depended on donors' knowing they will get something from the politicians in return for the money they give. However, with America now in crisis mode, there may be enough people who realize that a change in its political system is imperative and are willing to dig into their pockets to aid in the transformation. One can almost think of these contributions to the Civic Alliance as akin to charitable donations. Instead of subsidizing a museum or symphony orchestra, or trying to alleviate hunger in the third world, the contribution would go to engender clean, competent government in the United States.

Officeholders of the Civic Alliance will also not be allowed to form their own political action committees (PACs) to collect and disburse money, as this is obviously a breeding ground for corruption. The party, however, will set up organizations handling specific functions (administrative, educational, voter registration, and so forth) to which corporations and individuals can contribute to help the party, aside from campaign funding. People familiar with election laws will be called on to work out the details of how to structure these organizations.

Recruiting wealthy candidates who can finance their own campaigns for office on the Civic Alliance ticket would obviate the need for money in these instances. These individuals would have to commit to the party's rules and objectives. If they were victorious, they would not be beholden to any special interests since they would have received no funds or outside help in their campaigns. While there is nothing wrong with this scenario, the Civic Alliance would not want to be a party of the affluent alone and needs to have members and candidates from every economic level and all walks of life if it is to be effective. It will be necessary to ensure that all the party's candidates, no matter what their financial standing, receive adequate support when they run for office, which means aggressive fundraising within the party's restrictions.

Huge sums of money are currently spent on political campaigns, with each successive election demanding increased outlays. Every candidate seems to employ an army of advisers, consultants, and pollsters blanketing all the media in a blizzard of advertisements. While this may be productive at times, the volume of these announcements has adverse consequences in many cases, particularly the unrelenting attacks and negativity that some candidates favor. Civic Alliance candidates may be able to run persuasive campaigns less expensively by astute use of the Internet, dedicated volunteers and campaign workers, networking techniques, and word of mouth, getting more value for what they spend and requiring less money. The party will encourage innovation and experimentation by the candidates to cut costs as they run for office, but at the end of the day, whatever funding is needed by the candidates must be provided.

After Watergate, it was believed that furnishing presidential aspirants with public funds if they curtailed their spending would reduce corruption and the dependence on special interests for financing. But it turned out there were candidates who were unwilling to accept public money and adhere to the limits on spending, thinking it was too restrictive. It was truly astonishing to realize that presidential candidates were turning down the hundreds of millions of dollars they would receive through public funding. On the other hand, merely to be considered a serious contestant currently entails raising at least $100 million as an "entry fee." This is another commentary on the sad state of the nation's political system, which is unable to sever the ties between the fundraisers and those running for public offices. In February 2011, the House Republicans passed legislation to end public funding for presidential candidates.[35] This move would enhance the value of contributions from corporate donors and wealthy individuals. It remains to be seen whether it will make it through the Democratic-controlled Senate.

Individual donors are presently allowed to contribute $4800 to each contestant for federal office, $2400 for the primary and $2400 for the general election.[36] However, lobbyists, special interests, and people who can bundle contributions by soliciting from friends and family are the ones who are truly valued by the candidates and political parties, as they are the ones who can deliver huge sums of cash. The candidates who are willing to play ball with the lobbyists receive the largest contributions. Of course, as we have seen, some candidates are better able to harvest funds from individuals, including multiple small donations online that add up. The question Americans must ask is whether proficiency at fundraising makes a person more qualified in any way for the presidency or for any political office. The Civic Alliance wants to change the current paradigm for campaign fundraising and end the connections between the lobbyists, special interests, and elected officials.

## Endowment of the Civic Alliance

Endowment of a political party is a new and unique concept and needs to undergo thorough legal scrutiny to solidify its validity. Currently, there is a $30,400 limit that an individual can donate to any national political party committee per calendar year as defined in the Bipartisan Campaign Finance Reform Act of 2002.[37] Establishing a foundation of some sort and structuring the process in a particular way might be necessary to allow this strategy to be used. If the funds were employed to defray the regular expenses (the operating costs) of the party and did not finance political campaigns, large contributions to an endowment might be deemed satisfactory. Another possible plan might be for the endowment to be devoted to a public education function under the aegis of the Civic Alliance. One of the major roles this new party should play is to educate Americans about the political process and the problems facing the nation.

If public service announcements and infomercials created by the Civic Alliance did not endorse or oppose any candidates, they might pass muster with the Federal Election Commission even though they would be promoting Alliance objectives.

Other ways to make an endowment work for the party would have to be explored by creative attorneys, remaining within the bounds of legality. Depending on the size of the endowment, its yield could make fundraising less onerous. With the cost of political campaigns continuing to escalate, a reliable source of funds for other party functions would be extremely beneficial. For example, an endowment of $500 million would produce $35 million at a 7 percent return. An endowment of $5 billion would deliver $350 million annually.

Affluent individuals would have to be convinced that giving a portion of their capital to the Civic Alliance would be a worthwhile social investment, not a waste of their money. Men like Bill Gates and Warren Buffett have contributed billions of dollars to try to reduce various illnesses and poverty in Africa. In June 2006, Buffett announced a donation of $31 billion to the Bill and Melinda Gates Foundation, whose objective is to cure the world's major infectious diseases.[38] Wouldn't it be valuable if they used their money to attack partisan conflict, corruption, and inadequacies in the American political system by supporting a new party dedicated to repairing that system, when anything that government does or doesn't do affects the rest of the world? Currently, both the left and the right have a coterie of extremely wealthy supporters who pour money into Republican and Democratic coffers, ideological think tanks, candidates, and special campaign funds which may or may not be anonymous, to foster their beliefs. Just a few of the prominent names are Charles and David Koch, Richard Mellon Scaife, and Sheldon Adelson on the right, and George Soros and Herbert and Marion Sandler on the left; there are numerous others in both camps. What are needed now are some extremely wealthy Americans who would be willing to support the moderate political center and the rebirth of pragmatism as the path the nation should follow to establish effective government.

Not only would the endowment format or foundation have to

pass muster with the Election Commission, but taxes on any contri-butions would also be an issue. At present, there are no tax deduc-tions allowed for donations to political parties, though there might be for an educational foundation or similar organization. Sharp legal minds could probably decipher all the ramifications of this program and find a way to make it work, though undoubtedly the Republican and Democratic parties would try to keep this from occurring. And they might also try to develop their own endowments. leading to an escalation in the quest for funds.

Mayor Mike Bloomberg of New York would be an ideal per-son to found and help finance a centrist third party, with his term as mayor coming to an end. Though his name has been mentioned as a possible independent presidential candidate, he has disavowed any interest in running. He has said, in fact, that he would like to devote the remainder of his life to philanthropy. However, as a man who has been tremendously successful in business and in politics, he would be an excellent choice to take on the challenge of organizing a third party and making it work. He has the administrative ability, the moxie, and the practical approach to problems to build a func-tioning party from scratch, just as he forged his business empire. In addition, he would probably be able to recruit other businessmen and politicians with a similar vision to support the party. With the backing of Mayor Bloomberg and other wealthy individuals, funds would be available to launch the party on a sound financial footing. The larger the number of financiers and politicians present at the outset, the stronger the party would be. The Civic Alliance, or a similar entity, would be a unique gift for these men and women to give to America, different from the usual philanthropic endeavors. Bloomberg has been employing his media properties to dissemi-nate opinion pieces reflecting his ideas to influence the national political debate.[39] Why not support for a political party that takes a pragmatic approach to problems as a way to transform politics?

Bill Gates and Warren Buffett would also be excellent found-ing figures for the Civic Alliance. Aside from the financial boost they could provide, as successful businessmen they could be help-ful from an organizational standpoint in generating new ideas and shaping policy. People like Bloomberg, Gates, or Buffett on board would also give the Civic Alliance instant credibility. A financier like Pete Peterson, who has been fighting for years to make the government fiscally responsible, could fill the same role. In fact, there are many other Americans of similar standing whose support would aid the Civic Alliance immeasurably. The right "white knights" with the financial resources, intelligence, business acumen, and perseverance could help create and nourish this third party, and quickly make it competitive with the established two parties.

## Potential Presidential and Vice-Presidential Candidates for a Third Party

National elections are scheduled in 2012, including a presidential contest. Though the Civic Alliance would hope to run a slate of candidates for various offices from top to bottom in all geographic regions, it would be a major challenge for this new entity to be able to do so in such a short time frame. However, using the Internet and social networks does make it possible. The way the party is started, and how close it is to 2012, will likely determine the range of candidates that it fields. If it becomes too difficult to mobilize a full slate of nominees in 2012, the party might select a few elections to contest in districts or states that seem open to its message. This could be followed with a more comprehensive list of candidates for offices in 2014 and then the full range of candidates in 2016, including the presidency. At some point, there will have to be enough party members to step forward and run for office at every level of government.

Since there is no functioning nationwide third party to support a presidential bid by a top-tier candidate in 2012, the possible choices for this office are purely hypothetical. Nevertheless, there are many well-known figures who would make admirable nominees with the potential for a successful run. Having a credible candidate for president during the early phases of the Civic Alliance's development would lend the party respectability, whether or not that person was victorious, demonstrating that the party was going to be a major player on the political scene.

There is no reason to differentiate between candidates for president and vice president, as qualifications for one office should qualify that person for the other, with candidates for either position being of the same caliber. This is because the office of vice president recently has been given more power and responsibility in the executive branch than in the past, when the post was almost ceremonial. The job of president has grown ever more complex and is freighted with too many important roles not to hand some to the vice president. This began to happen during the Clinton and Bush administrations with Gore and Cheney, and is also true with Obama and Biden. But it is likely the office will be expanded even further. While the relationship could be formalized legislatively, it would probably be better left to the discretion of the president, or through an agreement between presidential and vice presidential candidates prior to their run for office.

A sampling of potential centrist third-party candidates for president or vice president follows. These are merely examples of individuals the Civic Alliance could support for high office. Their strengths and leadership qualities vary.

Colin Powell has both the experience and *gravitas* to be a serious contender for the presidency, and is also a moderate held in affection by much of the American public. In addition to his time as Secretary of State, he has been Chairman of the Joint Chiefs of Staff, National Security Adviser, and has held various military posts. Some, however, would view him negatively because of his support for the invasion of Iraq and his unwillingness to resign from the government to disassociate himself from President Bush's policies. In the past, he has rejected feelers from both the Republicans and Democrats about a possible presidential bid for personal reasons, one of which was opposition from his wife. But Powell is an old soldier and deeply patriotic, who believes in duty and obligation. He is fully aware of America's problems, both domestically and internationally.

Powell is too moderate to ever wrest the Republican nomination from control of the conservatives and the Democrats have enough of their own candidates, including Obama's probable bid for reelection in 2012. If Obama were to withdraw for any reason, Powell might find an independent challenge appealing, running without an established party's political baggage in an attempt to clean up the mess in Washington and return the country to fiscal sanity. Powell's great popularity and America's willingness to elect him to the presidency were affirmed in an exit poll taken after the 1996 election.[40] If Powell had been the Republican candidate instead of Bob Dole, he would have handily defeated Bill Clinton and Ross Perot in that race. Even though Clinton beat Powell in a survey among black voters, Powell would have received 53 percent of the white votes compared to 33 percent for Clinton. Powell's age, however, is a factor against his candidacy, as he was born in 1937.

Chuck Hagel, the former Republican senator from Nebraska, served as an infantryman in Vietnam, was wounded, and received two Purple Hearts in that conflict. Though a "prairie conservative," Hagel has proven to be pragmatic on most matters and has vigorously questioned the rationale for the Iraq war and its conduct. Prior to the invasion, he was skeptical about the need to fight the war on terror there, foresaw the difficulties of the aftermath, and the potential cost to the United States.[41] Throughout the time the United States was in Iraq, he favored Congressional oversight of the war. He said, "To question your government is not unpatriotic. To not question your government is unpatriotic."[42] Because of his willingness to speak out regarding the war and his disagreement with Bush, Hagel lost any chance he might have had of obtaining the Republican presidential nomination in 2008. He also voted against a number of Republican domestic measures in the Senate that he felt were ill advised, including a farm bill with special perks for corporate agriculture. In March 2007, he declined to formally enter the race for president to "concentrate on domestic and global concerns,"[43] and in September announced that he would not run again for the Senate.

Hagel is conservative but not partisan, principled, and against imposing values on people. He has said that religion should be a purely private matter and not worn on one's sleeve. As part of his political philosophy he wants "fiscal restraint at home and restraint in the use of American power abroad."[44] Some of the other reasons he would garner support as a third-party candidate is that he is a realist who thinks things through before he acts. He is intellectually curious and reads extensively, but is also known as a straight talker who says what is on his mind. The erosion of individual rights in the war on terror and the lack of consensus before acting on international problems are some of the issues that trouble him. His independent streak and commonsense approach to resolving problems would make him an excellent candidate for office of a centrist third party.

Mark Warner, a senator and a former governor of Virginia, would also be an able candidate for high office on the Civic Alliance ticket. A moderate Democrat, he governed well in a Republican state with the opposition in control of the legislature. Warner campaigned actively across the state for a tax hike he thought was necessary to close a $6 billion budget shortfall, willing to take an unpopular stance and work with the Republican legislature in a nonpartisan manner. He was subsequently elected senator in 2008. In spite of his push for a tax increase, he remained well liked and admired throughout the state, with an 80 percent approval rating when he left office in 2006,[45] stepping down after four years because Virginia law does not permit a governor to run for consecutive terms. In fact, his appeal helped Tim Kaine, another Democrat, get elected as his successor. Warner, a successful businessman before entering politics, is quite affluent, having helped start the cellular phone company that evolved into Nextel. In a run for president, he would be able to gather funds from venture capitalists and people in the high-tech field whom he knew in his previous career. Warner is attuned to the need for America to improve education and upgrade its economy to compete in a global world. He is young, dynamic, and attractive, and able to communicate well with the middle classes and small-town America.

Evan Bayh, after considering the race for president on the Democratic ticket in 2008, withdrew before becoming an official candidate.[46] Another centrist Democrat, he was a senator from Indiana before retiring in 2010 and a former two-term governor in a

Republican state. Though he is not well known outside of the Midwest, the *Wall Street Journal* described him in 1992 as "a genuinely fiscally conservative Democrat."[47] In 1998, he received 64 percent of the vote when he ran for the Senate, the largest margin ever for a Democratic candidate in Indiana, and was reelected in 2004 with 62 percent of the vote. He was a member of the Senate Centrist Coalition and previous chairman of the Democratic Leadership Council, another centrist group. Initially, he voted to authorize the Iraq war in the Senate, but subsequently became a critic because of the absence of a coherent plan by the Bush administration and the failure to find weapons of mass destruction. In 2004, he voiced a lack of confidence in Secretary of Defense Rumsfeld and asked for his resignation. After the victory by the Democrats in the 2006 midterm election, Bayh warned of defeat ahead "if the party pursues an ideological course."[48] He wanted the Democrats to be wary of the partisanship that had characterized the Republican regime in Washington, which he felt the electorate had rejected. He is a pragmatic moderate with appeal in both the red and blue states, with a history of attracting independents and voters from both parties.

Mike Bloomberg, as we have mentioned, would be an excellent founding member for a centrist third party. Though he will be seventy in 2012, he would also be an able presidential or vice-presidential candidate. An adept administrator, he is a political moderate, has no ideological bias, and is practical in his approach to problems. In addition, he is incorruptible, in need of no funds from lobbyists or special interests in any run for office he might make. Bloomberg was a Democrat who became a Republican prior to his initial bid for mayor, realizing that he could never win the Democratic primary but could be nominated on the Republican ticket. Then in the general election, he was able to take the mayoralty in an aggressive and well-funded campaign. Reelection to his second term was easier, since his approval rating was high. His run for a third term was closer, however, as the public was unhappy about his support for overturning the term-limits law.

In dealing with the disparate groups in the city, Bloomberg has been an effective conciliator, and there has generally been labor peace and racial harmony during his administration. He has also actively backed centrist candidates from both parties in various elections. In June 2007, Bloomberg announced a switch in his affiliation from the Republican Party to independent. This would make it simpler if he ran for the presidency[49] since any attempt would have to be as an independent or third-party candidate.[50] Though Bloomberg would be a viable candidate given his resources and moderate stances, he continues to deny any interest in the job. Indeed, a run in 2012 might split the vote sufficiently to allow a far-right Republican to capture the presidency. On the other hand, if he won enough Electoral College votes, he could become a presidential kingmaker. In all likelihood, Bloomberg will not proceed unless he believes he has a legitimate shot at winning, which will depend on whom the other parties choose as their candidates.

General Wesley Clark was valedictorian of his class at West Point and a Rhodes Scholar at Oxford, earning a master's degree in economics.[51] As a second lieutenant infantryman in Vietnam, he won the Bronze Star, Silver Star, and Purple Heart during his tour of duty. After a long and illustrious career in the Army, including a period as the Supreme Allied Commander of NATO forces in Europe and oversight of the operations in Kosovo, he retired as a four-star Army general. Perhaps not politically battle-hardened and ready for bruising combat, he briefly entered the 2004 Democratic primary race, then withdrew and supported John Kerry. Because of his centrist views, there are some who believe that Clark could have joined the Republicans as easily as the Democrats for his foray into politics, though he was critical of the Bush administration's performance in Iraq. During the midterm election of 2006, Clark himself and his political action committee aided a number of Democratic candidates. Far from a juggernaut in terms of fundraising, he did not pursue the Democratic presidential nomination for 2008. However, with his generally moderate positions, Clark would be a reasonable candidate for office on the Civic Alliance ticket.

Sam Nunn, a former Democratic senator from Georgia, is centrist and pragmatic, and well versed in foreign affairs and national defense issues. As a senator, he was chairman of the Armed Services Committee and the Permanent Subcommittee on Investigations. Currently a major force behind the Concord Coalition to restore fiscal sanity to the federal government, he is also co-chairman of the Nuclear Threat Initiative, a charitable group devoted to lowering the worldwide threat from weapons of mass destruction.[52] After twenty-four years in the Senate, he retired to a busy life of public service in 1996. In addition to the activities noted above, he is also chairman of the board of the Center for Strategic and International Studies in Washington and a professor of international affairs at Georgia Tech. Aside from his age—Nunn was born in 1938—he is another person who would be a superb choice for a cabinet post or major office for the Civic Alliance.

Lincoln Chafee, a former Republican senator from Rhode Island, had a moderate to liberal record while in the Senate, losing his seat in 2006 in the Democratic tide in spite of a high approval rating from the voters.[53] A strong environmentalist, he is considered socially liberal while fiscally conservative in the old New England GOP mode. Unlike most Republicans, he opposed tax cuts while there was a large budget deficit and the nation was at war. He was the only Republican in the Senate not to support authorization for the Bush administration to lead the United States into the war in Iraq. He left the Republican Party in 2007 and ran and won the race for governor of Rhode Island in 2010 as an independent. He would be an able centrist third-party candidate for a major office. Given his election as an independent, along with his moderate views, he could play a role as a founding member of this new party.

In addition to the individuals noted, there is a host of other politicians from both the Republican and Democratic parties who seem suitable as members of the Civic Alliance, some of whom would be excellent candidates for higher office. They should be approached to join the new party soon after its formation or as founding members. These include moderate Republicans in the Senate such as Olympia Snowe and Susan Collins of Maine, Richard Lugar of Indiana, and Lindsey Graham of South Carolina, all of whom have shown a willingness at times to work with Democrats on important legislation. Centrist Democrats in the Senate include Michael Bennet and Mark Udall of Colorado, Mary Landrieu of Louisiana, Claire McCaskill of Missouri, Ben Nelson of Nebraska, Bill Nelson of Florida, Jeanne Shaheen of New Hampshire, Tom Carper of Delaware, Herb Kohl of Wisconsin, Jim Webb of Virginia, and Mark Begich of Alaska. Independent Senator Joe Lieberman from Connecticut might be another possible convert. Unfortunately, some of the Senators mentioned above are not running for reelection.

While the count of Blue Dog Democrats in the House was greatly diminished in the 2010 elections, there are still a number in office who are centrist in orientation. On the Republican side of the aisle, there are only a few who might be considered moderates. In addition to these House members, the Civic Alliance should also seek to recruit those centrists and moderates from both parties who have lost in recent elections, or have retired from federal or state offices. Republicans, former Governor of Florida Charlie Crist, former Congressman Tom Davis of Virginia, and former Congressman Mike Castle of Delaware would all fit into the above category and could play important roles for the Civic Alliance. Former Republican Governor Jon Huntsman of Utah, who served as President Obama's Ambassador to China and is now running for the presidency on the GOP ticket, also appears to be a moderate who would mesh well with the Civic Alliance if he does not get the Republican nomination.

Many of the political figures mentioned would feel quite comfortable in a centrist party that was pragmatic and non-ideological. Unlike most of their peers, they do not appear to be bound by dogma and seem to be relatively untainted by corruption or political scandals. None of them, however, have declared any interest in leaving their current political domains and joining a third party. But perhaps if they were convinced that this party was a credible alternative to the Republicans and Democrats that could attract voters and possibly get its candidates elected to office, they might well be willing to cast their lot with this new organization, work for it, and even run for office on its ticket. These are all intelligent people and surely recognize that America is in trouble, that its political system is dysfunctional, and that the needs of its citizens are not being met.

They must know that far-reaching changes to the political status quo are necessary, and that a centrist third party might provide the required shake-up. The new entity's credibility will be the stumbling block that must be overcome.

The increasing length of the races to capture the Republican and Democratic nominations for president and the high level of spending may also generate support for third-party candidates who are more low-key and not dependent on outrageous sums of money. Though a quest for the presidency previously consumed a year of a candidate's time (or even less in the distant past), at least two years of continuous effort are now required. This demands a large and potent organization, and constant fundraising and combat with other party members. The fact that many states are moving the dates of their primary contests forward into early February and January favors those candidates who can afford to flood the airways with advertising blitzes as the primary elections approach.[54] These early primaries are a distraction for incumbent presidents, who have to take time away from their duties to campaign, unable to focus on the business of running the country. The lengthy primary schedule also affects other officeholders who are unable to pay complete attention to their jobs as senators, governors or members of Congress. The personal campaigning that was previously prevalent in states like New Hampshire and Iowa, and could give an underdog a boost, may no longer be as relevant. In a true sense now, money talks, rather than the candidates themselves. Many good men and women who would make fine candidates do not have the stomach to compete in this environment and may have difficulty financing lengthy and increasingly expensive campaigns capped by this wave of early primaries. Some of them might be attracted to an alternative vision of a run for office offered by the Civic Alliance which is less in-your-face and less costly, with an emphasis on the Internet.

## Recruitment and Durability

In addition to presidential candidates, the Civic Alliance will have to recruit men and women to run in congressional and senatorial races, as well as for offices at every governmental level. It is important for the party to have a strong national footprint to convince the public that it will have a permanent presence, which should translate into greater support and more votes. Competent party executives, particularly national and state chairmen and their deputies, will also be required to ensure that the party functions efficiently and is up to the challenge that the Republicans and Democrats will mount. It is likely the Civic Alliance will be able to find many seasoned executives and politicians among the ranks of the established parties who are disillusioned with their current organizations. Outsiders new to politics from the corporate and academic worlds will also fill these roles. Both Republicans and Democrats hope that if a new party arises, it will not survive long, since they know that durability will be the key to this party's success and they will pull out all stops to destroy it.

The Republicans have been alienating moderates both in and out of the party for years, the disaffection made worse by the recent pernicious influence of the Tea Party. The Civic Alliance can provide a legitimate alternative home for moderates, where they will feel comfortable participating in the political process. As Kevin Phillips describes in *American Theocracy*, the Republicans are to a great extent becoming the party of the religious right with no room for dissenting views, especially on social issues.[55] The party is fervently pro-life and against same-sex marriage to the point where these are the defining political issues for many of its members. And social conservatives have teamed with economic conservatives and Tea Partiers within the GOP to demonize centrists and moderates who disagree with them, labeling them with a pejorative acronym, RINOs— Republicans In Name Only—implying that only those who hew to the most conservative economic and social beliefs are true Republicans. The Tea Party and the conservatives in the party have also engaged in internecine warfare with moderates, running against centrist incumbents in primaries and not actively supporting them in the general elections, wanting them to take positions further to the right.

The extent of the transformation that the Republican Party has undergone in recent years is most evident in New England, the fount of moderate Republicanism. Starting with the abolitionist Republicans of the mid-nineteenth century, the party in New England has always been socially moderate to liberal while fiscally conservative, and was politically dominant in the region for most of the last century and a half. It was the party of Main Street and Wall Street and the Episcopal and Presbyterian churches. Senators and congressmen from these six states were overwhelmingly Republican. This can be contrasted with the composition of the current House. After the 2010 election only two of twenty-two congressmen from the region were Republicans despite the party's overwhelming victories throughout the United States driven by the Tea Party and conservatives. Republican moderates now occupy a shrinking sliver of the party's territory, their small numbers marginalizing their ideas even further. In reality, the Republican Party is no longer a home for moderates and centrists, and the chances of their changing the party's stance on social and economic issues are almost nil. Many of them have stayed with the GOP because they see no alternative, since a party's support and structure is a necessity in American politics. The Civic Alliance would be happy to provide these discontented politicians with a new domicile, where moderation and pragmatism are the guiding principles.

While the ideological schism in the Democratic Party is not quite as wide as in the Republican Party, there is a still significant distance between far-left liberals like House Minority Leader Nancy Pelosi and centrists like Senator Jim Webb of Virginia in terms of policy priorities. Many leftist bloggers are particularly venomous in their diatribes against centrist Democrats. Some on the left have been willing to contest centrist incumbents in the party primaries because they are not "true" Democrats. Even if the incumbent wins, it is more difficult to mount an effective campaign in the general election, as attacks against him or her have provided ammunition to opponents. An interesting dynamic, however, played out in the Connecticut senatorial election in 2006. A liberal, Ned Lamont, challenged centrist Joe Lieberman in the Democratic primary, and won an impressive victory, using Lieberman's support of the Iraq war as a lever. Because Lieberman had previously been considered a sure winner in the general election, no Republican figure of stature had chosen to run against him. Thus, when he decided to mount an independent campaign for the Senate after losing the Democratic primary, Lamont was his major opponent, with a token Republican candidate on the ballot. In the general election, the centrist Lieberman was victorious. He had emphasized his moderate credentials and autonomy from party ideologues, garnering votes across party lines and from independents. Lieberman is now caucusing with the Democrats in the Senate and retains his seniority and committee appointments, but has stated that his victory was "a declaration of independence from the politics of partisanship . . . and he will be beholden to no political group."[56] (He is not running for reelection in 2012.)

Aside from Lieberman's backing of the Iraq war, he and other centrist Democrats would find a more comfortable habitat in the Civic Alliance Party, where common sense and practicality will trump ideology. No single issue will be used as a litmus test to determine whether a person is suitable for membership. It is more important that the individual's worldview and general beliefs are compatible with the kind of political changes the party would like to initiate. There are many disaffected Democrats both in and out of office who are uneasy with the party's leadership and tendency to fall back on long-standing party dogma when confronting new challenges, rather than addressing them in an open-minded way. Most of them would be comfortable with the philosophy of the Civic Alliance.

The Civic Alliance will try to enlist all the Democrats and Republicans who want to transform themselves into new champions of integrity and pragmatism. America needs men and women who want to look at themselves in the mirror and be happy at their reflections, not wondering about who they have become and what they are doing in the name of service to their parties. If the Civic Alliance is successful in recruiting these individuals, the Republican Party will become even more conservative while the Democrats shift more to the left. The balance of political power may lie with the Civic Alliance, which will be able to set the agenda and see to it that the necessary actions are taken to move the ship of state through whatever rough waters lie ahead.

In addition to moderates who are willing to defect from the Republican and Democratic parties, the Civic Alliance must actively proselytize among independent voters and those citizens who have become disengaged from politics. They are needed both as members and possible candidates willing to run for office. It is important to recapture those who have lost interest in the political process, persuading them that they can play a role and make a difference in how America is governed. New blood reinvigorates politics and government. Some of it can be transfused from the business and academic communities, but political "dropouts" must also be brought into the fold. Though Republican and Democratic officeholders who join the Civic Alliance may convert and sign the Oath of Ethical Conduct, as career politicians they may not be able to generate the innovative ideas and transformative thinking that America must have to compete in a rapidly changing world. Alternative mindsets and different viewpoints that exist within the nation must be used. It is worth remembering that the Founding Fathers were not professional politicians.

As noted before, there is a paradox in the American political system that has not yet been resolved. In order to win the Republican or Democratic primaries, a candidate usually has to be strongly partisan and parrot an ideological line. Yet to win the general election, the candidate has to be more moderate and appeal to centrist voters. An article in *Political Science Quarterly* in 2005 stated:

> the more lawmakers worry about winning the swing vote, the more actively they will cultivate images of moderation and nonpartisanship. . . . Winning these voters over means establishing a reputation for independence and nonideological position-taking.[57]

Since a candidate cannot contest the general election without winning his or her party's primary, partisanship takes precedence with most party members, leaving the majority of centrist voters to choose the lesser of two evils rather than someone who reflects their views. The Civic Alliance will offer these moderate voters the alternative they have been seeking.

There are already centrist political groups who are raising money and trying to influence government policy with a pragmatic approach to the nation's problems. Some of them might be willing to associate with the Civic Alliance Party, or help in various ways if their objectives coincide with those of the Alliance. Recruitment among their contributors might also yield a good return in augmenting the party's membership. One group with bipartisan credentials is the Concord Coalition, which has been working to induce Congress and the federal government to be fiscally responsible and bring the budget deficit and national debt under control. Moderate Republicans and Democrats play large roles in the leadership of this organization. A number of other centrist political groups could be of organizational assistance to the Civic Alliance, some with specific goals like preserving the environment or supporting scientific research, that would meld well with the party's agenda. But the party should not get entangled with groups that focus on emotionally discordant social issues, either for or against abortion rights, or same-sex marriage. While these are important and have resonance among certain segments of the population, getting involved with these would be like stepping on land mines and could blow the Civic Alliance apart. For the time being, Alliance members can agree to disagree on these issues, and not approach them in a formal fashion with legislation or executive orders that will distract from the difficult tasks at hand.

An organization called "No Labels" was formed in December of 2010 to try to overcome the hyper-partisanship and polarization that is now the defining characteristic of American politics.[58] Their motto is "No Labels. Not Left. Not Right. Forward." This group is not trying to form a new party but may support candidates in the current party primaries who hold moderate views rather than rigidly partisan ones, men and women who are willing to work across party lines to get things done. A number of well-known politicians, Republicans, Democrats and independents alike, are involved with the movement. They include Mayor Mike Bloomberg of New York, former Senator Evan Bayh of Indiana, Senator Kirsten Gillibrand of New York, Mayor Antonio Villaraigosa of Los Angeles, former

Florida Congressman Joe Scarborough, and the political strategists David Gergen and Mark McKinnon, as well as a host of others. Though the overall list has more Democrats than Republicans, there is significant Republican representation. The main problem with this initiative is that the founders believe the Republican and Democratic parties, or at least many of their members, can be transformed and their orientations brought back toward the center. Given the current political climate and the level of venom on both sides of the aisle, this belief is questionable. In addition, no consideration is being given to reining in the rampant corruption in the two parties and severing the connection between the politicians and the special interests and lobbyists. The only way change will come about is with a completely new centrist party that is free of corruption, offering Americans a real alternative to the parties in power. Perhaps if some of the members of No Labels come to this understanding, they will be able to work with the Civil Alliance to bring about the required metamorphosis in American politics.

## A Third Party of the Right

In October of 2007, a coalition of conservative religious leaders in a secret meeting said they would explore abandoning the Republicans and running a third party candidate for president in 2008 if Rudy Giuliani won the Republican nomination.[59] They said they did not want to consider supporting anyone who was not strongly pro-life and did not condemn homosexuality. In the 2010 midterm elections, the most conservative supporters of the Republican Party were the Tea Party members, who had a strongly populist bent and to whom economic issues, such as balancing the budget, seemed more important than the social issues. Thus far, the Tea Party appears more interested in gaining control of the Republican Party than breaking away to form a new party of the right. How this will play out in the future is uncertain. However, a third party of the far right would siphon votes from Republican candidates and make more Democratic victories likely, reducing conservative power. Because of this scenario, it is unlikely that a national conservative third-party movement will come to fruition. But if the Tea Party does coalesce into an actual political party and runs candidates, it might make it easier for a centrist party to mobilize votes and win elections.

## Campaign Tactics

Given the Civic Alliance's objectives of reforming the two-party system and the process of governing, the way the party conducts its campaigns will play an important role in convincing the public it is serious about ethics and integrity. Negative campaigning, attack ads, and dirty tricks have made America's citizens skeptical about the motivation and sincerity of the established parties, with many people loath to participate in the elections and vote for candidates on either the Republican or Democratic slates. Their cynicism and reluctance to vote is not healthy for American democracy and reinforces the bad behavior of the nation's politicians, who believe they will not be held accountable for their actions. The Civic Alliance must set higher standards as their candidates run for office, forswearing attack ads and abusive campaign tactics. Their focus should be on matters of policy and explaining to the voters where Alliance candidates stand on the issues and why—straight talk, and the issues without spin.

This does not preclude describing ethical infractions or corrupt behavior by political opponents or the opposition parties if the information is factual, for this is certainly something voters should realize when they make their decisions. Other candidates' obduracy and unwillingness to compromise is also fair game. Politicians should be answerable as well for what they have said and what they have done. However, there should be no innuendos or inferences about conduct if they are of questionable origin, or attempts to smear candidates with lies or exaggerations. Only the facts. And no robo-calls or push-polls increasingly employed by political parties in recent elections. If lies and falsehoods regarding Civic Alliance candidates are spread by Republicans or Democrats (or by associated anonymous groups), this misinformation should be immediately pointed out to the voting public, emphasizing its origin without responding in kind. Use of the Internet, Facebook, and Twitter can spread the messages of the Civic Alliance quickly. To reclaim alienated citizens for the political process, they must be made to feel they are voting for honest candidates who are running virtuous campaigns.

Creating a third party will take energy, commitment, and perseverance. With the American political system unable to function effectively, the nation needs politicians who are flexible and pragmatic, able to understand and deal with a complex new world; men and women who are free of ideological constraints, unencumbered by ethical shortcomings and independent of special interests. They will be found only in a new third party that is appreciative and supportive of integrity, competence, and a sensible approach to governing.

Many Americans feel that politics and principles are incompatible. The Civic Alliance will aim to change that perception.

> Complaints are everywhere heard from our most considerate and virtuous citizens . . . that the public good is disregarded in the conflicts of rival parties, and that measures are too often decided, not according to the rules of justice and the rights of the minor party, but by the superior force of an interested and overbearing majority.
> —James Madison, *The Federalist Papers*[60]

## References

[1] Niccolò Machiavelli, *The Prince*, Bantam-Dell, New York, NY, 2003, (originally published in 1513), 31.

[2] Gordon S. Black and Benjamin D. Black, *The Politics of American Discontent*, John Wiley and Sons, New York, NY, 1994, 62.

[3] Ibid., 11.

[4] John Avlon, *Independent Nation: How Centrists Can Change American Politics*, Three Rivers Press, New York, NY, 2004, 2.

[5] David Brooks, "The Middle Muscles In," Op-Ed, *New York Times*, November 9, 2006, A33.

[6] Dan Balz and Jon Cohen, "A Political Force With Many Philosophies," Washingtonpost.com, July 1, 2007, A01.

[7] Ted Halstead and Michael Lind, *The Radical Center*, Anchor Books, New York, NY, 2001, 3–4.

[8] Joe Klein as quoted in Micah L. Sifry, *Spoiling for a Fight*, Routledge, New York, NY, 2002, 71.

[9] Steven J. Rosenstone, Roy L. Behr, and Edward H. Lazarus, *Third Parties in America*, Princeton University Press, Princeton, NJ, 1996, 3.

[10] Marjorie Randon Hershey, *Party Politics in America*, Pearson-Longman, New York, NY, 2005, 40.

[11] Bibby and Maisel, 81.

[12] Micah Sifry, *Spoiling for a Fight*, Routledge, New York, NY, 2002, 9–10.

[13] Bibby and Maisel, 7.

[14] Lisa Jane Disch, *The Tyranny of the Two Party System*, Columbia University Press, New York, NY, 2002, 128.

[15] *Webster's New Twentieth Century Dictionary, Unabridged Second Edition*, William Collins, New York, NY, 1979, 331.

[16] Ibid., 48.

[17] "Phrygian cap," en.wikipedia.org/wiki/Phrygian_cap.

[18] Hershey, 26–28.

[19] Daniel Galvin, "How to Grow a Democratic Majority," OpEd, *New York Times*, June 3, 2006, A13.

[20] Rosenstone, Behr, and Lazarus, 188.

[21] Lev Grossman, "Time's Person of the Year: You," December 13, 2006, www.time.com/time/magazine/printout/0,8816,1569514,00.html.

[22] Ron Fournier, "Internet gives voters the edge," HotSoup, MSNBC.com December 12, 2006, www.msnbc.com/id/16325750/from/ET/print/1/displaymode/1098/.

[23] Adam Nagourney, "Politics Faces Sweeping Change via the Web," *New York Times*, April 2, 2006, 1.

[24] Nicholas Confessore, "An Uneasy Alliance," *New York Times,* November 12, 2006, Week in Review, 5.

[25] David D. Kirkpatrick and Aron Pilhofer, "Donors Linked to the Clintons Shift to Obama," *New York Times*, April 16, 2007, A1.

[26] Associated Press, "Obama raises $25 million, rivals Clinton in fundraising," *USA Today*, April 4, 2007.

[27] David D. Kirkpatrick, "Candidate's Pleased to Remember This Fifth of November," *New York Times*, November 6, 2007.

[28] Alex Williams, "The Future President, on Your Friends List," *New York Times*, March 18, 2007, Sec. 9, 1.

[29] Jim VandeHei, "From the Internet to the White House," Washingtonpost.com, May 31, 2006, A04. www.washingtonpost.com/wp-dyn/content/article/2006/05/30/AR2006053001139.html.

[30] Ibid.

[31] Unity08—A People's Movement To Take Our Country Back, www.unity08.com/.

[32] Joshua Green, "Surprise Party," *The Atlantic*, January/February, 2007, 115.

[33] Ibid.

[34] Patrick Healy, "To '08 Hopefuls, Media Technology Can Be Friend or Foe," *New York Times*, January 31, 2007, A15.

[35] Editorial, "Trashing the Lessons of Watergate," *New York Times*, February 27, 2011, Week in Review, 7.

[36] Federal Election Commission, "Contribution Limits 2009–2010, www.fecgov/pages/brochures/contriblimits.shtml.

[37] "Campaign Finance 101," www.vote-smart.org/resource_govt101_07.php.

[38] Donald G. McNeil, Jr. and Rick Lyman, "Buffet's Billions Will Aid Fight Against Disease," *New York Times*, June 27, 2006, A1.

[39] Zachary Abrahamson, "Bloomberg 'privately conceding' no W.H. run," Politico, March 1, 2011, http://www.politico.com/news/stories/0311/50409.html.

[40] Martin Plissner, "Ready For Obama Already," *New York Times*, OpEd, February 7, 2007, A19.

[41] Joseph Lelyveld, "The Heartland Dissident," *New York Times*, February 12, 2006.

[42] Chuck Hagel, "A Conversation with Senator Hagel on the Middle East and U.S. Foreign Policy," [Prepared Remarks], Council on Foreign Relations, November 15, 2005, www.cfr.org/publication/92201.

[43] Jeff Zeleny, "Senator From Nebraska Says No To Presidential Bid, For Now," *New York Times*, March 13, 2007, A16.

[44] Ibid.

[45] Matt Bai, "The Fallback," *New York Times*, March 12, 2006, magazine.

[46] Adam Nagourney, "Indiana Senator Leaves 2008 Presidential Field," *New York Times*, December 17, 2006,

[47] "Evan Bayh," http://en.wikipedia.org/wiki/Evan_Bayh.

[48] Mike Glover, "Bayh warns against ideological agenda," Associated Press, http://news.yahoo.com/s/ap20061204/ap_on_el_pr/bayh2008.

[49] Diane Cardwell and Jennifer Steinhauer, "Bloomberg Severs G.O.P. Ties, Fueling Further Talk of '08 Bid," *New York Times*, June 20, 2007, A1.

[50] John Heilemann, "His American Dream," *New York Magazine*, December 11, 2006, 28.

[51] "Wesley Clark," http://en.wikipedia.org/wiki/Wesley_Clark.

[52] "Sam Nunn," http://en.wikipedia.org/wiki?Sam_Nunn.

[53] "Lincoln Chafee," http://en.wikipedia.org/Lincoln_Chafee.

[54] Adam Nagourney, "Big States' Push for Earlier Vote Scrambles Race," *New York Times*, January 25, 2007, A1.

[55] Kevin Phillips, *American Theocracy*, Viking Press, New York, NY, 2006.

[56] Jennifer Medina, "Liberated Lieberman Likely to Be Courted by Both Sides," *New York Times*, November 8, 2006, 7.

[57] Peter Trubowitz and Nicole Mellow, "Going Bipartisan: Politics by Other Means," *Political Science Quarterly*, Fall 2005, 436.

[58] Luisita Lopez Torregrosa, "No Labels Speaker David Gergen in NYC: The Country Is on the Edge," Politicsdaily, December 11, 2010, http://www.politicsdaily.com/2010/12/11/no-labels-political-group-aims-to-combat-hyper-partisanship/.

[59] David D. Kirkpatrick, "Guiliani inspires conservative threat of a third party race," *International Herald Tribune*, October 2, 2007, 5.

[60] James Madison, *The Federalist Papers*, No.10, New American Library, New York, NY, 1961, (originally published 1787–1788), 54.

CHAPTER 4

# America's Domestic Challenges
### (Origins and Current Status)

It is a common failing of men not to take account of tempests during fair weather.

—Machiavelli, *The Prince*[1]

And Jacob said, swear to me this day; and he sware unto him: and he sold his birthright unto Jacob. Then Jacob gave Esau bread and pottage of lentils; and he did eat and drink, and rose up, and went his way.

—Genesis 25:33, 34

Analysis of America's current problems reinforces the pressing need for a third political party. Many of these problems have resulted from poor management by the established parties as well as their unwillingness to make hard decisions that have potential political consequences. While some of these domestic challenges arose from circumstances beyond Washington's control, others were caused by errors of omission where things that should have been done were not, and still others by errors of commission where the actions taken were wrong and mistakes were made. These difficulties did not arise overnight and can be traced to multiple administrations. Indeed, most are the culmination of decades of misguided policies, denial, and neglect, overseen by both Republican and Democratic presidents and Congresses controlled by both parties. Political gain rather than long-term needs has determined much of the nation's policies, with planning focusing on immediate requirements. Both parties have been reluctant to tell the electorate the truth about what the future holds, offering simplistic solutions to complex problems. Because of the self-serving nature of America's political parties, the nation is in trouble and a change of direction is necessary. This will require sacrifice by citizens to accomplish that change.

Trying to fit America's challenges into neat categories is like trying to tease the strands of a spider's web into discrete pieces, since so many of them are interconnected and addressing one affects others. There is unemployment, economic growth, the trade deficit, energy policies, relations with various countries, and environmental policies, all linked together. This survey divides problems into areas that seem closely related.

## The Recession, Unemployment, and Economic Growth

According to economists, the recession of 2009 has come and gone. But individuals, families, and businesses have been left devastated in its wake. In many cities and towns, one would never know the recession was over, with the twin hardships of joblessness and home foreclosures taking their toll on formerly middle-class citizens as well as those chronically impoverished. The rate of unemployment in the United States has been particularly troubling, hovering at nine percent or above with no signs of abating in the near term. Even more upsetting is the number of the chronically unemployed, unable to find a job after six months or more of searching. And it appears that many of these individuals may never work again.

In discussing unemployment, long-term trends have to be considered as well as those jobs that have disappeared because of the recession itself. For decades now, America has been in the process of selling her birthright to other nations for the equivalent of a cup of porridge, as multi-national corporations have transferred a large portion of the US industrial base to countries with cheaper labor costs to expand their profits. During this period, Washington has been unwilling or unable to stop the flow. Because of this shift, America is no longer a manufacturing dynamo but has been transformed into a services-oriented economy with many of its factories and plants shut down. (In 1953, 28.3 percent of the nation's GDP was derived from manufacturing.[2] This dropped to 15.5 percent in 1996 and 11.7 percent in 2007.[3] However, in 2007, manufacturing still accounted for 60 percent of American exports and was a major driver of productivity.)

With US factories being offshored, the loss of American jobs has gone from a trickle to a torrent. Initially, this involved mainly workers with few skills and limited education, though their wages had been sufficient to lift them from poverty to the middle class. Their jobs in the garment industry and textile mills went to shops in Bangladesh, Pakistan, Turkey, Mexico, and Central America, as well as China. In the last twenty years, highly skilled and high-paying union jobs have also vanished, with employees forced to accept work at lower wages as their grip on middle-class status also slipped away. More recently, the ax has been falling on the service sector, on call center personnel, and educated white-collar workers, their jobs outsourced to India and Eastern Europe. Included are many back-office financial workers, software developers, computer programmers, copy editors, and other positions that don't require face-to-face contact. According to Alan Blinder, who served on the White House Council of Economic Advisors from 1993 to 1994 and was Vice Chairman of the Federal Reserve from 1994 to 1996: "We have so far barely seen the tip of the offshoring iceberg, the eventual dimensions of which may be staggering."[4]

Besides the loss of income for those directly affected, it has also made many of them feel vulnerable in ways that are new to America. They are constantly distressed about being outsourced, downsized, or being laid off, or being fired without cause and unable to find comparable jobs. Education, which some felt would protect them indefinitely, is no longer a shield from adversity. Of course, if they worry about job security, or their wages are lower, they are less likely to spend money, especially on nonessential items, and this hurts the economy. In order to make ends meet, families now need two earners, or one earner may have two or even three jobs. What once brought in some discretionary income is now barely enough to hold onto a lifestyle with few indulgences.

As long as the economy was growing, there were enough jobs

domestically to keep the American unemployment rate low, though the quality of the jobs kept declining and salaries for the majority of the population remained static or also declined. With the recession, the cushion of jobs disappeared, those with less education and older workers the hardest hit. There are also many who go through job retraining programs to find work in different fields and after six months or a year of struggle discover there are no positions in their new area of expertise. The middle class, with its work ethic and striving for material success and security, has been the backbone of America. If they are dispirited and beaten down, it will cast a pall over the nation, no matter how much corporate profits soar and how much extra income is flowing into the coffers of the wealthy.

Though American businesses have rebounded since the onset of the recession, worker salaries have not followed. With labor markets weak, workers have less bargaining power in terms of wages. And many companies in the United States have not been plowing their profits back into domestic ventures, choosing instead to invest greater amounts overseas. Henry Ford believed that paying his workers a decent wage was a good policy for his company and for America, because that would allow them to buy his cars and other products, bolstering the economy. But now because of a dearth of high-paying jobs the American economy is driven by the spending of the more affluent,[5] rather than the great mass of wage earners.

Though the government has to share responsibility for the recession because of its lack of oversight and regulation, along with the banks and mortgage companies that took unconscionable risks, the question after the fact is how to help the economy grow and generate jobs. Although as of July 2011 the stock market had regained some of its luster and American corporations were again profitable, Washington has been unable to lift the economy to the degree necessary to make a dent in the unemployment level. The Republicans and Democrats in Congress cannot agree on the mechanisms to turn things around, with the former favoring major tax cuts and the latter wanting increased government spending. The $787 billion stimulus package approved by Congress in February 2009 contained some measures that should have appealed to both parties, but was passed despite almost unanimous nay votes from Republicans, who were unhappy with the government spending. The bill included $288 billion in tax cuts, as well as $224 billion for extended unemployment benefits, education, and health care, and $275 billion for job creation with Federal contracts, grants, and loans.[6] It was estimated that this legislation would produce 900,000 to 2.3 million jobs. In fact, Obama's economic advisors predicted that the stimulus would help the economy enough to keep the jobless rate below 8 percent, a gross miscalculation that provided ammunition for its opponents.[7] Most economists agreed, however, that it did stabilize the economy and possibly prevent a depression, and some argued that the stimulus had simply been weaker than what was needed.

With the persistently high unemployment rate and lagging economy, the Republican congressional victory in the election of November 2010 was almost preordained. The question afterward was how Congress would work with the president to boost the economy and cut unemployment. In the lame duck session before the newly elected officials took over, a compromise was worked out between the administration and Republicans in what the White House labeled the 2011 stimulus plan. It included continuation of the Bush tax cuts for everyone for two years, a $5 million exemption for the estate tax with a 35 percent rate above that, the extension of unemployment insurance for an extra year, a payroll tax cut, various tax benefits for low-income families, and allowing businesses to expense all 2011 investments.[8] Liberal House Democrats were unhappy with the compromise because of the extension of tax cuts for the wealthy. They threatened to try to block it, though the bill was designed to help middle-class and lower-income families as well as the affluent. Eventually, enough Democrats joined Republicans to ensure its passage. The fact that it would increase the deficit over the short term was downplayed by both parties. The new House Republicans in 2011, however, are focusing on cutting the deficit rather than further government measures to reduce unemployment.

In addition to the recession's impact on individuals, families, and businesses, the governments at state, county, and municipal levels have been hard hit by the decline in revenue as a result of lower sales, income and property taxes. Generous pension and health benefits to public sector workers along with inadequate contributions to the funds that support these benefits have also been responsible for shortfalls. Budgets have been balanced temporarily through fiscal tricks and borrowing, putting more pressure on future governments to come up with the increased funding that will be needed. While some municipalities may go bankrupt, this is not an option for states, some of which face severe financial difficulties.[9] Cutting spending or raising taxes is not a desirable solution during a recession and how these budget deficits and debts will be managed remains to be seen. Where Republicans have controlled the levers of government there have been attempts to limit the power of public service unions in spite of their agreeing to financial givebacks.

~~~

As of July 2011 the federal government had failed in its attempts to ameliorate the effects of the recession because the two political parties could not resolve conflicts over the steps needing to be taken. The Federal Reserve made a number of moves from a monetary standpoint to assist the economy, but these had been insufficient without adequate fiscal measures from the federal government. Ideological blinders had again kept the two parties from cooperating for the good of the nation. Among other failings, there was not enough emphasis on infrastructure projects, where federal dollars could have been used to provide jobs and would have had long-lasting effects benefiting the economy. In addition, the stimulus did not provide enough support for new industries that would have enhanced job growth and made the nation more competitive globally; this applies particularly to green industries such as alternative energy production. There is no reason that Chinese companies should dominate solar energy and that Chinese and Europeans companies should dominate wind energy. There is no reason there are no high-speed rail lines in the United States when they ubiquitous in China, Japan, and Europe.

## Globalization, the Trade Deficit, and the Economy

For decades, American jobs have been migrating abroad, with the United States now borrowing huge sums from other countries to pay for the goods once made here, reflected in the nation's exploding trade deficit. In return, these countries, particularly China and Japan, buy United States treasury bonds, helping to keep interest rates low and the American economy on an even keel. This also lowers the renminbi and yen compared to the dollar, aiding the exports of China and Japan. In addition, foreign corporations who have amassed capital are able to acquire assets in the United States. Even some strategic assets are now in the hands of foreign entities, such as companies that manufacture products vital to the America's military. America is also kept in thrall to the countries that own its debt, for if they decide to withdraw their money, interest rates will jump and the nation's economy will be sent into a tailspin.

Though part of the loss of America's manufacturing capability may have been inevitable, the process might have been delayed or managed by the Federal government in a way of greater benefit to the nation, and some of it might never have happened at all. The metamorphosis of the United States from a manufacturing to a service economy took root shortly after World War II, when its industrial proficiency and productivity were unrivaled. At that time, other nations were suffering from the aftermath of the war, with economies ruined, buildings and factories destroyed, and infrastructure smashed. Simultaneously, the Soviet Union was emerging as an adversary. The US needed to strengthen Japan, Germany, and the rest of the free world to have them as allies in the Cold War, which meant helping them rebuild their shattered industries. With the Marshall Plan and other assistance, America aided the European nations in their recovery from the war's devastation to forge modern competitive economies. Similarly, with American help, Japan progressed over the next several decades from defeated mendicant to industrial power. By the 1980s, in fact, there was concern that Japan would overtake America as the world's largest economy and that the United States would be unable to compete with this rising

Asian giant. It is now obvious these worries were overblown; by the '90s, Japan had suffered a major economic downturn. But America has continued to run a trade deficit with Japan, along with Korea, Taiwan, and more recently China, with the latter now the major holder of US debt. How did America get to this point?

In its desire to court Japan, the United States made some crucial mistakes, and repeated the mistakes with other Asian nations. First of all, the US discounted the fact that these countries began with much cheaper labor costs than the United States, manufacturing inexpensive goods of low quality for the US market. Secondly, the US also ignored the fact that they were able to build plants and factories at home that contained the latest technology, since their industries were essentially starting from scratch while much of America's industrial base was older and less efficient. Beginning with cheap plastic toys and similar goods, Japanese corporations moved into technically advanced niche products such as cameras, optical goods, and machine tools, which Americans readily consumed. Over time, their lower-grade cars and televisions improved and America began importing them in greater numbers. At one point, they were equal to American products, then surpassed them in quality, yet still remained less expensive than equivalent goods of US origin. Thirdly, America allowed them to develop their products slowly over a number of years, going from lower to higher quality, while their home markets were protected from competition.

In other words, America permitted them to sell cheaper and poorer-quality goods in the United States as they gradually improved their products, while America could not export its better products to them in any quantity. Either the tariffs and taxes were too high or American access was restricted, stifling the development of US industries. And absurdly, American capital (the money spent on their products) went to construct modern plants and factories in the Asian countries that were more productive than America's, to better compete against America. Eventually, both Japanese and Korean companies were also able to use American money to build auto plants in the United States, employing non-union, less expensive workers to assemble their cars. In 2006, as GM and Ford downsized and closed plants, Toyota and Kia announced plans to manufacture their cars in states the American companies had abandoned.[10] And even as GM and Chrysler were driven into bankruptcy, more Japanese and Korean automobile factories were being built in the US. The story of the American industrial decline has not been simply one of losing out to other countries in the free trade that American politicians lionize, but losing out because of stupid trade, where the government and politicians of both parties allowed the wool to be pulled over their eyes.

Clyde Prestowitz described the machinations of "Japan Inc" in his book, *Trading Places,* in 1988:

> The social and industrial structure of Japan [has] made it an extremely difficult market to penetrate; furthermore, the Japanese government views industrial performance as akin to national security and pours enormous energy into ensuring that its industry is the world leader. By comparison, the United States has been relatively easy to penetrate. Its open society makes for an open market that has welcomed foreign goods and foreign businessmen . . . the United States does not view industry as a matter of national security as Japan does. . . . While the United States embraces Adam Smith, the seventeenth century prophet of free trade, and has concentrated on consumption as the main economic engine, Japan has focused on production and dominance of key industries that will enhance its strategic position.[11]

Japan was able to achieve its objectives because of the cooperative efforts of government, corporations, labor, and the general population, orchestrated by MITI (The Ministry of International Trade and Industry). The United States perceived power mainly in military terms and did not attach enough importance to economic power and the support of its industries. Because of its almost religious belief in free trade, open markets, and the avoidance of government interference in commerce, the United States failed to protect its own interests, not even enforcing trade laws when they were clearly violated.[12] Both political parties and all the post-war administrations, with amazing folly and shortsightedness, must share the blame for this inability to understand the economic conflict that was in progress and to take effective action. In addition, by allowing Japan to be protected by the American military shield, that nation had to spend only a tiny percentage of its GDP on its defense forces, while the US spent huge amounts that were diverted from more productive areas of its economy.

American money has also subsidized China's economic growth to a large degree, again with the transfer of United States industry and technology to mainland China because of myopic government policy and the inability of both political parties to protect America's interests. Of course, the lobbyists for corporations anxious to use Chinese labor to enhance their profits played a large role, using contributions to convince lawmakers that what was being done would benefit America. Now China's economy is second only to America's and is predicted to overtake the US and become the world's largest economy by 2027.[13] While China's rise may have been preordained, United States compliance accelerated its growth, losing more manufacturing and more middle-class jobs in the bargain. As with Japan, the US has frequently neglected to object to China's breach of trade laws, or to bring China before the World Trade Organization for its transgressions.[14]

Although on occasion Washington has subsidized industries or acted in a protectionist manner, it was for specific political reasons and not as part of a long-term, well-defined plan. Examples include President Bush's help for the steel industry and Congressional support for farm subsidies, tariffs, and quotas on agricultural products.[15] American antidumping laws, to prevent foreign products from being sold in the US below cost, are also used to block competition from foreign companies to benefit special interests domestically.[16]

Of course, the reasons for the decline of American companies and the rise of Asian producers are more complex than what is outlined above. For instance, in the auto industry, the "Big Three" auto companies (GM, Ford, Chrysler) were saddled with pension and health care costs for their workers and retirees (legacy costs) that their foreign competitors didn't have. These were estimated to be as high as $1500 or more per vehicle before the manufacturing process even started, putting GM, Ford, and Chrysler at a major disadvantage. In addition, the design of Japanese and Korean vehicles, more than American vehicles, had the sex appeal and pizzazz that inspire consumers to buy. Although the quality of American vehicles was not as good as the Japanese for a long time, in the last few years the gap has closed. The *Wall Street Journal* reported that the problem for GM and Ford was that they were not designing "vehicles that Americans want to pay 'Toyota' money for,"[17] and that Toyota's engineering and development systems were simply better than theirs. Prior to GM and Chrysler's bankruptcies in 2009, the auto companies lost tens of billions of dollars, shed tens of thousands of jobs, and shut dozens of plants.[18],[19] At the same time, Asian auto companies were opening new technology centers in the Detroit area and were hiring skilled engineers and designers, many of whom had been laid off by the American firms.

American auto manufacturers were also asleep at the wheel in not paying attention to the price of gasoline. For too long, the Big Three pushed gas-guzzling SUVs instead of developing fuel-efficient smaller cars like hybrids, hydrogen-powered vehicles, and electric cars. They also ignored the new generation of diesel engines that conserve fuel and are cleaner and more powerful than the last generation. Perhaps executives of the Big Three were too complacent, drawing their high salaries without any linkage to the success of their companies. Even after gas climbed to $3.50 a gallon in 2007, auto executives lobbied Congress not to raise mileage standards, heedless of the country's need to conserve oil and the public's increasing appetite for high-mileage vehicles.[20]

Currently virtually all American consumer electronics are imported. Although new technology that evolved in the last decade produced various types of high-definition TVs, there are few significant US players in the game. The majority of the nation's appliances are imported as well, along with most of its digital cameras. Interestingly, many of the patents and much of the work behind some of these devices occurred in the United States, but the manufacturing was sent abroad, with new factories built by American and foreign corporations. The computer industry was once an American stronghold, developing new chips, software, and new types of computers, and manufacturing these models in the United States. Now Asian nations command an increasingly larger portion of this market, including keyboards, monitors, printers, storage devices, and various peripherals and accessories. US-based multinational corporations like Dell and Hewlett-Packard, with strong American brand names, do much of their manufacturing in Asia, and IBM sold its computer business to a Chinese firm, Lenovo, to concentrate more on services.

American companies are also transferring advanced technology to China, resulting in helping the Chinese compete against them. Sometimes these transfers are instituted with loans from Washington. In one egregious example, the Export–Import Bank of the United States made a preliminary agreement to support with loans Westinghouse Electric Company's bid to construct nuclear reactors for China.[21] It was hoped that this would generate American jobs and reduce the trade deficit. But China would be receiving the latest nuclear energy technology, which it could duplicate to power its factories. In addition, a British company owned Westinghouse and was planning to sell it to Toshiba of Japan, so the profits from this venture would not even return to America. The most modern automobile plants are now being built by the world's major automakers in China, to compete against each other and Chinese corporations.[22] Chinese engineers have been able to copy these factories and the newest models for their own companies, shortcutting the development process. This has also happened with Gamesa, a Spanish manufacturer of wind farms, that set up its business in China.[23] It was forced to use Chinese companies to make at least 70 percent of its content and had to train their workers to produce these parts. The Chinese companies subsequently manufactured the complete mechanisms and now control 85 percent of their domestic market. The Chinese government is currently urging these companies to export to foreign markets, helping them with various subsidies. And similar sequences have been occurring with other high-tech industries that entered the Chinese market. Industrial polices won't even be considered by the rigidly free-market USA, but it is losing the battle for the global marketplace to countries that follow these practices.

America used to be a major shipbuilding power, but now this work is performed in Korea and some European nations (with the exception of military vessels, still in American hands). And American companies and sailors do not operate commercial ships. The United States was once the premier producer of steel in the world, but currently much of its steel is imported, and some of the nation's largest domestic steel companies are foreign owned. Almost all of America's clothing and shoes are made in other countries, with once-flourishing mills in the South and Northeast now gone. Most toys and games are imported as well. It must be kept in mind that nearly 60 percent of the goods sent from China to the United States are from American or non-Chinese companies,[24] and it is likely the statistics are similar for goods imported to the US from other developing nations.

Globalization means that capital, manufacturing, and employment migrate to places where labor is cheapest. American membership in the World Trade Organization (WTO) and the free-trade agreements negotiated with other countries have enhanced this process. But during the last several decades when the transformation of the global economy was occurring, Washington did not advocate American interests strongly enough, often acquiescing to lobbying from its trading partners or from various multinational corporations. It also did not protect some of its strategic industries. Free trade should not be a one-way street. It was foolish for the government to open American markets to goods that other countries produced cheaply, while not insisting that their markets be open to US products. These nations also had policies supporting developing industries and protecting them from foreign competition. Chinese manufacturing companies can obtain land free or at cut-rate prices from local officials to build factories, then get low-cost loans from government-supported banks for construction. Then, once a product is ready to be sold abroad, export subsidies from the government along with government protection from rival imports ease the path.

Manipulation of currency prices has also contributed to America's trade deficits and difficulty competing against foreign manufacturers. Over the years, Japan's central bank has consistently purchased dollars to keep the value of the yen low, to promote its own products and undercut American goods. China has refused to float the renminbi, its national currency, to allow the market to decide its worth, repeatedly saying it will do so in the future when it is more developed. Meanwhile, it has run up an annual trade surplus with the US of well over $200 billion in each of the last six years.[25] As of 2006, China's exports to the US were nearly six times as large as US exports to China.[26] America allowed China to join the World Trade Organization to help promote free trade, but how can the economic relationship between it and the rest of the world be considered free when China sets the value of its currency to maximize its competitiveness and insure a trade imbalance in its favor?

In addition, the United States has not insisted on the protection of its intellectual property rights, allowing foreign companies to pirate its software, movies, and music without paying for them. Billions of dollars are lost in this type of thievery, with China by far the greatest culprit. The Business Software Alliance (a software industry lobby) believes that over 90 percent of the software employed in China is unlicensed.[27] Books, scientific texts, and pharmaceuticals are also copied and reproduced without regard to legal ownership. Patented manufacturing techniques are stolen as well to produce items that compete with the countries and companies that developed them. America's huge trade deficit with China could be reduced if Washington was more insistent on American rights to have open markets to allow the US to trade its products without impediment, and ensure that its intellectual property is respected. China and the United States are in a symbiotic relationship, with each needing the other for both economies to flourish.

The bottom line remains that America's industrial base is disappearing and it no longer manufactures much of what it requires, increasing its dependency on other countries, squandering its financial resources, and losing millions of middle-class jobs. The US trade deficit has to be significantly pared and it needs better balance in trade with its partners. America's multinational corporations, however, don't want to alienate China and other "developing" nations. They want to use their low-cost labor and they see opportunities to sell products in their growing markets, indifferent to the problems they might be creating in America. The US government seems reluctant to rock the boat because of its reliance on China for a vast number of goods and the financing of its deficit.

An article in *Foreign Affairs* in 2005 by David H. Levey and Stuart S. Brown noted:

> Until 1989, the United States was a creditor to the rest of the world . . . Chronic current account deficits ever since have given the United States the largest net liabilities in world history. Since foreign claims on the United States ($10.5 trillion) exceed U.S. claims abroad ($7.9 trillion) the net international investment position is now negative: $2.6 trillion at the start of 2004, or −24% of GDP.[28]

It has certainly grown larger since 2004. Though the volume of America's exports has continued to rise over the last twenty years, it has not kept up with the boom in imports. The decrease in America's national savings rate has also played an important role in its deficit.[29] Sherle Schwenninger asserted in an essay several years ago:

America and its trading partners are locked in co-dependency. In the short term this co-dependency has worked reasonably well: our principal partners lend us money to buy their cheaper goods with a strong dollar. In return, they have access to a stable market for their products, enabling their economies to grow at an impressive rate . . . But current account deficits and international debt do matter; they represent real claims on US assets by foreign individuals and corporations—claims that will eventually need to be repaid.[30]

As of March 2006, China had surpassed Japan as the largest holder of foreign reserves.

In sum, globalization has benefited American consumers,

the multinational corporations, and their executives and affluent stockholders while hurting middle-class workers, damaging the economy with the loss of well-paying manufacturing jobs, and accelerating the growth of the nation's trade deficit. While all this was happening, America's political leaders were asleep at the wheel or influenced by lobbyists to look the other way.

## Income Inequality, Excess Compensation, and Corporate Corruption

Inequality is inherent in the capitalist system, where those who are smarter or were born into the right family or work harder or take more risks can make more money and have more material goods. Most people accept that individuals who have greater responsibility or perform at a higher level or are more valuable to society should receive more compensation than their peers. Yet there are limits to how much inequality can be tolerated in any society, particularly if the acquisition of wealth is perceived to have been accomplished unfairly. This may include corrupt practices, bending or breaking the rules, or even hereditary riches. Some of the most affluent may also showcase their money in ways that provoke anger along with envy. As Mickey Kaus noted in *The End of Equality*:

> ... is it the gnawing sense that, in their isolation, these richer Americans not only are passing on their advantages to their children, but are coming to think that those advantages are deserved; that they and their children are, at bottom, not just better off but better?[31]

During Colonial times and the first half of the nineteenth century, the gap between the wealthy (mostly large landowners and successful merchants) and the average citizen (mainly farmers and tradesmen) was much smaller than today. The industrial revolution and growth of the railroads were responsible for a widening gulf between the rich and middle class in the era of the robber barons and in the Roaring Twenties. The Depression along with the estate tax and progressive income tax reduced the disparity significantly.

Over the last quarter-century however, with marginal tax rates lowered, the disparity has again been increasing, the magnitude of difference greater than it has ever been. Financial rewards from the performance of the American economy have not been dispersed through every level of society. The most affluent have benefited disproportionately, while little has filtered down to the middle- and lower-income groups. In fact, these groups are falling further behind as real wages have stagnated, and they have little money to invest in order to derive income from bond yields, dividends, or capital gains.

From 1966 to 2001, the median wage in the United States rose only 11 percent.[32] Income related to the increase in productivity during this period went more to the top one percent of households than to the entire bottom 50 percent.[33] Even those in the 90–99th percentiles had only a minimal increase, while those in the 99–99.9th percentiles saw their income jump dramatically. In 2005, the most affluent 300,000 Americans made as much as the bottom 150 million.[34] The income gap was almost double that existing in 1980. Economists suggest these figures actually underestimate the true difference in inequality, as only about 70 percent of business and investment income, which goes mainly to the wealthy, is accurately reported.[35] The disparity in income between corporate executives and their workers and the excessive compensation for investment bankers and financiers has been responsible for most of the inequity. A chief executive in one of the top one hundred corporations in America in 1977 made about fifty times the pay of its average worker.[36] Thirty years later, these CEOs made about 1100 times the wages of an average employee. For the average worker the remuneration for a hard day's work may be just enough to keep his or her head above water. Yet they see others, sometimes because of drive and effort, but often through connections and luck or manipulation and chicanery, earn enough discretionary income to keep hundreds or thousands of people clothed, fed and housed.

Though the financial industry, the energy sector, and high-tech companies have the largest annual payouts for their officers, virtually all corporations have been rewarding their top executives with increasingly high salaries. The mantra "a rising tide lifts all boats" has not proven to be true. And the financial industry provides the highest salaries by far. When including all jobs in a sector, from janitors and secretaries to executives and managers, the average weekly pay in investment banking was ten times that of other industries in 2007—$8,367 versus $841.[37] Wall Street pay broke a record in both 2009 and 2010[38] in spite of the damage these firms had done to the economy and the need for government bailouts. Financial firms twenty-five years ago generated about one-seventh of the profits of all businesses in the US.[39] By 2009, it was more than a quarter and had been as high as a third at the height of the boom in 2006. The best and the brightest from the nation's universities have been choosing careers in the financial industry to reap some of these profits instead of in science or engineering, where the nation has a significant need. Yet it has been said that "much of what investment bankers do is socially worthless."[40] Whereas in the past their capital was used to fund businesses and produce useful goods, money is now transferred among complex financial instruments that generate profits for the bankers, but do not otherwise serve a purpose. The Wall Street firms have become trading houses more than investment banks. What happened in the last decade was massive redistribution of wealth to people who did not create value, but simply moved assets around.

Furthermore, the CEOs of many corporations choose the compensation committees and boards of directors who decide executive remuneration and who have particularly benefited from corporate largesse. In 2005, the average American CEO paycheck was almost $11 million with about $5.6 million in exercised stock options.[41] Many CEOs earned much more, a number of them above the $100 million range. While compensation was once supposed to be tied to company performance, this idea has been mostly abandoned. In good times and bad times, executive compensation keeps rising, even while many of these corporations slash pensions and health care benefits, lay off workers, and sometimes flirt with bankruptcy. Clive Crook in *The Atlantic*, describing corporate governance, noted

... pay schemes that rewarded chief executives generously when share prices were soaring continued to do so as prices tanked. CEOs fired for incompetence, leaving injured companies and distressed investors behind them, sometimes walked away with multimillion-dollar payments.[42]

The CEOs and top executives of the investment banks whose bungling was responsible for the huge losses that precipitated the recent recession, men such as Charles Prince at Citigroup, Stanley O'Neal at Merrill Lynch, Richard Fuld at Lehman, and Angelo Mozilo at Countrywide, received hundreds of millions of dollars in compensation for their ineptitude.

In addition to their salaries, CEOs and high-level corporate executives have been given huge packages, including stock options, bonuses and pensions, special retirement plans, and golden parachutes if the company is taken over. There has been an outcry over backdating and preferential pricing of stock options for executives in a host of corporations, providing them with even greater compensation without risk.[43] On top of this, executives have gotten enormous perks from the use of corporate jets, membership in exclusive clubs, living expenses while traveling, and more. Shareholders, though supposedly owners of the corporations, exert little influence over executive pay, with corporate regulations written to keep them on the sidelines and out of the executives' hair. Proxy voting and shareholder meetings are rigged to allow CEOs and corporate boards to maintain control and set their own salaries, thwarting the wishes of those people who supposedly employ them. And the compensation achieved by hedge fund managers and private equity personnel dwarfs that of American CEOs.

Though there have always been differences in wealth and standards of living among US citizens, those who struggled were sustained with the belief that America was a meritocracy and that anyone could rise to the top based on intelligence, competence, and drive. Whether these perceptions were valid doesn't matter, as they infused Americans with optimism about their ability to transcend origins and status to realize whatever their dreams might be. This is in the process of changing (aside from high-tech savants) as an aristocracy of wealth is developing, its members having the power and ability to shape the world to fit their needs and expectations. Fairness and equity are no longer catchwords for US legislators as they write the laws that guide American lives, particularly in the realm of taxes and finances.

Blatant corporate corruption has also cast a shadow across America as arrogant executives who believe they are immune to internal criticism or outside the arm of the law manipulate earnings and cook the books to guarantee their earnings and stature. Reports of misbehavior by these titans of industry are in the newspapers and on television every day, feeding citizens' cynicism about society and feelings of impotence. Though many of these white-collar criminals are eventually brought to justice, many others evade punishment or receive a light slap on the wrist, able to retain their ill-gotten gains and opulent lifestyle through the use of high-profile lawyers. For the American system to function well and its citizens to feel secure, it is important that individuals in positions of power, like corporate executives or politicians, know that any corruption or criminal actions will be punished to the full extent of the law.

## Poverty and the Minimum Wage

In 2005, according to the Census Bureau, 12.6 percent of America's population, 37 million people, lived in poverty.[44] For a family of four, this was defined as an income below $19,971; for a single person, below $9,973. In 2009, after the recession had hit, the poverty rate was 14.3 percent, encompassing almost 44 million people.[45] Though there are no simple answers to the problem of poverty, the federal government has not aggressively tried to find solutions. Congressional leaders seem to believe that by keeping poverty out of the public eye, it may be erased from public consciousness and cease to be an issue.

There are many reasons why the poverty rate has remained high, even as corporate profits and productivity continue to increase along with individual wealth. Certain human characteristics create a poor underclass in all societies, no matter how interventionist the government may be. These include various types of addiction (drugs, alcohol, gambling), mental illness, dysfunctional families, and individuals with low or borderline intelligence. In America, superimposed on these is an educational system that fails a large segment of its population, the flight of jobs abroad, lack of access to health care for many people, and a high cost for others that in itself may impoverish them. Poverty rates also show racial differences, with 24.9 percent of African Americans, 21.8 percent of Hispanics, 11.1 percent of Asians, and 8.7 percent of non-Hispanic whites living in poverty in 2005.[46]

In spite of the level of poverty in the United States, the minimum wage has been kept low by Congress under pressure from lobbyists for agricultural interests, restaurants, hotels, and the maintenance and construction industries. The increase to $7.25 per hour over two years in 2007 was the first boost in over a decade,[47] while inflation and the cost of living rose steadily, and taxes of the most affluent were reduced. This means that someone working a forty-hour week can now earn $290 weekly, or $15,080 a year, before taxes, Social Security, and Medicare, wages that keep a family of four below the poverty line. Some city, state, and local governments, frustrated by the lack of federal action, have passed minimum wage laws covering workers within their jurisdictions. However, these are not the answer to the problem, as they will spawn a host of complex regulations that will hurt businesses and make these locales less competitive.

## Budget Deficits, the National Debt, Pork, and Tax Policy

America's enormous annual federal budget deficits and rising national debt portend a bleak and difficult future for the nation if they are not brought under control. More than any other issue, this is what galvanized the Tea Party movement. As is true with any household, no government can keep spending more than it takes in. The financial markets will not countenance this type of behavior and its currency will fall in value, heightening the risk of inflation. Interest rates will also have to rise to entice financial institutions and others to buy its bonds. Higher interest rates will lead to a decline in GDP and recession, or worse. The last Bush administration did not appear to understand these economic facts of life and continued to cut taxes and increase spending. Though some of the expenditures were due to the Iraq War, national security, and Hurricane Katrina, domestic initiatives also played a role, like the Medicare prescription drug bill and various earmarks written into legislation. Former Federal Reserve Chairman, Alan Greenspan, warned about the dangers of huge budget and trade deficits,[48] but was essentially ignored. Since the recent recession, various fiscal stimuli have increased the budget deficits significantly. However, most economists agree that this was necessary in the short-term to reinvigorate the economy.

Because of the annual budget deficits, the national debt limits have been raised regularly by Congress as the amount America owes keeps climbing. In March 2010, it was $12.6 trillion and as of December had added another trillion.[49] As the financier Peter G. Peterson noted:

> There are long-term tradeoffs to be faced: between economic security and national security, between retirement security and national security, and between today's taxpayers and tomorrow's taxpayers. As yet, however, the leaders of the two major political parties have hardly mentioned these tradeoffs, much less discussed them seriously.[50]

To compound the problem, America's declared national debt does not include unfunded liabilities of tens of trillions of dollars to meet the obligations of its Social Security and Medicare programs, government pensions, and veterans' benefits.

How did America get to this level of debt? Though the problem started with World War II, until 1980 the amount it owed was kept below $1 trillion, which appeared to be manageable. The growth of the national debt began accelerating during the Reagan years in the early '80s and has been rising since, aside from a time in the late '90s during Clinton's tenure, when it stabilized and actually declined in inflationary terms. Bush came into office with a tax surplus of $5.6 trillion projected during the following decade, and economists were even talking about eliminating the national debt. But the Bush administration transformed this boon into a deficit of $2.6 trillion.[51] They accomplished this through tax cuts and additional spending, putting the country back on the path to penury. In the first two years of Obama's tenancy in the White House, the national debt rose over $2 trillion more, much of it due to initiatives to end the recession. And in spite of the Deficit Commission's recommendations to lower the budget deficit and the national debt, as of July 2011, no significant action had been taken. In fact, the compromise tax proposal passed by Congress at the end of 2010 further increased the budget deficits by extending the Bush tax cuts. When the need to raise the debt limit by early August 2011 arose to avoid default by the US, Republicans and Democrats fought bitterly over how to accomplish this goal, with the former unwilling to increase any taxes and the latter reluctant to cut entitlement spending.

Interestingly, it is the Republican Party that professed to be fiscally conservative when out of power that must bear the onus for most of America's national debt. Under Bush, through the end of 2005, federal spending grew 33 percent, double the rate of the Clinton years, outpacing every president since Lyndon Johnson.[52] President Bush and members of his administration claimed repeatedly that their tax cuts would pay for themselves, but in fact they did not, according to an analysis from the Center on Budget and Policy Priorities, an independent watchdog group.[53]Government revenues were substantially lower than the White House Office of Management and Budget had predicted prior to the passage of the 2003 tax cuts, as they were for the 2001 tax cuts, and the budget deficit and national debt ballooned. As Pete Peterson noted in his book, *Running On Empty*: "This administration and the Republican Congress have presided over the biggest, most reckless deterioration of America's finances in history."[54] In his book, *The Age of Turbulence: Adventures in a New World*, Alan Greenspan also harshly criticized Bush, Cheney, and the Republican-controlled Congress for "abandoning their party's principles on spending and deficits" and lacking fiscal discipline.[55]

Running a budget deficit is not always bad economic policy. In times of national stress, such as war or recession, it is not unreasonable for the government to spend more than it collects. Tax cuts can be beneficial in stimulating a dormant economy, encouraging consumption and spending, as people have more money in their pockets. Thus the increase in the deficit may have been necessary during the first two or three years of the Obama administration. When the crisis passes, however, plans have to be made to rein in the deficits with sound economic strategy rather than wishful thinking. This has not yet been done. To allow the tax cuts for the wealthy to continue at this time borders on the immoral, in view of the colossal government expenditures. Again, Pete Peterson:

> The Democrats and Republicans . . . have found only one important way to compromise, and this is for both sides to take what they want (low taxing and high spending) and send the bill to our kids. These two parties have launched America . . . . on a course of vast and mounting budget deficits which, if left unaltered, can only end in an economy-shattering crisis or crushing burdens on America's younger generations—or both.[56]

Cutting government spending seems a nearly impossible task, given the composition of the budget. Money allotted to the military and so-called entitlement programs like Medicare and Social Security encompass nearly 80 percent and are due to outpace economic growth and inflation. These are essentially off the table in terms of reducing expenditures because of the political storms that any discussion would generate. This leaves domestic discretionary spending, less than 20 percent of the budget, as the area to be attacked by those who want to be perceived as deficit hawks. Included under this umbrella are education programs, scientific research, the space program, the environment and national parks, and support for cultural institutions. Though there are efforts to pare small amounts from various programs, there has been no attempt to address the major areas of expenditures. And in addition to government spending disclosed in the budget, there are also supplemental items requested from Congress. These emergency spending bills avoid the normal budget and appropriation procedures, obscuring the true costs from the public.

With America's borrowing mainly from abroad, just funding the interest payments on the national debt further increases the debt and takes money away from programs that would benefit the country. Interest on $14 trillion at 3 percent is $420 billion annually that is essentially wasted. This will be a great weight holding back succeeding generations of Americans, as the nation's wealth is slowly drained away by its profligacy and winds up in the hands of foreign creditors.

~~~

As noted earlier, pork is defined as government spending on pet projects favored by individual senators or congressmen that benefits constituents or special interest groups. It can be part of the regular budget bills or supplementary bills and can also be inserted surreptitiously into voluminous unrelated bills as so-called "earmarks" by legislators, concealed from the public and not debated by their colleagues (though 2007 ethics reform mandates transparency). When the bill is passed, the pork is approved as part of it, with funds disbursed to the particular recipient. Some legislators claim that they are best able to determine the needs of people in their district and that there is nothing wrong with the process of pork. Many earmarks are also done as favors for special interests. Nonetheless, many of these projects are wasteful, frivolous, or unnecessary, bolstering the legislator at home but not serving the needs of the country.

The $286 billion transportation bill in 2005 had 6371 "special projects" inserted at a cost of $30 billion more than the president sought.[57] The energy bill that year was $12.3 billion, twice as much as the administration had wanted. The conservative Citizens Against Waste estimates that pork projects by Congress, with the Republicans in control of both houses, soared from less than 2000 per year in the mid-1990s to nearly 14,000 in 2005.[58] In the 2005 budget, $67 billion was spent on earmarks.[59] Some of the most blatant pork programs were allocated for Alaska; one for $250 million to build a bridge similar to the Golden Gate, linking an airport to the town of Ketchikan with a population of 14,000.[60] Another $230 million was designated for a bridge between Anchorage and an undeveloped port area. In 2009, with the Democrats in control of Congress, there were 9,287 pork projects in the Omnibus spending bill, costing almost $13 billion.[61]

Legislators also fund military programs costing tens of billions of dollars or more designated for planes, ships, or weapons systems that the military has not asked for and does not want. However, they provide jobs or support industries in that legislator's district, or help special interests to whom the legislator is beholden. These may be payback for campaign assistance, or even for bribes. Some earmarks are comical, such as financing a teapot museum in Sparta, North Carolina, and hundreds of other similar projects.[62] Whatever the rationale, pork and earmarks are unnecessary spending that raise the federal deficit further. It seems to make little difference which party is in control. Though one of the Tea Party's signature issues was its opposition to earmarks, fifty-two members of the Congressional Tea Party caucus requested more than $1 billion in earmarks during fiscal year 2010.[63] After much wrangling, the Republican leaders in Congress in 2011 prohibited the use of earmarks for two years.

Farm subsidies are a recurring theme in federal legislation that is expensive but cannot be eliminated because of the backing of farm state legislators. In these programs, the tens of billions of dollars that are dispensed annually, mainly to corporate farmers, do not help small family farms and contravene trade agreements.[64] Again, neither Democratic- nor Republican-controlled Congresses seem able to reform a system that makes payments to farmers who bank sizeable profits. (And subsidies are antithetical to the free market lauded by American politicians.) The subsidies also encourage production of foods that are unhealthy—grains instead of fruits and vegetables—contributing to the epidemic of obesity in America. Yet free-trade advocates and those railing against government handouts can't seem to overcome the farm state politicians on the issue of subsidies.

In addition to the federal budget deficits, most of the individual states have budget deficits of their own, ranging from minimal to major. The primary cause is a significant decrease in revenue as a result of the recession, but previous financial gimmicks are also playing a role. Failure to fund pension obligations of public service employees in the past is also putting pressure on state governments, as is the rise in health care costs. While asking state workers to pay more for their benefits seems a reasonable path, cuts to education funding through firing of teachers and larger class sizes is a serious mistake, sacrificing the children's and the nation's future. Though there is an aversion to raising taxes, at times it may be necessary to keep essential services, like education, at a high level of performance.

~~~

America's tax codes have evolved over many decades, with new laws and revisions of old laws piled one upon another as Congress has changed its mind, adjusted, and compromised in different sessions about the ways it wants to collect revenue to run the federal government. Its rules and regulations now run to thousands of pages of jargon and bureaucratic language requiring a special interpreter to understand. Even experts at the Internal Revenue Service have difficulty deciphering all of its facets and ramifications, while the average citizen may be completely befuddled. Federal taxes include personal income taxes, estate taxes, capital gains taxes, and other taxes on passive income like dividends. There are also corporate income taxes, various other corporate taxes and fees, sales taxes on certain products such as gasoline, tariffs and import duties, licensing fees for use of the broadcast spectrum, other usage fees, drilling and mining rights, royalties and so forth.

There is general agreement that the tax code should be simplified, and at various times, congressmen and government officials have trumpeted the need for this. Indeed, President Obama has placed tax reform on his to do list for 2011, though actually getting it done may prove to be another story. One concern is how to handle the Alternative Minimum Tax (AMT), which takes a substantial bite out of many middle-class households. Originally passed in 1969 to try and insure that the truly wealthy would not avoid taxes through shelters and creative accounting, it did not make adjustments for inflation and in 1986 further changes were enacted eliminating common deductions. The result has been that those earning what are modest incomes now are falling under its provisions. Like the law of unintended consequences, the rich are now little affected by the AMT, the burden falling mainly on the middle class. Both parties have vowed on a number of occasions to right this inequity, but have yet to come up with a solution. Given the problem of America's surging budget deficits, whatever proposals for overall tax reform are generated must consider ways to increase government revenue, a move that is certain to create conflict between the two parties.

The extension of the Bush tax cuts last year in a compromise move by the Obama administration and Republicans has also been disquieting. Though the measures that provide relief for the middle class appear reasonable, it seems foolish to add to the budget deficits by giving the wealthiest citizens tax breaks. In addition to lower income tax rates, changes in the estate tax will also benefit the most affluent. The Bush administration had heralded their tax cuts as necessary to stimulate the economy, but the economy had actually done much better during the Clinton years with higher rates. Bush's decrease in taxes on investment income alone put an extra $500,000 on average into the pockets of those with incomes of more than $10 million,[65] with a bonus averaging over $150,000 to those earning more than $1 million.[66] Supporters of these cuts said they would spur job growth, investments, and consumer spending. But if consumer spending were important, why weren't more of the cuts focused on the poor and middle classes? (The top one percent received 36.7 percent of the tax cut.[67]) The 2001 tax cut was followed by another one in 2003 favoring the affluent, and President Bush obtained yet another one in 2006. These were in spite of spiraling government expenditures, the large annual deficit, and the growing national debt, none of which seemed to bother the president or the Republicans in Congress then.

Reforming the estate tax has also been a matter of some contention between the parties, with Republicans always referring to it as the "death tax" and asserting that it is ruinous to small businesses and family farmers who must sell assets to pay the tax. Yet there is no evidence it significantly affects these groups. They are being used as stalking horses by anti-tax ideologues who want to permanently terminate the estate tax on the super-rich, the ones who would benefit most from this measure, again ignoring the budget deficit and national debt. The tax cutters also claim the estate tax is tantamount to taxing earnings twice, though much of the assets in estates of the most affluent comes from real estate, capital gains, dividend and interest income, rather than wages. Estate taxes actually affect only a tiny percentage of the total population; their elimination would preserve a great quantity of money for a very few individuals and families, with average savings of about $800,000 accruing to about one in 6,000 estates.[68]

With many special interests pushing for tax preferences and compliant Congressmen willing to play ball (in return for campaign funding and other support), it has been difficult to craft tax legislation that is fair and equitable. In this regard, many Democrats and Republicans act similarly. Senator Charles Schumer of New York, a liberal Democrat, came out in favor of tax breaks for hedge fund and private equity executives in 2007, insisting there was no relationship between his stance and the outpouring of campaign funds for him and the Democrats by the hedge fund industry.[69] Fund managers claim that the "carried income" on the enormous profits they make should be taxed at the capital gains rate of 15 percent instead the ordinary income tax rate of 35 percent, a difference that could mean billions of dollars to the government. Though people in the hedge fund and private equity industries do not place any of their own money at risk to warrant capital gains designation, Schumer agreed to resist any increase in their taxes.

Corporate taxes in the United States are also in need of a major overhaul. While the federal rate of 35 percent is among the highest in the world, virtually no businesses actually pay that rate. Various loopholes and deductions allow companies to pay much less, many below 20 percent and some in the single digits.[70] These include major corporations such as General Electric, Prudential, Southwest Airlines, Carnival Cruises, and more. This makes for a system that impedes economic growth, as companies search for ways to avoid taxes rather than doing what makes the most economic sense. Corporate lobbyists who want the tax rate lowered, at the same time are unwilling to phase out the special deductions and loopholes their clients now enjoy.

## Pension Reform and Social Security

Pension reform is another important issue America's political parties have been unwilling to address. Many pension plans have been underfunded by corporations over the years to boost their bottom lines, using creative accounting to meet government guidelines for the required contributions. The federal government has an insurance program, similar to that in banking, that guarantees corporate pensions if the plans pay an annual premium. As corporate bankruptcies increased, many pension plans were found to be severely deficient in financing and unable to meet their obligations. This left the government holding the bag for payments to retired employees from these companies. Since government pension benefits are capped at much lower amounts than the retirees were supposed to receive, many faced a change in lifestyle or a return to work.

The corporations that underfunded their pension plans sometimes did it legally by using projections for returns on investment that were improbable though still acceptable, but at other times were fraudulent. Some corporations declared bankruptcy merely to rid themselves of the millstones of pension plans that had become too costly, dropping the load on the government. Mary Williams Walsh observed in the *New York Times*:

Loopholes in the federal pension law allowed United Airlines to treat its pension fund as solid for years, when in fact it was dangerously weakening. . . .These loopholes give companies ways—all perfectly legal—to make their pension plans look healthier than they really are, reducing the amount of money the companies must contribute.[71]

According to the Pension Benefit Guaranty Corporation, the United pension fund had a deficit of $8.3 billion in 2004.

Additionally, the insurance premiums that support the pension system have been insufficient to bail out all the failed plans, even at the lower level of payout the government provides. Because of the financial burden, more and more corporations have been eliminating pensions completely, switching to 401K plans and other savings vehicles. But Congress has dropped the ball by not providing oversight for pension plans, not penalizing corporations that underfunded their programs, and not insisting on adequate insurance premiums to cover the costs of failed plans. To do that would mean bucking the corporations and their lobbyists—who are big campaign contributors.

An even greater problem may lie with the states, municipalities, counties, school districts, and so forth, that have also been deficient in funding their pension and health plans for prospective retirees.[72] Oversight of these programs has been lacking as well and the extent of the liabilities is unclear in many instances. Estimates of the deficits for these public agency plans run as high as $3 trillion, with taxpayers on the hook.[73] Public service unions of teachers, firefighters, policemen, administrative employees, and others negotiated these benefits over the years with politicians who wanted their support, disregarding the potential for future debacles. Now there are major battles in a number of states and municipalities, as public employee unions fight to preserve their collective bargaining rights against government officials who want to break the unions.[74] While some overreaching by the unions undoubtedly occurred, the fact that the politicians did not make sufficient contributions to the health and pension plans has been generally disregarded.

~~~

Social Security is another financial dilemma that has been left in limbo by Republicans and Democrats despite promises to reform a program that is on a track to insolvency. Originally conceived as a social insurance program in 1935, the retirement age when workers could receive benefits was set at sixty-five, with recipients then expected to live about twelve years more.[75] By 2040, however, workers will survive nearly twenty years after retirement or even more depending on medical advances. This reality cannot be ignored. As Pete Peterson notes in his book, *Gray Dawn*:

> Global aging will become the transcendent political and economic issue of the twenty-first century . . . renegotiating the established social contract in response to global aging will soon dominate and daunt the public policy agendas of all the developed countries.[76]

It is not only that people will be living longer after retirement; there will be more of them as well. About 12.5 percent of Americans are currently sixty-five or older.[77] In another twenty-five years, over 20 percent of the nation's population will have passed that milestone. Besides having more old people, America will also have proportionately fewer younger workers to support the Social Security system because of a drop in the birth rate over the last seventy years. In 1950, for each Social Security beneficiary there were sixteen workers. By 1999, there were slightly more than three.[78] The immigration of young people to America has slightly strengthened Social Security, counteracting to some extent the impact of families having fewer children. But it is estimated that by 2020 there will be only two workers for each person receiving benefits. In Europe and Japan, the demographics are even more dire, with a lower birth rate and more restrictions on immigration undermining their social insurance systems.

Though the two political parties have been aware of the looming Social Security crisis for years, they have been unable to reach any consensus on corrective measures, which will involve some sacrifice and pain. When the shortfall will occur and how draconian the numbers will be is uncertain. But certainly at some point in the future, funds will be exhausted, necessitating drastic reductions in payouts to beneficiaries. The deficit could reach tens of trillions of dollars or be significantly smaller, but some action to prevent the deficit is required. President Bush's plan to privatize a portion of Social Security[79] was ideologically based, looking for the market to generate additional income for retirees, though many economists felt it would not work. The plan did not have the backing of a majority of Americans and did not make it through Congress.

The quandaries with Social Security and the pension systems are even more critical because America's citizens have neglected to save on their own. The baby boomers who will soon be retiring will require additional income from their savings that won't be there, making them dependent on Social Security and pensions for their daily living expenses. Perhaps their indifference reflects the conduct of a government that seems to be willing to live on credit as well. Americans' lack of personal savings also increases the country's need for foreign sources to service the national debt, with the interest paid going abroad rather than to American citizens. The historian Niall Ferguson describes a paradox regarding savings:

> The average American has an income of about $40,000 a year and . . . a personal savings rate of zero. The average Chinese earns around $1500 per year but has a personal savings rate of 23 percent of his income—and is lending a large chunk of these savings, via the People's Bank of China, to the average American.[80]

The recent recession wiped out even more of Americans' savings, but as citizens worry about their ability to retire and to survive future economic crises they are increasing their rate of saving. In May 2009, the household savings rate was 6% compared to 0% a year earlier.[81]

## Education and Science

The quality (and quantity) of education experienced by America's children and adolescents is another reason for the country to be concerned. The United States is destined to become a second-rate economic power unless the failings of its educational system can be reversed. Almost one third of all of America's students do not gradu-ate from its public high schools, but nearly one half of Latinos and African Americans.[82] College enrollment and completion rates are also dropping, connected in large part to increased costs.[83]

Standardized tests at every grade level have consistently shown that Americans perform poorly in comparison to students of other nations in all parameters of knowledge, but particularly in math and science. Only six percent of Americans achieve ad-vanced proficiency in math.[84] Even the brightest students do not fare well, the top five percent ranking only twenty-third of twenty-nine nations whose students were tested.[85] The majority of the pupils in American schools do not reach educational milestones in reading, English, math, and science, and that does not even consider familiarity with history, geography, and current events that are necessary to forge responsible citizens. Incredibly, test-ing also reveals that a large percentage of US college graduates are not fully literate and lack basic abilities in writing and math. Businesses complain that many high school and college graduates do not have the required skills to perform their jobs and have to receive remedial training. As further evidence of America's edu-cational breakdown, a large percentage of its citizens do not un-derstand simple concepts in science.[86] Only 40 percent accept the theory of evolution, with only 13 percent understanding what a molecule is. Only about half of Americans know that humans did not exist at the time of the dinosaurs, and 20 percent believe that the sun revolves around the earth.

All of the above are signs of the bankruptcy of America's edu-cational system. The blame for this must be shared by the schools, the administrators, the teachers, parents, and pupils as well as local, state, and federal governments. Part of the problem is money, as local school boards and many state governments restrict funding for education, guided by referenda and citizen pressure to reduce taxes. Teachers' unions have also balked at innovative changes, afraid they will be burdensome for their members and might have financial repercussions. They have also been resistant to rewarding teachers on the basis of merit instead of seniority, and removing teachers who perform poorly. Unfortunately, the lack of accountability and good metrics makes it difficult to correct the structural flaws and know exactly where to put the nation's money and muscle to work. Instead, there is the prevailing image of many of America's children glued to the television or playing video games three or four hours a night rather than doing homework, reading, or trying to master something new. Recently, teachers have been demonized as part of the public's reaction against public service unions, although teacher salaries are far from excessive.

At the college level, tuition and fees have been rising constantly, even at public universities, making it more difficult for many students to afford a higher education. State governments have been less willing to subsidize education and many students find grants and loans to pay for college harder to obtain or requiring higher interest rates.

President Bush's attempt to set standards and improve achievement, particularly for minority students, with the No Child Left Behind Act generated mixed support both in and out of the schools. To receive federal funding, schools had to meet certain guidelines and have highly qualified teachers in every classroom.[87] Annual testing from grades three through eight devised by the states was supposed to be used to gauge progress. However, many states tried to bolster scores by designating teachers as highly qualified without objective measures of their ability and using student testing that was far from rigorous. For example, Tennessee's testing of eighth-grade students in math showed 87 percent performing at or above the proficiency level.[88] Similar federal tests a few months later revealed that only 21 percent were proficient. Mississippi declared 89 percent of its fourth-grade students proficient in reading, but only 18 percent were so designated on federal testing. The differences in results occurred because states did not employ stringent tests to ascertain student progress. Gauging improvement with these state standards, in order to determine federal funding, neither made students truly proficient nor advanced the educational process.

Presidents George H.W. Bush and Bill Clinton both believed that national standards and national testing in the public schools were important to reform America's educational system.[89] President George W. Bush, however, and his Republican majority in Congress did not seek that objective "because it was contrary to the Republican philosophy of localism. Instead, he adopted a strategy of '50 states, 50 standards, 50 tests'—and this approach did not significantly improve student achievement."[90] Local officials and congressmen also pressured the Department of Education to be more lenient in interpreting the rules, though this neutralized the rationale behind the law. Some educators also believe that schools focused on teaching to the tests, rather than trying to improve overall learning and acquisition of knowledge.

Another effect of the No Child Left Behind law was that in an attempt to qualify for federal funds, many school districts placed less emphasis on programs for gifted children as they tried to raise the test scores of those who were performing poorly. Though this may have been seen as egalitarian by some, it was an extremely shortsighted policy, since the nation's gifted children are the ones who have the most potential to help America compete against the rest of the world. Many parents are spending out of their own pockets for special programs for their smart children who are not being challenged by the usual classes in school.[91]

The dearth of competent teachers also plays a major role in the disappointing achievements of America's students. While there are many bright, dedicated teachers who have chosen the profession for idealistic reasons, a large proportion are not well trained nor properly motivated enough to serve as catalysts for the learning process. In general, teaching at a primary or high school level is not a career choice for smart, ambitious college students, as it provides only meager salaries and little prestige, in spite of the critical function it plays.

Under Secretary of Education Arne Duncan, the Obama administration has moved to correct some of the problems of No Child Left Behind. Using a $4 billion grant program called Race to the Top, the Department of Education has tried to use funding to motivate the states to try novel strategies to improve student performance in the public schools.[92] It is too early to say if this approach has been successful, and many of the difficulties created by No Child Left Behind remain in place. Too many schools have been labeled as failing because of lack of student proficiency in math and reading, even though they have shown improvement.

America's educational weakness has grave implications for both society and the individuals unable to gain basic skills. Lack of educational attainment by early adulthood is in general a marker for an unsuccessful life, with years of schooling a fairly reliable predictor of the level of later affluence. Yet as bad as it may be for individuals, the toll educational failure will take on American society as the nation tries to maintain its position in this new knowledge-based world is even higher. The growth of the Internet and the rapid development of various kinds of software allow work related to information processing to migrate to those countries with the technical expertise. In *The World is Flat,* Tom Friedman describes changes in the twenty-first century: "Companies have never had more freedom, and less friction, in the way of assigning research, low-end manufacturing, and high-end manufacturing anywhere in the world."[93] There have been many reports of the vast numbers of students in Asia who, starting in grade school, work twelve hours a day to learn as much as they can, battling with their peers for positions in the most prestigious universities. Are America's children adequately prepared to compete in this new globalized world with their cousins in India, China, Korea, and all the other nations that value education and expect proficiency from their students?

The United States takes deserved pride in the vitality of its economy, which forms the foundation of our high quality of life, our national security, and our hope that our children and grandchildren will inherit ever greater opportunities. That vitality is derived in large part from the productivity of well-trained people and the steady stream of scientific and technological innovations they produce. Without high quality, knowledge intensive jobs and the innovative enterprises that lead to discovery and new technology, our economy will suffer and our people will face a lower standard of living.[94]

These words come from *Rising Above the Gathering Storm,*

the executive summary of a report by a panel of experts from the National Academies, that deals with the critical need to strengthen America's scientific competitiveness or suffer the consequences.

In addition to its general educational deficiencies, America is not generating enough scientists, mathematicians, and engineers. Of the graduates who received doctorates in engineering from American universities in 2005, 58 percent were foreign nationals and only 42 percent were American.[95] On an undergraduate level, 36 percent of Germans obtain degrees in science and engineering, 59 percent of Chinese, 66 percent of Japanese, but only 32 percent of Americans.[96] Part of the problem is the lack of a foundation in these areas during early schooling. Many instructors also don't invest these subjects with enough excitement and passion to make their students want to learn more and continue in advanced classes. In addition, American society does not attach enough cachet to careers in these fields and provides no financial incentives for them. Its materialistic young people want to go into investment banking or hedge funds rather than mathematics or science.

Another impediment may be the restrictions imposed by local school boards on the teaching of science. Creationism, intelligent design, and pseudoscience have been pushed by those who wish to remove or at least downplay evolution and the big bang theory, both of which are important aspects of modern science. Students need to know the prevailing ideas in scientific disciplines if they are to understand and be successful in these fields. A number of politicians, including former President George W. Bush and John McCain, have stood behind the teaching of intelligent design in the schools to court religious voters, even though it is without scientific basis. The federal government is also making it more difficult for America to keep pace in the current high-tech world by cutting back on basic research. In the face of European and Asian nations increasing their funding for research, Washington foolishly is reducing its funding. Basic research pays off in the distant future, sometimes with products and sometimes with knowledge that can help Americans live better lives. The US economy is bound to feel the effects of the decline in research. The proportion of patents granted to American scientists has already begun to fall compared to those of other nations. In addition, government financing for research helps to train and sustain young scientists who might otherwise select different fields. Diminished support is extremely shortsighted.

Because of 9/11, Washington is putting up barriers to foreign scientists and engineers who want to immigrate to America to study at its universities or work for its corporations. With stringent visa requirements in place, many students who have been unable to come to America have chosen European or Asian institutions instead. Perhaps the Immigration and Naturalization Service doesn't speak to the Commerce Department and is not aware of the country's acute need for these individuals. Not only do these scientists and engineers help with research and developing new technology, they also play an important role in the universities as teaching assistants. It has been estimated that 62 future patent applications are gained for every 100 foreign students who obtain PhDs in science or engineering at American universities.[97] As America graduates fewer and fewer of its own scientists, it becomes ever more critical that it attract and retain foreign scientists to fill the vacant positions.

## Energy Policy, Global Warming, and the Environment

The energy expert, Daniel Yergin, noted in 2006:

> The renewed focus on energy security is driven in part by an exceedingly tight oil market and by high oil prices, which have doubled over the past three years. But it is also fueled by the threat of terrorism, instability in some exporting nations, a nationalist backlash, fears of a scramble for supplies, geopolitical rivalries, and countries' fundamental need for energy to power their economic growth. In the background, but not too far back, is renewed anxiety over whether there will be sufficient resources to meet the world's energy requirements in the decades ahead.[98]

The same issues remain in 2011.
The United States has needed a sound energy policy since the

nation was rocked by the Arab oil embargo in 1973, when oil prices quadrupled and a fuel shortage followed. The embargo was lifted in March 1974, but it drove inflation in America for years afterwards, with ballooning interest rates and economic turmoil. In 1979, during the Iran hostage standoff, a second oil crisis occurred. There were some minor shortages caused by disrupted Iranian supplies, but much of that was covered by increased production from other OPEC countries. Nevertheless, a panic ensued, with skyrocketing prices for gasoline and long waits at the pumps, as in 1973. Many administrations and Congresses, both Republican and Democratic, have come and gone since these crises, with an occasional nod in the direction of conservation, alternative fuels, or increased production, but America still doesn't have a sensible, comprehensive, long-term energy policy.

Dependence on foreign oil places America in a precarious position, constantly at the mercy of the countries that supply it. Many of these nations, such as Iran or Venezuela, are unfriendly and apt to do what they can to cause America pain. In addition, some of the money spent on Saudi Arabian oil goes to funding terrorist organizations that are America's sworn enemies, with the Saudis countenancing religious leaders who rail against the West and the United States. The Russian resurgence, with a leadership that opposes many US initiatives, also derives its power from oil and gas. And when oil jumps from $20 to $40 a barrel to over $90, it is equivalent to a foreign tax imposed upon American industries and consumers. Electricity, heating, and transportation costs all increase. Businesses have less to invest in upgrading their operations and individuals have less to spend on products and services. In addition, the ballooning trade deficit is at least partially the result of oil prices. The United States is held hostage as well to nature's whims, as when hurricanes in the summer of 2005 damaged the oil platforms in the Gulf of Mexico and prices soared. So why hasn't anything been done to lessen our need for oil? The auto industry and oil companies have combined through intensive lobbying and campaign contributions to both Republicans and Democrats over the years to maintain America's thirst for oil, defeating initiatives in

Congress or at the National Highway Traffic Safety Administration (NHTSA) that might have led to greater energy independence. In 1975, the Energy Policy and Conservation Act shortly after the Arab oil embargo set corporate average fuel economy (CAFÉ) standards for new passenger cars, with strict penalties for non-compliance.[99] New-car fleet fuel economy was only 12.9 mpg in 1974, and CAFÉ called for boosting that to 27.5 mpg by the model year 1985, with light trucks going to 20.7, SUVs included in the category of light trucks. But when the price of oil declined and the sales of smaller cars softened, Detroit petitioned the NHTSA to relax standards— and they did. American manufacturers fought against increased CAFÉ standards because they felt their sales would suffer, and that Japanese car makers who were producing vehicles with better mileage would benefit. Of course, by not adapting at that time, the American companies caused self-inflicted injuries that are only now starting to heal.

Subsequently, attempts to raise CAFÉ standards for all vehicles or light trucks were rebuffed by Congress or the NHTSA, and in 1996, Congress essentially froze the standards. A study by the National Academy of Sciences in 2001 . . . concluded it was possible to achieve more than 40 percent improvement in light truck and SUV fuel economy over a 10–15 year period at costs that would be recoverable over the lifetime of ownership.[100]

But Congress did not act to increase the standards for either light trucks or passenger cars. Though SUVs have been the best sellers for American companies over the last two decades, they have also been the biggest gas guzzlers. Detroit did little to improve their fuel economy. Now with oil prices spiraling ever higher, SUVs are less attractive and American companies have lost market share to Asian manufacturers, whose vehicles get superior mileage. The Big Three had about 80 percent of the American auto market in April 1985. Their share had dropped to under 43 percent by January 2009.[101] (The percentage rose, however, with Toyota's image problems as well as the earthquake and tsunami in Japan in 2011.)

Surprisingly, President Bush in his economic stimulus plan in 2003 suggested tripling the equipment deduction available for small business owners and professionals from $25,000 to $75,000, allowing the largest and most luxurious SUVs and trucks to become fully deductible.[102] The Economic Stimulus Package as part of the Jobs and Growth Act was passed by Congress in May 2003, increasing the deduction to $100,000 per vehicle. Instead of buying cars for professional use that might have gotten 30 mpg, this legislation encouraged businessmen to purchase SUVs that would get 15 mpg or less, with Hummers averaging only 10 mpg. These tax breaks for the largest and least fuel-efficient SUVs were totally contrary to the government's supposed goal of lowering fuel consumption and America's dependency on foreign oil. They also increased greenhouse gases. Not surprisingly, they did benefit American automobile manufacturers and oil producers, and were a startling triumph for the lobbyists in these two sectors. Though the law was changed the following year after media criticism, a $25,000 depreciation expense was allowed to stand along with a 50 percent bonus deduction, which still covered most of the costs of the large SUVs.

In March 2006, the NHTSA heightened fuel economy standards for SUVs, pickup trucks and minivans, but the change was only a modest difference phased in over a number of years and excluding the largest pickups.[103] In May 2009 President Obama finally raised the CAFÉ standards significantly for cars and trucks, mandating major increases in mileage requirements by 2016.[104] Mileage standards for cars would gradually rise to 39 mpg and light trucks to 30 mpg, with the current average at 25 mpg. Greenhouse gases would also be reduced, along with foreign oil imports.

Both parties must share the blame for amazingly poor judgment and neglect in failing to formulate an energy policy for decades that would have freed America from living under a sword of Damocles—its vulnerability from being dependent on foreign oil. Fearful of losing jobs, the automotive unions lobbied the Democrats while their bosses were lobbying the Republicans against proposals that would conserve fuel. The oil companies also lobbied against conservation measures, pushing instead for subsidies for increased exploration and production. Though freezing of the CAFÉ standards by the government may have helped American manufacturers in the short run, they had a negative long-term effect. The Japanese and Koreans worked on developing more fuel-efficient cars, while Detroit built bigger and more powerful SUVs. The strategy of American carmakers was certainly not intelligent, but the government did them no favor by agreeing to their demands and not advocating fuel efficiency as a priority.

Similarly, there has been no requirement for the utilities and other major corporate consumers of fuel to cut usage significantly and employ alternative sources of energy. Coal-burning plants provide a large portion of the power that American utilities generate, with domestically-produced coal relatively cheap. These plants do not require importing foreign oil, but they create huge volumes of carbon dioxide emissions, acid rain, and other pollutants. Private companies for the most part manage their problems in ways that cost the least money, so they can increase their profits. They do not pursue expensive protracted solutions unless they are forced to by the government through penalties, or aided by incentives. However, no meaningful federal initiatives have been forthcoming to cut the utilities' use of hydrocarbon fuels.

For America to deal with its dependency on foreign oil, there are three possible approaches, none of which would be sufficient in itself. The first is to increase domestic production of oil by trying to recover more of it from old secondary wells and allowing drilling in new areas. However, this requires exploration in environmentally sensitive regions like the Arctic National Wildlife Refuge in Alaska and coastal regions of the continental shelf, and would yield only temporary increases. Another option may turn out to be shale oil, which, over the last several years has been found to be extremely plentiful in the US, though there appear to be some questions about pollution from the production process ("fracking") that need to be answered. Finding new sources of oil in other parts of the world would raise global supplies, but again would provide only short-term relief.

The second approach is to expand the use of alternative fuels, including ethanol, electric and hybrid technology, hydrogen-powered engines, and natural gas. America has abundant sources of relatively cheap natural gas that can be used to replace expensive imported foreign oil, but there has been no concerted effort to encourage the development of vehicles that use natural gas as fuel, along with the stations necessary to supply them. To run the nation's homes and industries, greater use of solar technology, wind power, thermal power, hydroelectric power, clean coal technology, and nuclear energy plants could all have played a role. But America has made minimal progress in these areas. The use of natural gas as a source of fuel for power plants, however, has been increasing.

The third arm of energy independence is fuel conservation, a possibility that has been sadly neglected by legislators. An emphasis here might produce considerable results over time, with government incentives and perhaps a little arm-twisting of both corporations and the general public. A nod toward conservation did come from the stimulus package (The American Recovery and Reinvestment Act of 2009), which included a $4.3-billion home energy credit to increase energy efficiency.[105] This provided tax deductions for energy-efficient windows and doors, improved furnaces and air conditioners, insulation, and so on, but it was not a major initiative.

Connected to the nation's energy problems are environmental issues such as global warming that present a long-term threat to the planet. The overwhelming consensus among scientists who deal with climate and weather is that global warming has already begun, resulting from ever-increasing greenhouse gas concentrations caused by human activity.[106] This has caused melting of the polar ice caps, the Greenland ice shelf, and glaciers in mountainous areas around the world. How much the temperature will rise in the future and how rapidly is uncertain, but it is likely an increase in sea level will flood low-lying coastal areas and many islands at some point. As Ruth Greenspan Bell noted in *Foreign Affairs*:

> Most climatic models now predict continued deterioration, but the signs that are currently visible, such as the thawing of the permafrost, lack the drama of airplanes piercing the World Trade Center. Like the frog in the pan of heating water that does not notice the temperature rising until it is too

late, human beings have been lulled into believing that they have many years to deal with climate change. When dramatic changes finally do occur, it will be too late for remedial action.[107]

Greenhouse gases like carbon dioxide trap the heat from sunlight in the earth's atmosphere and prevent its reflection back into space, warming the planet. About 85 percent of the nation's energy needs come from burning fossil fuels and the United States, with the world's largest economy, is responsible for about 25 percent of the world's carbon emissions, though it has only five to six percent of the world's population. Half of America's electric power comes from coal-burning generators, with a significant increase of these plants in the planning stage or under construction.[108] China's use of coal as a major source of energy has also greatly elevated pollution and $CO_2$ emissions, and will only get worse as its economy grows. Although the world's second-largest economy, China is now the largest producer of carbon dioxide.[109] Similarly, India burns coal for energy as do other developing nations. Why hasn't America been working toward the objective of reducing its energy use and carbon emissions?

Starting with rejection of the Kyoto Protocol and the appointment of lobbyists and oil industry personnel to high posts in sensitive government agencies, the Bush administration signaled its disdain for environmental issues. Though the Kyoto Protocol was seriously flawed, there was no attempt by the US government to revise or amend it, or to offer new proposals. Members of the Bush administration consistently downplayed the evidence for global warming and the dangers that might follow, not permitting dissent from that stance. Dr. James Hansen, a renowned climatologist and NASA scientist who is the director of the Goddard Institute for Space Studies, said in March 2006 that "political operatives in the agency's press office were trying to censor his views on global warming."[110] Other scientists at various government agencies described similar attempts to suppress their professional beliefs.

Virtually across the board, the Bush administration ignored environmental concerns when making policy decisions. This stance affected sales of mining or timber rights on Federal land, enforcement of pollution rules, completion of toxic cleanup at contaminated superfund sites, maintenance of clean air and water standards, control of acid rain, limitation of arsenic levels in water, and management of the national parks and forests. Whenever questions arose as to how to handle problems, the Bush administration decided in favor of commercial interests and businesses against the public interest. These decisions were often made by former lobbyists for the industries involved, or people who worked for these industries.

Though President Obama issued an executive order that would reduce greenhouse gas emissions by the federal government and pledged to other nations to reduce total emissions from the United States by 2020, there is yet to be definitive legislation to codify that commitment. With Republican control of the House after the 2010 elections, and with many of the new representatives denying the existence of global warming, it is unlikely that significant legislation in this area will be forthcoming.

## Health Care

The latest attempt at health care reform, the Affordable Care Act, was passed by Congress in March 2010 over Republican resistance in both houses and signed by President Obama. It was designed to provide health care for the uninsured through various mechanisms, but will not be fully implemented until 2014. Measures were included in an attempt to control escalating medical costs and the Congressional Budget Office did predict some savings, though this assumption has been challenged by a number of economists. Since its passage, Republicans have been trying to overturn the act through the legal system, attacking the individual mandate to purchase insurance as unconstitutional. Whether or not the ACA is reversed, the health care system needs a more aggressive strategy to check skyrocketing costs as the government, private industry, and ordinary citizens cannot live with the constant increases in the price of care.

Health care expenditures were responsible for 17.3 percent ($2.5 trillion) of the nation's GDP in 2009, with estimates it will reach close to 20 percent in ten years.[111] Medical bills have been a major cause of bankruptcy and home foreclosures. Comparable percentages of GDP for health care were 10.7 percent in Germany, 9.7 percent in Canada, and 9.5 percent in France.[112] In addition, employer-based health insurance premiums in the US increased 119 percent from 1999 to 2008 and were projected to further double by 2020.[113] The nation spends over four times as much on health care as it does on national defense. Though medical care consumes a greater percentage of America's GDP than that of any other nation, American life expectancy and infant mortality lag behind the average of other industrialized countries.[114] And over one-sixth of its population does not have health insurance (though the ACA aims to change that).

With the huge sums it pays out, America does not get an adequate return on its investment because of a markedly inefficient and fragmented system. The government has allowed entities at every level who are driven by profit to control their sectors of the system, each of them taking their piece of the pie and running up the tab. This includes insurance companies, hospitals, physicians, imaging centers, pharmaceutical companies, clinical laboratories, home health care businesses, nursing homes, physical therapy units, and other organizations. Over the last decade, the health insurance industry has been consolidating through mergers and acquisitions, with larger companies dominating the major markets and able to determine pricing and access.[115] This has not fostered competition and cost constraints. The recent legislation on health care reform does not seriously address the complexities and inefficiencies in the system, and may in fact make them worse.

Overhead and administrative costs have been estimated to consume 15 to 25 percent of the nation's health care dollar. Americans are also being over-treated and many receive what might be termed "excessive care." The Center for Evaluative Clinical Sciences at Dartmouth Medical School believes that

> . . . 20 to 30 percent of health care spending goes for procedures, office visits, drugs, hospitalization, and treatments

that do absolutely nothing to improve the quality or increase the length of our lives—but which nonetheless drive up costs. At the same time, the type of treatment that offers clear benefits is not reaching many Americans, even those who are insured."[116]

Evidence is given to support these assertions, showing that "the supply of medical services rather than the demand for them determines the amount of care delivered."[117]

If the Center's estimates are valid, between overhead costs and unnecessary care, 40 to 50 percent of health care spending (many hundreds of billions of dollars) is not being used productively.

The Medicare Prescription Drug Program passed in 2003 to help seniors pay for drugs is another example of something that should be simple made extremely complicated for political reasons. With a multiplicity of convoluted plans and deductions offered, even the standard plan was Byzantine and difficult to understand.[118] Rather than the seniors who need the coverage, the main beneficiaries were the pharmaceutical and health insurance companies, whose lobbyists played a major role in formulating the legislation.[119] With greater coverage for drugs becoming available, pharmaceutical makers raised prices sharply in the first quarter of 2006 to maximize their profits, greatly outstripping the inflation rate.[120] In addition, funding the Medicare drug program required a major increase in federal spending, as the government's share of prescription drug costs soared from two percent in 2005 to 27 percent in 2006.[121]

One wonders why Americans are willing tolerate an expensive, inefficient system that does not deliver the goods. Perhaps they have been brainwashed over the years by various health care interests telling them how good they have it, and how any modifications will cause problems and interfere with their care. Americans have been led to believe they receive the best health care in the world, and for the very affluent that may be true. For most patients, however, it is another story, being rushed in and out of doctors' offices, with little time for discussion, and a lack of preventive services. Meanwhile, the poor, who have no insurance, receive their care in hospital emergency rooms. In addition, a surfeit of specialists and a lack of primary care physicians add to the problem.

Excluding the Affordable Care act, there were six attempts to introduce some type of universal health insurance during the past century, all meeting with failure. Admittedly, some of the proposals were outlandish and unworkable, but there were sensible suggestions in the medical and health care literature that never got any traction. The most important reason for their failure is that they were opposed by powerful special interests, the same ones influencing public opinion, who did not want to see any change. Politicians were reluctant to offend these players, who contribute large sums of money to them and can attack them in the media. Time and again, the specter of socialized medicine was raised when change was suggested, implying government control of all aspects of care and with it, reduced quality. In 2006, Massachusetts passed health care reform legislation to provide coverage for 90 to 95 percent of state residents who lack medical insurance[122],[123] But problems regarding cost and access have developed with Massachusetts's program. The Affordable Care Act has similarities to the Massachusetts legislation and it is likely to run into the same kinds of problems.

Unfunded future liabilities for Medicare are estimated to run into trillions of dollars. In addition, runaway health care expenses for employees make American products less competitive, with many large corporations and small businesses hurting because of these costs.[124] This escalation cannot go on indefinitely without overwhelming the American economy. The Affordable Care Act does not appear to be the vehicle to resolve the issue of cost.

## Immigration

The dilemma of illegal immigration is another matter that has stymied Congress, opening fault lines between the two parties and within the Republican Party that make it difficult to negotiate a solution. In today's world, America needs secure borders to protect itself from terrorists and to limit the entry of illegal drugs and immigrants. This means that the nation cannot permit people without proper documents to enter the country at will. To some citizens and many members of Congress, this is the only concern. But America must realize that to criminalize and deport an estimated 13 million undocumented immigrants already living and working in its midst would be an impossible logistical feat. Aside from the task of finding all the immigrants who have melted into communities throughout the nation, it would be necessary to incarcerate them for a period of time, bring legal proceedings against them, then transport them by air or sea to their original homes. The sheer number of personnel this would entail and the cost of the operation make this a fantasy and not a solution. The government has to find a way to give immigrants a path to legality and citizenship, imposing some sort of penalty because they broke the law when they came to America. The "amnesty" law passed in 1986, which was supposed to end the problem of illegal immigration, was totally ineffective, as politicians against immigration point out.[125]

There are also sectors of the economy dependent on immigrant labor that must be considered in any new legislation. Many agricultural enterprises, landscapers and builders, hotel and restaurant industries, meat and poultry processing plants rely on immigrants in order to function. Though there are federal laws requiring employers to verify their workers' documents to exclude "illegals," the laws were generally disregarded and the penalties relatively minor until August of 2007, when the Bush administration began a crackdown on the hiring of undocumented immigrants, causing employers to howl in protest.[126] This policy has continued under Obama with a beefing up of border security as well.

America must also acknowledge the impact any legislation might have on its neighbor, Mexico, which has been dependent on illegal immigration as a safety valve. It has too many young people and not enough jobs, and the country would experience social upheaval if the US closed its doors completely. This would not be good for Mexico and would not be good for America. Workers in the United States are also a major source of foreign exchange for Mexico and its economy might collapse without it. The North American

Free Trade Agreement (NAFTA) was partially responsible for increasing illegal immigration by making American agricultural products from corporate farms cheaper than those of Mexican farmers. When these farmers could not make a living from their land, they migrated to the United States.

Most of the immigrants who come to America are hard working and industrious, seeking a better life. Many of them pay taxes and Social Security, though they are not eligible for benefits. They bring a certain energy that is helpful to the US economy and fill low-paying jobs American citizens are reluctant to take. Many economists believe, however, that immigrants may depress wages for American workers on the low end of the scale.[127] Their willingness to do particular jobs for less money makes employers place a certain value on the work and they are hesitant to pay more to Americans doing the same or similar jobs. Undocumented immigrants also require services that are borne by local and national taxpayers, such as schooling for children, health care costs, and welfare payments.[128]

In 2006, President Bush pushed for a compromise bill on immigration, tougher on border security while allowing immigrants who were here for a certain length of time to receive legal status and a path toward citizenship. But Republicans in the House refused to consider any measure that would legalize undocumented immigrants. Ultimately, a bill was passed to build "a fence" along seven hundred miles of the border with Mexico, though funding was appropriated for only about half.[129] A plan to deal with the illegal immigrants already within the country was never enacted. In May 2007 a bill was worked out between a group of Republicans and Democrats in the Senate,[130] but was ultimately rejected because of vehement opposition to "amnesty." States then pursued their own programs for handling immigrants within their borders, with no uniformity in terms of the law. Subsequently, there was support for Congress to pass what was called the Dream Act, allowing those undocumented immigrants who served in the armed forces or were attending college to be eligible for accelerated citizenship.[131] This was again blocked in the Senate in December 2010, when there were not enough votes to overcome a Republican filibuster. Thus, after years of debate and political maneuvering, there is still no definitive policy about how to deal with the illegal immigrants who have established roots within America.

## Infrastructure

Politicians in the federal and state governments have long deferred the maintenance and upgrading of the nation's infrastructure, with dire consequences in New Orleans from Hurricane Katrina in 2005. Though made worse by incompetent management from government officials, the inadequacy of the levee system was mainly responsible for the disaster that occurred. The Army Corps of Engineers had previously estimated that $2.5 billion was necessary to construct levees to withstand a grade five hurricane,[132] and had made that recommendation to Congress. But funding was never appropriated. Other instances highlighting the neglect of America's infrastructure were the collapse of a major highway bridge in Minneapolis in 2007 and the rupture of a giant underground steam pipe in New York City. The American Society of Civil Engineers gave the nation's infrastructure a cumulative grade of D in 2005, because of the overall state of disrepair and deterioration.[133]

Infrastructure includes roads, bridges, tunnels, mass transportation, railroads, ports, airports, dams and levees, electrical plants and transmission lines, phone and communication systems (broadband), pipelines and refineries, many of which are slowly crumbling and all of which are vital to the economy. Government and private industry share the task of building and maintaining the infrastructure, with federal, state, county, and municipal governments all playing roles. Investing in new elements of infrastructure involves large outlays with ongoing maintenance costly as well. Because of America's budget deficits and the desire of many politicians to cut taxes, the upgrading of the nation's infrastructure to meet the needs of population and economic growth has not been forthcoming, with maintenance often delayed or shunted aside. When Congress does appropriate money for infrastructure it is often for pet projects through earmarks, rather than what government engineers believe should have priority.[134] The American Society of Civil Engineers estimated in 2009 that $2.2 trillion was necessary in the next five years to prevent further disintegration of the nation's infrastructure.[135] An earlier report suggested that about 13,000 fatalities occur each year because of highway disrepair alone.[136]

Without the preservation and necessary expansion of highways, bridges, and tunnels, slowdowns and traffic jams will occur more often, with untold numbers of productive hours lost, millions of gallons of gasoline wasted, and pollution levels raised. In 2000, the Texas Transportation Institute estimated that congestion in 75 urban areas cost drivers nearly $70 billion in lost time and fuel.[137] Disregard of mass transit will force even more vehicles onto the roads. Insufficient refinery capacity will escalate gasoline and heating oil prices and cause shortages at times. Inadequate numbers of electrical plants and transmission lines will result in reduced electrical supplies, blackouts, and brownouts. And with imports rising, port capacity must grow to handle more ships, and airports must be enlarged to manage increased volumes of air traffic. The Environmental Protection Agency noted that bottlenecks at American ports cost the nation $200 billion every year.[138]

The failure to fund Amtrak and the national rail system adequately is another foolish move. When Amtrak was formed, it was left with an outmoded infrastructure that results in breakdowns and frequent problems. Without an upgrade into a modern rail system, Amtrak will never be a reliable, alternative means of travel to the air and roads, similar to those in the industrialized nations of Europe and Asia. Amtrak needed between $2 and $4 billion dollars a year for capital expenditures to bring it up to snuff, according to Department of Transportation analysts in 2006.[139] Congress and the White House offered $600 million.

The electrical grid is also at risk because America lacks a national agency to supervise a deregulated industry, in which utilities often purchase power from distant generating plants delivered over lengthy transmission lines with various complex links. Human operating errors or natural disasters can lead to major blackouts with economic impact. Regional control groups are not designed to deal with these problems, nor can they plan for augmenting the grid on a national level.

Though the United States was sixteenth in the world in terms of broadband connectivity in 2005, the federal government has made no move to help correct this deficiency.[140] With the importance of the Internet and online activities to the economy, Korea, Japan, and a number of European countries have pushed high-speed broadband access for businesses and individuals, while America did not. The Baby Bells were supposed to have provided this as outlined in the 1996 Telecommunications Act, but never did. Optical fiber is required for this instead of the old copper lines and it is expensive to institute. It is vital, however, for American competitiveness.

Many state legislatures have also avoided spending on infrastructure. Some have sold off elements to private firms, which then become responsible for upkeep and can charge consumers usage fees, making a profit while covering maintenance. *Barron's* noted that "America's toll roads, better known for political patronage than for strong business and financial management, suddenly are hot assets."[141] *Barron's* believed the push for privatization was motivated by both financial and political considerations, since about $92 billion was needed each year for maintenance alone on bridges and highways, not counting the costs of upgrading them. Of course, foreign firms are doing much of this buying, and the question remains whether they will put American convenience and safety above profits. Ports and even some airports are also coming under the control of foreign corporations. Is this another example of our nation selling its birthright for a cup of porridge? Why can't federal, state, and local governments also manage these assets and make a profit?

While America does little to correct its infrastructure deficiencies, its competitors in Asia and Europe are forging ahead with high-speed trains, new roads, broadband connectivity, and whatever is needed to support their economies. When the United States government had the opportunity to fund infrastructure repairs and new construction with its economic stimulus program in

2009, few projects resulted. Politicians in the two parties have no vision regarding the future needs of the nation in the context of a cutthroat global economy.

(This chapter and the next discuss the many challenges America faces. The amount of text devoted to each one is not necessarily proportional to its importance.)

## References

[1] Niccolò Machiavelli, *The Prince*, trans. Daniel Dommo, Bantam Classics, New York, NY, 2003 (originally published in 1513), 90.

[2] Richard McCormack, "Manufacturing continues to shrink as a percentage of U.S. economic activity," All Business, June 26, 2006, www.allbusiness.com/manufacturing/computer-electronic-product-manufacturing/1182847-1.html.

[3] Sherle Schwenninger and Samuel Sherraden, "Manufacturing and the US Economy," New American Foundation, July 13, 2009, www.newamerica.net/file/manufacturing_report.pdf.

[4] Alan S. Blinder, "Offshoring: The Next Industrial Revolution?" *Foreign Affairs*, 2006, Vol. 85, No. 2, 114.

[5] David Leonhardt, "The Economics of Henry Ford May Be Passé," *New York Times*, April 5, 2006, C1.

[6] Kimberly Amadeo, "Economic Stimulus Package," About.com guide, November 16, 2010. http://useconomy.about.com/od/candidates and the economy/a/obama_stimulus.htm.

[7] Stephen Gandel, "Obama's Stimulus Plan: Failing by Its Own Measure," Time.com, July 14, 2009, www.time.com/time/printout/0,8816,1910208,00.html.

[8] "New Stimulus Plan," December 12, 2010, http://newstimulusplan.com/2011_Stimulus.html.

[9] Michael Cooper and Mary Williams Walsh, "Mounting Debts by States Stoke Fear of Crisis," *New York Times*, December 4, 2010, A1.

[10] Micheline Maynard and Jeremy W. Peters, "2 Asian Automakers Plan Ventures in 2 States Left by U.S. Carmakers," *New York Times*, March 13, 2006, C1.

[11] Clyde V. Prestowitz, Jr, *Trading Places*, Basic Books, New York, NY, 1988, 13.

[12] Ibid., 22.

[13] Bloomberg News, "China Overtakes Japan as World's Second-Biggest Economy," August 16, 2010, www.bloomberg.com/news/print/2010-08-16/china-economy-passes-japan-s-in-second-quarter.

[14] Keith Bradsher, "To Conquer Wind Power, China Sets the Rules," *New York Times,* December 15, 2010, A1.

[15] Peter Hakim, "Is Washington Losing Latin America?" *Foreign Affairs*, January/February, 2006, 49.

[16] N. Gregory Mankiw and Phillip L. Swagel, "Antidumping: The Third Rail of Trade Policy," *Foreign Affairs*, July/August 2005, 107.

[17] James Womack, "Why Toyota Won," *Wall Street Journal*, February 13, 2006.

[18] Alex Taylor III, "Inside GM's bankruptcy filing," CNN Money.com, June 3, 2009, http://cnnmoney.printthis.clickability.com/pt/cpt?action=cpt&title=MotorWorld%3A+Ins.

[19] Chris Isidore, "Chrysler files for bankruptcy," CNNMoney.com, May 1, 2009, http://cnnmoney.printthis.clickability.com/pt/cpt?action=cpt&title=Chrysler+filing+for=b.

[20] Edmund L. Andrews, "Auto Chiefs Make Headway Against a Mileage Increase, *New York Times*, June 7, 2007, C1.

[21] Excerpt from Joseph Farah's G2 Bulletin, "U.S. Backs China Nukes," World Net Daily, March 19, 2006, www.worldnetdaily.com/news/printer-friendly.asp?articleID=49354 Also reported on CNN News.

[22] Keith Bradsher, "Thanks to Detroit, China Is Poised to Lead," *New York Times*, March 12, 2006, Business, 1.

[23] Keith Bradsher, December 15, 2010.

[24] Neil C. Hughes, "A Trade War with China?" *Foreign Affairs*, July/August 2005, 94.

[25] Foreign Trade Statistics, "Trade with China 2010," www.census.gov/foreign-trade/balance/c5700.html#2010.

[26] C. Fred Bergsten, "China's Trade Surplus with the United States," Congressional testimony, March 29, 2006, Peterson Institute for International Economics. www.iie.com/publications/papers/bergsten0306-al.cfm.

[27] David Lague, "China Begins Effort to Curb Piracy of Computer Software," *New York Times*, May 30, 2006, C3.

[28] David H. Levey and Stuart Brown, "The Overstretch Myth," *Foreign Affairs*, March/April 2005, 3.

[29] Martin Feldstein, "The Return of Savings," *Foreign Affairs*, May/June 2006, 87.

[30] Sherle R. Schwenninger, "America's Suez Moment," *The Real State of the Union*, New American Books, New York, NY, 2004, 45–46.

[31] Kaus, Mickey, *The End of Equality*, Basic Books, New York, NY, 1992, 17.

[32] Ian Dew-Becker and Robert J. Gordon, "Where did the Productivity Growth Go?" Paper presented at the 81st meeting of the Brookings Panel on Economic Activity, 2005:2, www.brookings.edu/es/commentary/journal/bpea.

[33] Ibid.

[34] David Cay Johnston, "Income Gap Widening, Data Shows," *New York Times*, March 27, 2007, C1.

[35] Ibid.

[36] Eduardo Porter, "How Superstars' Pay Stifles Everyone Else," *New York Times*, December 26, 2010, 1.

[37] David Cay Johnston, "Pay at Investment Banks Eclipses All Private Jobs by a Factor of 10," *New York Times*, September 1, 2007, Business, C1.

[38] Liz Rappaport, Aaron Lucchetti, and Stephen Grocer, "Wall Street Pay: A Record $144 Billion," *The Wall Street Journal*, October 11, 2010.

[39] John Cassidy, "What Good Is Wall Street?" *The New Yorker*, November 29, 2010, 49–57.

[40] Ibid.

[41] Scott DeCarlo, "What the Boss Makes," Forbes.com, 4/20/06, www.forbes.com/2006/04/20/ceo-pay-options-cz_sw_0420ceopay.html.

[42] Clive Crook, "Executive Privilege," *The Atlantic*, January/February 2006, 151.

[43] Eric Dash, "Inquiry Into Stock Option Pricing Casts a Wide Net," *New York Times*, June 19, 2006, C1.

[44] U.S. Census Bureau News, August 29, 2006, Public Information Office.

[45] "About Poverty—Highlights, U.S. Census Bureau, www.census.gov/hhes/www/poverty/about/overview/index.html.

[46] Ibid.

[47] Stephen Labaton, "Congress Passes Increase in the Minimum Wage," *New York Times*, May 25, 2007, A12.

[48] Heather Timmons, "Greenspan Points to Danger of Rising Budget Deficits," *New York Times*, December 3, 2005, C3.

[49] Mark Knoller, "National Debt Up $2 Trillion on Obama's Watch," CBS News, Political Hotsheet, March 16, 2010, www.cbsnews.com/8301-503544_162-20000576-503544.html.

[50] Peter G. Peterson, "Riding for a Fall," *Foreign Affairs*, September/October 2004, Vol. 83, No. 5, 111–112.

[51] Jonathan Rauch, "The New Nixon," *The Atlantic*, July/August 2005, 27.

[52] Edmund L. Andrews, "80% of Budget Effectively Off Limits to Cuts," *New York Times*, April 6, 2006, A22.

[53] Richard Kogan and Aviva Aron-Dine, "Claims That Tax Cuts Pay For Themselves Is Too Good To Be True," Center on Budget and Policy Priorities, March 8, 2006, www.cbpp.org/3-8-06tax.htm.

[54] Peter G. Peterson, *Running On Empty*, Farrar, Straus and Giroux, New York, NY, 2004, xxv.

[55] Edmund L. Andrews and David E. Sanger, "Former Fed Chief Attacks Bush on Fiscal Role," *New York Times*, September 15, 2007, A1.

[56] Peterson, *Running On Empty*, 4–5.

[57] Robert B. Reich, "An Economy Raised on Pork," *New York Times*, September 3, 2005, OpEd, A21.

[58] Ibid .

[59] Sheryl Gay Stolberg, "What's Wrong With a Healthy Helping of Pork?" *New York Times*, May 28, 2006, Week in Review, 4.

[60] Heather Lende, "Alaska's Road to Nowhere," *New York Times*, August 20, 2005, OpEd, A13.

[61] Brian M. Riedl, "Omnibus Spending Bill: Huge Spending and 9000 Earmarks Represent Business as Usual," WebMemo, The Heritage Foundation, www.heritage.org/Research/Budget/wm2318.cfm.

[62] Bill Marsh, "Pork Under Glass? Small Museums and Their Patrons on Capital Hill," *New York Times*, April 30, 2006, Week in Review, 4.

[63] Reid Wilson, "Tea Party Caucus Takes $1 billion in Earmarks," *The Atlantic*, downloaded 12/16/10, www.theatlantic.com/politics/print/2010/12/tea-party-caucus-takes-1-billion-in-earmarks/67326/.

[64] David Herszenhorn, "Farm Subsidies Seem Immune to an Overhaul," *New York Times*, July 26, 2007, A1.

[65] David Cay Johnston, "Big Gains for Rich Seen in Tax Cuts for Investments," *New York Times*, May 4, 2006, A1.

[66] David Cay Johnston, *New York Times*, March 27, 2007.

[67] William G. Gale and Samara Potter, "The Bush Tax Cut: One Year Later," Policy Brief #101-2002, www.brookings.edu/printme.wbs?page=comm/policy/briefs/pb101.htm.

[68] David Cay Johnston, "A Boon for the Richest in an Estate Tax Repeal," *New York Times*, June 7, 2006, C8.

[69] Raymond Hernandez and Stephen Labaton, "In Opposing Tax Plan, Schumer Breaks With Party," *New York Times*, July 30, 2007, A1.

[70] David Leonhardt, "The Paradox of Corporate Taxes," *New York Times*, February 1, 2011, B1.

[71] Mary Williams Walsh, "Pension Loopholes Helped United Hide Troubles," *New York Times*, June 7, 2005, C1.

[72] Milt Freudenheim and Mary Williams Walsh, "The Next Retirement Time Bomb," *New York Times*, December 11, 2005, Business, 1.

[73] Tamara Keith, "Pension Woes May Deepen Financial Crisis For States," NPR, March 21, 2010, www.npr.org/templates/story/story.php?storyld124894618.

[74] Kate Zernike, "More Standoffs and Protests, Plus a Prank Call," *New York Times*, February 24, 2011, A20.

[75] Peter G. Peterson, *Gray Dawn*, Random House, New York, NY, 1999, 40.

[76] Ibid., 5.

[77] S. Burner, et al, "Nation's Health Care Expenditures Through 2030," *Health Care Financing Review*, Vol. 14, No. 1 (1992):4.

[78] David Rosenbaum, "Social Security: The Basics With A Tally Sheet," *New York Times*, January 29, 1999.

[79] "Strengthening Social Security of Future Generations," White House Web Page, www.whitehouse.gov/infocus/social-security/.

[80] Niall Ferguson, "Reasons to Worry," *New York Times Magazine*, June 11, 2006, 45.

[81] Rich Miller and Alison Sider, "Surging U.S. Savings Rate Reduces Dependence on China," Bloomberg, June 26, 2009, www.bloomberg.com/apps/news?pid=21070001&sid=Gg3KshLrpV8.

[82] Nathan Thornburgh, "Dropout Nation," *Time*, April 17, 2006, 32.

[83] Tamar Lewin, "Report Finds U.S. Students Lagging in Finishing College," *New York Times*, September 7, 2006, A23.

[84] Amanda Ripley, "Your Child Left Behind," *The Atlantic*, December 2010, 94–98.

[85] "Back to School, Thinking Globally," *New York Times*, September 6, 2005, editorial, A26.

[86] Nicholas D. Kristof, "The Hubris of the Humanities," *New York Times*, December 6, 2005, A27.

[87] "School Reform in Danger," New York Times, May 8, 2006, Editorial, A20.

[88] Sam Dillon, "Students Ace Tests, But Earn D's from U.S." *New York Times*, November 26, 2005, A1.

[89] Diane Ravitch, "Every State Left Behind," *New York Times*, November 7, 2005, OpEd, A23.

[90] Ibid.

91 Julie Bick, "It Pays to Have a Smart Child, but It Can Cost, Too," *New York Times*, January 22, 2006, 8.

92 Sam Dillon, "New Challenges for Obama's Education Agenda in the Face of a G.O.P. Led House," *New York Times*, December 11, 2010.

93 Thomas L. Friedman, *The World Is Flat*, Farrar, Straus and Giroux, New York, NY, 2005, 209.

94 "Rising Above The Gathering Storm," Executive Summary, National Academies Press, February 2006, www.nap.edu/books/0309100399/html/1.html.

95 Statistics from a table in *USA Today*, February 22, 2006, (source: American Association of Engineering Societies), 1.

96 Thomas L. Friedman, "Keeping Us in the Race," *New York Times*, November 16, 2005, OpEd, A23.

97 Stuart Anderson, "America's Future Is Stuck Overseas," *New York Times*, November 16, 2005, OpEd, A23.

98 Daniel Yergin, "Ensuring Energy Security," *Foreign Affairs*, March/April 2006, Vol. 85, No. 2, 69–70.

99 Robert Bamberger, "Automobile and Light Truck Fuel Economy: The Café Standards," Congressional Research Service, *Almanac of Policy Issues*, updated September 25, 2002, www.policyalmanac.org/environment/archives/crs_cafe_standards.shtml.

100 Ibid.

101 Josh Hakala, "Detroit Three's US market share at record low," mlive.com, February 4, 2009, http://www.mlive.com/auto/index.ssf/2009/02/detroit_threes_us_market_share.html.

102 Jim Walczak, "Free SUVs For Small Business Owners—Pros and Cons of New SUV Tax Break," About Automotive, 4Wheel Drive/Offroading, April 2004, http://4whelldrive.about.com/cs/drivingtipssafety/a/aa041.

103 Mathew L. Wald, "U.S. Raises Standards on Mileage," *New York Times*, March 30, 2006, C1.

104 Mike Allen and Eamon Javers, "Obama announces new fuel standards," Politico, May 18, 2009, http://dyn.politico.com/printstory.cfm?uuid=5481D758-18FE-70B2-A8AF6C70885AA5D5.

105 Sandra Block, "Stimulus package's tax credits reward home energy efficiency," *USA Today*, www.usatoday.com/cleanprint/?1292877295771.

106 Naomi Oreskes, "The Scientific Consensus on Climate Change," *Science*, December 3, 2004, Vol. 306, No. 5702, 1686.

107 Ruth Greenspan Bell, "What to Do About Climate Change," *Foreign Affairs*, May/June 2006, Vol. 85, No. 3, 106.

108 William Grimes, "The Promise and Problems of Those Dirty Black Rocks," book review of *Big Coal*, Jeff Goodell, *New York Times*, June 21, 2006, E10.

109 Laurence O'Sullivan, "Largest producers of Greenhouse Gas Emissions," Suite101.com, www.suite101.com/content/largest-producers-of-greenhouse-gas-emissions-a16611.

110 Warren E. Leary, "New NASA Policy Backs Free Discussion by Scientists," *New York Times*, March 31, 2006, A16.

[111] Ken Terry, "Health Spending Hits 17.3 Percent of GDP In Largest Annual Jump," BNET, February 4, 2010, www.bnet.com/blog/healthcare-business/health-spending-hits-173-percent-of-gdp-in-largest-annual-jump/1117.

[112] "Facts On Health Care Costs," National Coalition on Health Care, 2006, www.nchn.org/facts/cost.shtml.

[113] The Commonwealth Fund, "New Report: Employer-Sponsored Health insurance premiums Increase 119 Percent from 1999–2008; Projected to Double Again by 2020," August 20, 2009, www.commonwealthfund.org/Content/News/News-Releases/2009/Aug/Employer-Sponsored-Health-Insurance.

[114] Malcolm Gladwell, "The Moral_Hazard Myth–The bad idea behind our failed health care system," *The New Yorker*, Fact Issue of August 8, 2005, www.newyorker.com/printables/fact/050829fa_fact.

[115] Robert Pear, "Loss of Competition Is Seen In Health Care Industry," *New York Times*, April 30, 2006, 21.

[116] Shannon Brownlee, "The Overtreated American," *The Real State of the Union*, New American Library, New York, NY, 2004, 130.

[117] Ibid., 131–132.

[118] "Medicare Prescription Drug Coverage," *Medicare and You, 2006*, Official Government Handbook [for Connecticut and Rhode Island], 53.

[119] Louise M. Slaughter, "Medicare Part D—The Product of a Broken Process," *New England Journal of Medicine,* 2006; 354:2314–2315.

[120] Milt Freudenheim, "Drug Prices Up Sharply This Year," *New York Times*, June 21, 2006, C1.

[121] Julie Appleby, "Health care spending rises at blistering pace," *USA Today*, June 9, 2006, Sec. B, 1.

[122] Stuart H. Altman and Michael Doonan, "Can Massachusetts Lead The Way in Health Care Reform?" *New England Journal of Medicine,* 2006; 354:2093–2095.

[123] Robert Steinbrook, "Health Care Reform in Massachusetts—A Work In Progress," *New England Journal of Medicine,* 2006; 354:2095–2098.

[124] Paul Webster, "US big business struggle to cope with health-care costs," *Lancet,* 2006, 367:101–102.

[125] Rachel Swarns, "Failed Amnesty Legislation of 1986 Haunts the Current Immigration Bills in Congress," *New York Times*, May 23, 2006, A20.

[126] Julia Preston, "Farmers Call Crackdown on Illegal Workers Unfair," *New York Times*, August 11, 2007, A1.

[127] Nicholas D. Kristof, "Compassion That Hurts," *New York Times*, April 9, 2006, Week in Review, 13.

[128] Clive Crook, "The Benefits of Brutality," *The Atlantic*, May 2006, 38–40.-

[129] Carl Hulse and Rachel L. Swarns, "Senate Passes Bill on Building Border Fence," *New York Times*, September 30, 2006, A10.

[130] Carl Hulse and Robert Pear, "Immigrant Bill 15 Votes Short, Stalls in Senate," *New York Times*, June 8, 2007, A1.

[131] Julia Preston, "Immigration Vote Leaves Policy in Disarray," *New York Times*, December 19, 2010, 35.

[132] Andrew C. Revkin and Christopher Drew, "Intricate Flood Protection Long a Focus of Dispute," *New York Times*, September 1, 2005, A16.

[133] "A Bridge Collapses," *New York Times*, August 5, 2007, Week in Review Editorial, 9.

[134] John Tierney, "The Case for a Cover-Up," *New York Times*, September 10, 2005, OpEd, A17.

[135] Michael Cooper, "U.S. Infrastructure Is in Dire Straits, Report Says," *New York Times*, January 28, 2009.

[136] Louis Uchitelle, "Disasters Waiting to Happen," *New York Times*, September 11, 2005, Business, 1.

[137] Jonathan Rauch, "Taking Stock," *The Real State of the Union*, Basic Books, New York, NY, 2004, 72.

[138] "That Sinking Feeling," *New York Times*, February 21, 2007, Editorial, A20.

[139] "Railroading Amtrak," *New York Times*, May 26, 2006, Week in Review Editorial, 9.

[140] Thomas L. Friedman, "Calling All Luddites," *New York Times*, August 3, 2005, OpEd, A19.

[141] Andrew Barry, "Toll-Road Sales: Paying Up," *Barron's*, May 8, 2006, 17.

CHAPTER 5

# America's Challenges—National Security and Foreign Policy

The cause of America is in a great measure the cause of all mankind.

—Thomas Paine, *Common Sense*[1]

It is to be noted that in seizing a state one ought to consider all the injuries he will be obliged to inflict and then proceed to inflict them all at once so as to avoid a frequent repetition of such acts. Thus he will be able to create a feeling of security among his subjects and, by benefiting them, win their approval.

—Machiavelli, *The Prince*[2]

This chapter focuses on national security challenges, the performance of America's intelligence apparatus, the situations in Iraq and Afghanistan, and America's overall foreign policy. It should again be kept in mind that many of these areas are interconnected and that actions in one area can have repercussions in other domains. Although it is said that bipartisanship should be the norm where foreign policy is concerned and that disagreements between the parties should end at the water's edge, this is often not the case. The two parties still fight for political advantage in dealing with security and foreign policy issues, making it more difficult to show a unity of purpose to the outside world.

In his book, *The Rise and Fall of the Great Powers*, Paul Kennedy, a professor of history at Yale, describes the interrelationship between military and economic power and warns how excessive spending on armaments and military forces can lead to a nation's decline. He states:

> wealth is usually needed to underpin military power, and military power is usually needed to acquire and protect wealth. If, however, too large a proportion of the state's resources is diverted from wealth creation and allocated instead to military purposes, then that is likely to lead to a weakening of national power over the longer term.[3] . . . a top-heavy military establishment may slow down the rate of economic growth and lead to a decline in the nation's share of world manufacturing output, and therefore wealth, and therefore power.[4]

Is the United States overextending itself in terms of its military expenditures and hastening its decline as a world power? The US spends more on the military than all the other nations in the world combined.[5] Its involvement in two recent wars and its military spending have certainly contributed to its budget deficits and skyrocketing national debt. Joseph Nye, director of the Center for International Affairs at Harvard, sees America as "both the world's largest economy and its largest military power,"[6] and does not believe it is destined to decline because of overreaching and military overspending. He notes that worry about the deteriorating position of the United States has occurred periodically throughout its history and believes the current ruminations are no different.

## Intelligence Failures and Nuclear Nonproliferation

America's intelligence agencies have had a disappointing record since the end of the Cold War. During the '90s, they did not recognize advances in the Indian and Pakistani nuclear programs, and the US was unprepared when both countries exploded nuclear devices. Washington also lacked intelligence about the development of their delivery systems, missiles that could carry nuclear payloads to targets hundreds or thousands of miles away. The sale by the rogue Pakistani nuclear physicist A.Q. Khan of information about the production of nuclear weapons also caught America by surprise with no effective strategy in place to counter his efforts. North Korea's and Iran's nuclear programs appear to have been given large boosts by data supplied by Khan. It also seems likely that Pakistan's missile capability benefited from trading information with North Korea about its nuclear projects, allowing both countries to accelerate the production of weapons. Because of these failures of intelligence, one of America's major foreign policy initiatives, nuclear nonproliferation, has been unsuccessful and has led to continuing confrontations with North Korea and Iran.

During the Clinton years, with the Cold War over, intelligence cutbacks contributed to America's deficiencies. With no rival to challenge US military primacy, spending on intelligence was felt to be less critical. The initial terrorist attack on the US homeland, the first World Trade Center bombing in 1993, stunned the nation's intelligence agencies, though the Islamic fundamentalist perpetrators were later caught and sentenced to long prison terms. At that point, Al Qaeda was not seen as a danger to the United States, though the bombers were connected to that organization. Even after the embassy bombings in Kenya and Tanzania in August 1998, America did not fully understand the magnitude of Al Qaeda's potential threat. In retaliation for those attacks, Washington launched cruise missiles that struck the group's compounds in Afghanistan and a pharmaceutical company in the Sudan thought to have links to bin Laden, though in retrospect, that connection seems questionable. Aggressive intervention against Al Qaeda in Afghanistan was not pursued, although perhaps if there had been hard intelligence about what Al Qaeda was planning, the administration's response would have been more punishing.

The suicide bombing of the destroyer, the USS Cole, by Al Qaeda adherents in Yemen occurred in October 2000 as the Clinton presidency was drawing to a close, again without any foreknowledge by US intelligence. This event should have made the incoming Bush administration more attuned to the threat posed by Al Qaeda, but it did not seem to make a major impression on their national security team. Part of the problem may have been an unwillingness to accept concerns or priorities passed on by Clinton personnel.

The 9/11 attacks, of course, were America's most glaring intelligence failure. Although intelligence operatives picked up indications beforehand that Al Qaeda was planning actions on American soil, policy makers largely downplayed or disregarded these signs. Richard Clarke, the national coordinator for security, infrastructure protection, and counterterrorism from 1998 to 2003 under both Presidents Clinton and Bush, as well as other intelligence analysts, tried to warn major figures in the Bush administration about the dangers of Al Qaeda prior to 9/11, but these admonitions were minimized or ignored. Clarke's frustrations are described in his book, *Against all Enemies*. Among those who were briefed on Al Qaeda were Condoleezza Rice, Stephen Hadley, Paul Wolfowitz, Colin Powell, and Vice President Cheney,[7] none of whom reacted with a sense of urgency. Bob Woodward, in *State of Denial*, describes how George Tenet, the head of the CIA, and Cofer Black, a senior operative, met with Condoleezza Rice in early July 2001, warning of the likelihood of an Al Qaeda attack in the United States, but she did not follow through on the information.[8] In general, there was a feeling of disbelief by Bush officials that this ragtag bunch of terrorists was a danger to America. Indeed, before 9/11, Attorney General John Ashcroft was unwilling to make terrorism a top priority for the Justice Department and rejected any increased funding for counterterrorism efforts.[9]

After the end of the Cold War, America's intelligence agencies had difficulty adjusting to the new and unconventional enemy the country was facing. Robert Kaplan wrote:

> . . . the post-Industrial Revolution empowers anyone with a cellular telephone and a bag of explosives. America's military superiority guarantees that such new adversaries will not fight according to our notions of fairness: they will come at us asymmetrically, at our weakest points.[10]

While the hierarchical structure and fixed assets of the Soviets made monitoring fairly straightforward, the Islamic terrorists are composed of shadowy and evanescent groups that operate across national borders. An analysis of intelligence reform in 2006 noted:

The ability of the United States to defend itself depends on whether US intelligence agencies built for a different enemy at a different time can adapt.[11]

America spent huge sums on advanced technology for surveillance, such as satellites with very high definition and on eavesdropping on phone conversations from areas where terrorists might be hiding, but relatively little for human spies to penetrate terrorist cells. Human intelligence (HUMINT), the down-and-dirty work of collecting information from the sources, was badly neglected. In addition, the US failed to recruit enough people who spoke Arabic, Farsi, Pashto, and other relevant languages to work with the nation's intelligence organizations. Because of this, thousands of intercepted phone conversations were never examined for content.

Although before 9/11 some intelligence agents had considered the use of airplanes as weapons, they did not anticipate the scope of the attacks that occurred. There was never an attempt to strengthen lax security at the nation's airports, nor warnings to pilots and other personnel about terrorists commandeering airplanes. Concern by an FBI agent in the Midwest about Arabs taking flight training was dismissed by her superiors, who refused to allow her to follow up on her suspicions. There was also a lack of communication among intelligence agencies that prevented investigation of minor leads that might have been fruitful. In the decade prior to 9/11, there were twelve different reports by blue-ribbon panels with suggestions for intelligence reform, few of which were implemented.[12] During this period both the executive and legislative branches of government failed to act to overhaul the intelligence agencies.

The FBI was particularly inept and unprepared for dealing with the threat of terrorism before the attacks. Before the Millennium plot to blow up the Los Angeles airport in late 1999 was discovered, the FBI claimed there were no active cells of Al Qaeda in the US and no major threat within the country.[13] However, it had not mounted a thorough investigation before reaching that conclusion. The National Security Division of the FBI was directing its attention to Russian and Chinese espionage and the fifty-six field offices were concentrating on organized crime and drugs, with no surveillance of Islamic radicals. In addition, computer support and data systems for FBI operations were primitive or nonexistent, with many agents not able to access the Internet. Information acquired on terrorist activity was not transmitted to agents or offices or communicated to other agencies. Wiretaps and other data could go for weeks before being studied.

Immediately after 9/11, George Bush and top members of his administration began trying to link the bombing in some way to Iraq.[14] There were suggestions that Saddam Hussein had been trying to purchase uranium yellowcake from Niger, had been making centrifuges to separate uranium gas, and had mobile laboratories manufacturing biological weapons. These questionable pieces of data along with the knowledge that Iraq had used poison gas in its war with Iran and against its Kurdish population over ten years earlier were sewn together by neoconservatives within the administration to build support for the subsequent invasion. George Tenet backed the course taken by Bush, and although many others in the intelligence community disagreed with this assessment, their voices went unheard. Paul Pillar, national intelligence officer for the Near East and South Asia from 2000 to 2005, noted in an article in *Foreign Affairs*:

> In the wake of the Iraq war, it has become clear that official intelligence analysis was not relied on in making even the most significant national security decisions, that intelligence was misused publicly to justify decisions already made, that damaging ill will developed between policymakers and intelligence officers, and that the intelligence community's own work was politicized.[15]

The intelligence "stool" the Bush administration used to promote the Iraq War had three legs. The first was that Saddam Hussein had weapons of mass destruction (WMDs); the second was that he was intent on building nuclear weapons if he didn't already have them; the third was that Iraq was linked to Al Qaeda and the bombings on 9/11. There is no evidence that any of these assertions were true. No signs of WMD were ever found in Iraq, including nuclear, chemical or biological weapons or laboratories or plants for their manufacture. In addition, no proof of a connection between Al Qaeda and Saddam Hussein was ever revealed, or that Saddam was involved in any way with 9/11. It is quite unlikely, in fact, that Saddam and bin Laden would have been in bed together, given the secular nature of Saddam's regime and the religious fundamentalist roots of Al Qaeda. Aside from their hatred of the United States, they would have been natural enemies. Richard Clarke has asserted that "[b]oth the White House and the CIA must have known there was no 'imminent threat' to the US, but one claimed the opposite, and the other allowed them to do so uncorrected."[16]

Besides an overreliance on technology and a paucity of human capital, the fact that America has so many different intelligence agencies makes it difficult to coordinate information and assets, and diffuses responsibility for actions and missteps. There are sixteen acknowledged government intelligence and security organizations including the CIA (Central Intelligence Agency), NSA (National Security Agency), FBI (Federal Bureau of Investigation), National Reconnaissance Office, Defense Intelligence Agency, and multiple other groups under the aegis of the Defense Department, State Department, Energy Department, Justice Department, and the Department of Homeland Security.[17] This format guarantees redundancy and waste, not to mention turf battles among groups and bureaucratic inertia. In 2006, the government admitted to spending $44 billion annually on its intelligence agencies and employed nearly 100,000 people.[18,19] In an attempt to reform intelligence gathering, Congress placed all of these agencies under the nominal control of a director of the Office of National Intelligence who was expected to have the president's ear and also allocate funding, set priorities, and try to integrate the different groups and their missions. Currently, in 2011, Lieutenant General James R. Clapper, Director of National Intelligence (DNI), is the fifth occupant of that office in the five years since it was established.[20] This speaks to the difficulty in fulfilling the designated mission of the position.

Also in the mix of problems for America's vast intelligence apparatus is the fact that many important tasks are subcontracted out to private companies. These corporate entities are concerned not only with gathering information and protecting America, but with making a profit. Because of the outsourcing of jobs to the private sector,

> . . . less than half of the staff at the National Counterterrorism Center in Washington are actual government employees. The *Los Angles Times* reported that at the CIA station in Islamabad, Pakistan, contractors sometimes outnumber employees by three to one.[21]

According to recent information from an executive of the office of the DNI, 70 percent of the intelligence budget now goes to private contractors. While some ideologues want to privatize whatever government functions are possible, it makes these processes more expensive, ignores the inherent conflicts of interest, and may not receive proper oversight.

George Tenet resigned from the CIA in 2004. Under the leadership of Porter Goss, the agency was demoralized and in disarray, and Goss was fired in May 2006 after an eighteen-month tenure that was near disastrous.[22] A Congressman and former CIA agent prior to his appointment, Goss had never held major administrative positions. It was surmised that President Bush appointed him because of his loyalty as a Congressman and his support for Bush's assessments about Iraq. When Goss placed some of his cronies with no intelligence background in top jobs at the CIA, a number of experienced personnel left the agency, causing a crisis in many areas. Kyle Foggo, one of Goss's appointees who did have CIA credentials and was given the third-ranking position, was subsequently investigated for ethics violations and fired from his post.[23] Goss's successor as director, General Michael Hayden, who assumed the post in May 2006, was formerly head of the National Security Agency[24] and vowed to bring professionalism back to the CIA. Given his lack of experience with human intelligence, there were some misgivings about whether he would be able to revitalize the agency and reconstitute old-fashioned spying. There were also questions raised when President Obama appointed Leon Panetta to replace Hayden in February 2009, a man with a long history of government service, but no military or intelligence experience.[25] However, the killing of bin Laden in Pakistan in June 2011 was a major coup for the CIA and American intelligence.

Currently, Washington's most glaring intelligence deficits involve the nuclear programs in North Korea and Iran. America has been playing cat and mouse with North Korea since the US and Pyongyang signed an agreement in 1994 to halt nuclear weapons development (an accord known as the Agreed Framework) in return for deliveries of oil, the building of a light water nuclear reactor, and other aid.[26] In 1999, there was suspicion by US intelligence that North Korea was constructing a centrifuge facility, and in October 2002 the United States accused Pyongyang of concealing its program to enrich uranium to weapons grade and stopped the oil shipments.[27] North Korea ejected the international inspectors in retaliation and announced that it was reprocessing plutonium again, which it had supposedly halted in 1994.

Subsequently, North Korea apparently forged ahead with a nuclear weapons program on two tracks, using both plutonium and uranium, and setting off a low-level nuclear device in October 2006.[28] Pyongyang then asked for direct negotiations with the US to try to resolve the nuclear issue, but Washington refused one-on-one talks. Instead, America negotiated off and on with them as part of a group that included China, South Korea, Japan, and Russia that was unable to get Pyongyang to give up its nuclear weapons. In addition, North Korea tested a long-range Taepodong missile, and though it failed and crashed into the sea, the launching itself was a provocation that went forward despite warnings from all five of the negotiating countries.[29] The standoff with North Korea over nuclear weapons has persisted through the present, with intermittent posturing by the North and further hostile actions such as the sinking of a South Korean naval ship and artillery bombardment of a South Korean island in 2010.[30] The bottom line remains that US intelligence has been able to gather little information about North Korea's nuclear programs or military intentions.

Similarly, America is now confronting Iran over its nuclear objectives with a dearth of hard intelligence, though secret programs by Iran to enrich uranium and separate plutonium have been uncovered by the International Atomic Energy Agency (IAEA).[31,32] Iran has stated that its nuclear program is for research purposes and power generation, and has denied any interest in producing weapons. American intelligence agencies believe Iran is still probably several years away from the ability to build a bomb, but this is mostly educated guesswork and not based on hard data. Iran has spread its nuclear program over multiple sites to make detection more difficult and lower the risk of destruction if it is attacked. An attempt by the major European powers, the US, Russia, and China to negotiate a compromise with Iran has so far gone nowhere. Iran's hard-line president, Mahmoud Ahmadinejad, and the clerics in power have insisted that it has the right to carry on its nuclear activities and will continue its work no matter what inducements are offered. Though President Bush was reluctant to engage Iran in multilateral talks, he was pushed by the other negotiating nations to do so.[33] Obama has subsequently made overtures to Iran but has been equally unsuccessful.

Two events in late 2010 may have caused a temporary setback to Iranian efforts to craft a nuclear device and may have been orchestrated by Western intelligence agencies or the Israelis. The first was the insertion of malware, the Stuxnet worm, into the control software of Iran's atomic centrifuges, causing them to spin wildly and self-destruct.[34] The second was the assassination of a prominent nuclear scientist in Teheran and the wounding of a second by separate car bomb attacks. Though these incidents may delay the Iranian program, the US is hopeful that overt military intervention will not be necessary to deter Iran from acquiring a nuclear arsenal. Despite current control of the country by the mullahs, the Revolutionary Guards, and President Ahmadinejad, there is a large proportion of the population that appears to desire a more secular regime and it is possible they may eventually supplant the religious conservatives in power. There are also analysts in the United States who think that if the Iranians obtain nuclear weapons, a strategy of containment could work with them as it did with the Soviet Union, and that more aggressive measures may not be necessary.[35]

## The War in Afghanistan

The United States has been involved in Afghanistan since the 1980s, when it supported the mujahideen, who were fighting the Soviets. After the Russians were driven out, civil war ensued for years, with shifting alliances of warlords battling for territory and control of the lucrative drug trade. The Taliban attained power in 1996, subduing the warlords except in a few northern strongholds. Combat continued sporadically in these areas, but was basically at a stalemate. In the regions they governed, the Taliban demanded strict adherence to their interpretation of Islamic law, essentially eliminating culture, education, and women's rights. [36] Although the Afghanis were initially relieved the fighting had ended, the majority of the population was unhappy about the imposition of an Islamist regime, though terrorized into obedience. The Taliban also allowed Al Qaeda and Osama bin Laden to build training camps and recruit followers from all over the Muslim world to learn how to fight the West and the more moderate Islamic regimes.

From the outset of the Taliban's ascendancy, the United States was concerned about Al Qaeda's use of Afghanistan as a sanctuary, and members of the Clinton administration tried unsuccessfully to persuade the Taliban to expel them and hand over bin Laden. The destruction of Al Qaeda's camps by American cruise missiles after the African embassy bombings in 1998 was merely an inconvenience for Al Qaeda, and their activities continued with the acquiescence of the Taliban. Everything changed after 9/11, with President Bush determined to destroy all elements of Al Qaeda in Afghanistan, oust the Taliban from power, and install a government in Kabul friendly to the United States.

In 2001, less than a month after the 9/11 attacks, an American bombing campaign designed to destroy the Taliban's communications infrastructure and air defenses initiated the Afghan War.[37] Within days, British and American Special Operations Forces

(SOF) moved into the country and linked up with the Northern Alliance warlords. Subsequently, assisted by tactical assistance from these special operations forces directing American air strikes, the armies of the Northern Alliance were able to overwhelm the Taliban. Over a two-month period, they gained control of virtually the entire country, as Mazar-i-Sharif, then Kabul, then Kunduz fell. As the allied soldiers of Hamid Karzai with their American special forces approached the city of Kandahar on December 6 from the north, with an army of the Afghan warlord Gul Agha Sherzai advancing from the south, Mullah Omar and the other senior members of the Taliban withdrew from the city and disappeared, apparently heading for Pakistan.

The remnants of Al Qaeda, with bin Laden believed to be among them, were located in fortified caves in the mountains of Tora Bora. Sixteen days of combat ensued, ending on December 17 with Al Qaeda's defeat, though many of their fighters, including bin Laden and Zawahiri, were able to make their way into Pakistan. The failure to kill or apprehend bin Laden was a major failure of the Afghan campaign, resulting from the use of unreliable local soldiers to cut off his escape routes. Though advised by senior Army leaders to place two divisions of US troops on the Afghan-Pakistani border, Bush sent additional American forces into Afghanistan only after the Taliban and Al Qaeda leaders had fled.[38] The ramifications of the failure to capture or kill the Al Qaeda and Taliban leaders while they were vulnerable still resound today. Bin Laden's escape at Tora Bora was a big psychological boost for Al Qaeda, giving them greater credibility among the Muslim masses and aiding their recruitment efforts. And the Taliban were able to reconstitute their forces from their sanctuaries in Pakistan to restart the insurgency.

Under American guidance, a government was formed of the liberating Afghan forces, taking into account ethnic divisions and rivalries and the numerical breakdown of the different tribal groups. Hamid Karzai, a Pashtun (the largest tribe), was chosen as president. A parliament was also elected, dominated by tribal leaders and warlords, that was not always supportive of Karzai's goals. The government controlled Kabul and some of the large cities, but the small towns and much of the rural areas remained insecure, with marauders from the Taliban, criminal gangs, and local warlords still active. Unemployment was rife and the economy did not function well. Production of poppies and opium soared. By 2003, the Taliban insurgency had started again. With the attention of the Bush administration focused on Iraq, American and NATO troop levels were inadequate to stem the depredations of the Taliban forces, and much of the south and the eastern portions of the country were under their control. Whether because of intimidation or tribal alliances, the Taliban were supported by many of the local Pashtuns, blending in among them when confronted by superior military might, or retreating into Pakistan.

As the Taliban gained in strength, some additional American and NATO forces were committed to Afghanistan, but still not enough to stem the tide. Then in November 2008, Obama was elected president, with a Democratic base anxious to end the wars in both Iraq and Afghanistan. With the military leadership asking for further troops for Afghanistan and with the war in Iraq winding down, Obama agreed to an increase in US forces, an additional 30,000 bringing the total to 100,000 by the end of August 2010.[39,40] Including troops from NATO nations, nearly 150,000 were in the country.[41] Though placed strategically around Afghanistan, major swaths remained under Taliban rule. A US review of Afghanistan policy in December 2010 suggested that there was some progress in subduing the Taliban, particularly in the south, but that the insurgency remained potent. Taliban forces were still able to gather in Pakistan and infiltrate across the border to attack the Afghan army, police forces, civilian officials, government sympathizers, as well as Western troops. Learning from the Iraqi insurgency, they employed suicide bombers and improvised explosive devices and rockets, ambushing the military and soft targets. With their forays, they disrupted efforts at reconstruction and education and made civilians reluctant to cooperate with the Karzai government or the Americans. In addition, the Taliban were now active in the north of the country, which had previously been quiescent. However, it was believed that enough progress had been made to allow some withdrawal of troops to begin in July 2011. With the continued training of Afghan government forces by the Americans and NATO, it was expected that the bulk of the Western soldiers could exit by 2014, with Afghans then responsible for the country's security.

But whatever military successes may have occurred, it is necessary to measure them against the negative incidents and a litany of civilian failures. The use of targeted bombing to eliminate insurgents has resulted at times in civilian casualties, including women and children, inflaming Afghans against the Western intruders. In addition, nighttime raids to root out Taliban members meant searches of Afghan homes where women were present, ignoring local cultural norms and engendering more hostility. And despite American aid, the Afghan economy has remained unproductive, with high levels of unemployment helping Taliban recruitment.

Perhaps even more important has been the inability of Americans to reduce or eliminate the ubiquitous corruption and graft in the Afghan government and police, a major reason citizens turn to the Taliban. The Afghan presidential election in 2009 was notable for the degree of fraud found by international observers, raising questions about Hamid Kharzai's legitimacy.[42] The parliamentary elections in 2010 were similarly believed to be lacking in credibility, with diminished Pashtun representation and threats by some tribes to join the insurgency.[43] Afghan farmers also continue to grow poppies to produce heroin and opium, since it makes the most economic sense to them. With the drug trade generating great amounts of cash along with American aid money, top Afghan officials all take their slice of the pie, apparently including Hamid Kharzai's brother, Walid, the governor of Khandahar province (who was assassinated in July 2011), and other members of Kharzai's family. Building democratic institutions and a culture of accountability in a tribal society where illiteracy and religious fanaticism are rampant is even more difficult than finding and eliminating the enemy. As of July 2011, the situation in Afghanistan remained in flux with uncertainty over whether a stable functioning government and effective military would be in place by the time Western forces departed.

The outcome of the Afghan War, initially considered an American success, is now seen as inconclusive. By shifting the nation's efforts to Iraq in 2003, President Bush left the war in Afghanistan unfinished. US policymakers believed that America could do the job on the cheap and with a minimum number of troops. But America has never had enough personnel to control every region of this large country, and hoped that its Afghan allies would be able to take up the slack. The Taliban continue to use western Pakistan as their home base, able to move their forces into Afghanistan at will. Al Qaeda has also rebuilt itself in Pakistan, setting up camps and training new recruits.[44] The Pakistani territories where Al Qaeda is situated are virtually independent of the central government, the tribal authorities there sympathetic to the Taliban and Al Qaeda. Although the Pakistani military has launched military offensives to clear Islamic militants from Swat, South Waziristan, and other tribal areas, North Waziristan and some of the adjacent provinces remain infested.[45] America is using drone aircraft with tacit Pakistani approval to target the militant leadership and this is apparently taking a toll. However, Pakistani control over the entire tribal areas is needed to make success in Afghanistan more likely.

## Iraq

With American troop levels in Iraq in August 2010 down to about 50,000 from a peak of 170,000, their combat role appeared to have ended, with US forces being used primarily for training and support of the Iraqi military.[46] Though most Iraqis are happy to see the Americans leaving, there is concern among many, particularly the Sunni population, about major hostilities breaking out again when the Americans are no longer present. As of August 2011, a simmering insurgency persisted with Al Qaeda perpetrating suicide bombings and assassinations, though considerably below previous levels, to cow the Iraqi populace. While there has been some thought about having a contingent of the US military remaining beyond their exit date at the end of 2011, Prime Minister Nouri al-Maliki has stated that the Americans must go. (This may have been a negotiating ploy and may have also been used to assuage some of his hard-line Shia backers, such as the Sadr organization.) As the exit date nears, it is still possible that a sizable American force may be asked to stay. It would seem that for at least the next several years, the US military will be indispensable to the Iraqi military for logistics, transportation, and air support missions, since there is no significant Iraqi air force. And the US presence is a deterrent to any incursions by the Iranians.

The political situation in Iraq in March 2011 was tenuous at best, when Maliki formed another government after eight months of maneuvering.[47] All the major parties were included, but the participation of such opposing forces as the secular Iraqiya bloc of Iyad Allawi and the religious Shiite party of Moqtada al-Sadr, along with the Kurds, suggested that stability would be difficult to achieve.[48] The arrangements had a Kurd, Jalal Talabani, continue as Iraqi president with a Sunni, Osama al-Najafi, as the speaker of the parliament. Though Allawi is a Shiite, he and his party are backed by the majority of Sunnis. (Iraqiya won more seats than Maliki's party in the national election in 2010, but Allawi had been unable to form a coalition government.) And with Sadr and his followers included in al-Maliki's coalition, their strongly anti-American and pro-Iranian leaning could make the retention of American forces more difficult. Still to be resolved by the new government are the distribution of oil revenues and the Kurdish claim, contested by the Sunnis, to the oil-rich province and city of Kirkuk.[49] Until the issues of oil distribution and Kirkuk are settled, the Maliki government can be expected to accomplish little. And it is still unclear whether democracy has taken root in Iraq, or whether sectarian hatreds and violence will destroy it in the future.

There is still debate about why the United States became involved in Iraq and whether the war was managed appropriately. The senior Pentagon correspondent of the *Washington Post*, Thomas E. Ricks, states in his book, *Fiasco*:

> President George W. Bush's decision to invade Iraq in 2003 ultimately may come to be seen as one of the most profligate actions in the history of American foreign policy. . . . the US

government went to war in Iraq with scant solid international support and on the basis of incorrect information. . . . and then occupied the country negligently.[50]

Initially, Americans were told that war with Iraq was necessary because Saddam Hussein was a serious danger to the country, possessing weapons of mass destruction and in league with Al Qaeda, and that deposing Saddam was essential to the war on terror. As these assessments were proven false, the basis for the undertaking shifted to ridding the country of an evil dictator and bringing democracy to the Arab world. Paul Pillar noted, "The administration wanted to hitch the Iraq expedition to the 'war on terror' and the threat the American public feared most, thereby capitalizing on the country's militant post–9/11 mood."[51]

There was never a question in the minds of the American military that it could win a war in Iraq relatively easily and that the resistance of Saddam's soldiers would be minimal. But throughout the planning stage of the war, which began shortly after 9/11, through the invasion in March 2003, Secretary of Defense Donald Rumsfeld consistently tried to pare down the military's request for troops, consonant with his theory of how a modern army should work.[52] He wanted light, mobile forces that would strike quickly and surprise the enemy, winning the war with tactical advantages and the use of overwhelming air power. Though General Shinseki, General Zinni, and the planners at US Central Command (CENTCOM) believed that a force of between 300,000 and 500,000 would be required to seal Iraq's borders and pacify the country after the major battles were over,[53] Rumsfeld insisted that a much smaller force could do the job, probably 125,000 or even fewer,[54] and seemed indifferent to the logistical problems that might arise. Little thought was given to the insurgency and sectarian conflict that was to develop after "victory." The secretary of defense did not believe that peacekeeping and nation building were tasks for the American military. They would win the war and then the job could be handled by the State Department and the Iraqis themselves. When General Shinseki testified before the Senate Armed Services Committee in February

2003 and said several hundred thousand troops would be necessary to control Iraq after Saddam was toppled, Rumsfeld told reporters that "it was ludicrous to think that it would take more forces to secure the peace than win the war."[55]

Indeed, the opening phase of the war and the major battles were over in a matter of weeks, with Baghdad in American hands by April 10. But as the Iraqi power structure crumbled, with the police and soldiers no longer functioning, chaos reigned. Unguarded arms caches and armories were plundered, with huge stores of weapons and explosives winding up in the hands of private militias and budding insurgents. At the same time, foreign jihadis infiltrated Iraq through its porous borders ready to fight the infidel Americans. Larry Diamond, who had been a senior advisor to the Coalition Provisional Authority (CPA) in Baghdad noted in an article in 2004:

> In the immediate aftermath of the war, US troops stood by helplessly, outnumbered and unprepared, as much of Iraq's remaining physical, economic, and institutional infrastructure was systematically looted and sabotaged. And . . . the Bush administration compounded its initial mistakes by stubbornly refusing to send in more troops.[56]

America's inability to control the population and prevent disorder after the invasion were the most important factors in the guerilla war and sectarian conflict that was to follow. America was seen as uncaring and arrogant, and in the process of removing Saddam had brought ruin to their country.

Decisions made by the civilian head of the Coalition Provisional Authority, L. Paul Bremer, with little experience in Iraq or the Middle East,[57] further contributed to the chaos and stoked the insurgency. He ordered the disbanding of the Iraqi Army and an extensive de-Baathification process (removing Baath party officials from their positions), against the advice of General Jay Garner, the previous CPA chief, and the CIA station chief and a number of military men.[58] By not keeping the Iraqi military in organized units, America lost an opportunity to use them as force extenders for its own troops and to maintain order. If Iraqi soldiers had been retained on America's payroll, it would also have secured the allegiance of many of them. Instead, they became part of the problem, transformed into the backbone of the insurgency. It is true that the Iraqi Army was controlled by Sunnis and filled with Saddam loyalists, but the latter could have been weeded out, and the Sunni population would have felt less marginalized if the Army had remained intact. Similarly, by not allowing lower-level members of the Baath party to hold government jobs and participate in the political process, America fueled their enmity and their perception that they could only be second-class citizens in the new Iraq. Thus the chances of controlling sectarian conflict and establishing a nonsectarian democratic Iraq were made even less likely by the incompetent planning and management of the secondary phase of the war.

As the insurgency expanded from 2004 to 2007, American forces found themselves on the defensive, with Al Qaeda in Iraq and their Baathist allies appearing to strike at will. Shia militias targeted Sunnis and their families, killing some and forcing many to leave the country, others fighting back. In the midst of the conflagration, there was little that the Americans were able to do. After considerable debate in the US over the proper approach to Iraq, President Bush announced in early 2007 that there would be a "surge" in American troop strength to fight the insurgency, tamp down on sectarian violence, and restore order. Under a new commander in Iraq, General David Petraeus, the increased American forces were able to turn the tide against the insurgency and significantly reduce violence. Part of the success was due to the American-funded Awakening Councils, formed by some of the Sunni tribes who had previously supported the insurgency. There were pledges of integration into the Iraqi military to follow, along with other jobs. As the American began to leave the country, however, many of the promises had been unfulfilled.

Suicide bombings, assassinations, executions, and torture in the conflict between Sunnis and Shia are less prevalent now (August 2011) than previously, although they continue at reduced levels. Ethnic cleansing has changed the composition of many neighborhoods and towns. With the central government deadlocked and seemingly unable to solve the nation's problems, the people still feel insecure in their homes and on the streets. Again, Larry Diamond:

> In post-conflict situations in which the state has collapsed, security trumps everything. . . . Without some minimum level of security, people cannot engage in trade and commerce, organize to rebuild their communities, or participate meaningfully in politics.[59]

Among the most disheartening aspects in terms of the conduct of the war were the widespread civilian casualties from bombing and artillery fire. The shootings of noncombatants by American troops, and criminal acts at Abu Ghraib prison by American interrogators were highlighted repeatedly by the Arab media and certainly did not help the image of America. In addition, these events helped in the recruitment of jihadis throughout the Muslim world, ready to fight America and the West.

In early 2006, a chorus of criticism arose over the American military's willingness to accept the administration's objectives and reasons for the war without dissent, the planning for the war's aftermath, and the implementation of pacification. The refrain emanated most strongly from a group of retired generals, some of whom had been involved with the preparations for the war.[60] Five senior generals in addition to a number of senators and members of Congress joined in asking for Rumsfeld's resignation. But President Bush remained resistant until the Republican defeat in the elections of 2006, after which Bush required Rumsfeld to step down. In 2007, before the success of the surge, a number of other generals criticized Bush and the administration for mismanaging the war.[61,62] However, President Bush rejected calls to set a timetable for withdrawal of American troops,[63] Congressional Republicans sympathetic to the president's stance blocking legislation for withdrawal on several occasions.[64]

(Interestingly, some of the biggest supporters of the war, officials willing to send American soldiers into battle, were men who had opted out of the military themselves, or who avoided combat during the Vietnam War. These included Vice President Cheney, who managed to get serial draft deferments, and President Bush, who served in the Air National Guard.[65])

The loss of American lives and treasure in Iraq for a questionable cause highlights the danger when ideology drives policy. Neoconservatives in the Bush Administration were obsessed with removing Saddam Hussein from power and bringing democracy to the Middle East, blind to the fact that he was not a threat to the US and that his presence enhanced stability in the region. In addition to slanting intelligence to support the war, decision makers in the White House and Pentagon dismissed warnings about the likely aftermath of the war. Prior to the invasion, the policy of containment, with the use of sanctions, no-fly zones, and Kurdish autonomy, was working; furthermore, Iraq had no weapons of mass destruction. The civilians running the war, President Bush, Cheney, Rumsfeld, and their appointees, combined hubris with incompetence as they managed the planning, the campaign, the pacification, and reconstruction, ignoring advice from those with differing views.

As a consequence of America's failed policies, the major victor in the war is Iran. By removing Saddam and his Sunni-dominated military, the natural constraining force for Iran in the region was eliminated, significantly increasing its power and influence. The Iraqi Shia, who America helped to gain control of the country, can be expected to be friendly to their Iranian co-religionists. The Bush administration told American citizens that when its forces went into Iraq they would be greeted with flowers and hailed as liberators, but instead US soldiers faced a hostile population and roadside bombs. Americans were told that the income from Iraq's oil industry would pay for Iraq's reconstruction, but instead over a trillion dollars have been drained from America for the war and rebuilding projects, wasted money that increased the national debt.[66] Americans were told that invading Iraq would be a blow to Al Qaeda and make the country safer from terrorism, but instead the terrorist threat increased, galvanizing jihadists to fight against the US.[67] Americans should also remember that under Saddam, Iraq was a secular dictatorship where women had great freedom, with the ability to function in society and pursue careers, unlike the rest of the Arab world. Currently, under an Islamist pseudodemocracy, the rights of women are disappearing and sectarian conflict has made freedom of expression as deficient as under Saddam. Thus nearly everything the Bush team told Americans about what to expect after the invasion of Iraq has not come to pass.

## Homeland Security

Shortly after 9/11, in early October 2001, President Bush established the Office of Homeland Security by executive order. Its mission was "to develop and coordinate the implementation of a comprehensive national strategy to secure the United States from terrorist threats or attacks."[68] The attacks of 9/11 had revealed in stark relief the dangers America faced and how unprotected it seemed to be. It also marked an emotional turning point, as the nation's citizens suddenly became aware of their vulnerability. Previously, there had been a "fortress America" mentality, people believing the vast oceans on both sides of the country's landmass safeguarded them from the terrorism and destruction common in the "old world." In November 2001, the Transportation Security Administration (TSA) was created by Congress, also in response to the attacks on 9/11, and given responsibility for airport security. The color-coding risk advisory scale was devised in March 2002 to alert federal, state, and local authorities as well as the American public about the possibility of terrorist acts. However, no terrorist acts ever followed any heightened classifications and it appeared that it was being employed to provide cover for federal officials in case something did occur.

The cabinet-level Department of Homeland Security (DHS), a more powerful successor to the Office of Homeland Security, was established by Congress in November 2002, mandated to protect America from terrorist attacks and manage natural disasters. Created from the integration of twenty-two already functioning federal agencies, it had approximately 180,000 employees.[69] Some of the major agencies folded into the DHS included Immigration and Customs Enforcement, Transportation Security Administration, Customs and Border Protection, Citizenship and Immigration Services,

Federal Emergency Management Agency, and the Coast Guard. Tom Ridge was appointed as the first Secretary of the DHS, but following Bush's re-election in November 2004, Ridge resigned and the president nominated Federal Judge Michael Chertoff for the position. According to its critics, the Department of Homeland Security did not perform well under Ridge or Chertoff, with the degree of risk not significantly reduced in many domains. Congressional auditors noted in September 2007 that the Department had not fulfilled even half of its performance expectations in the four years since its inception.[70] Many of these difficulties continue to await resolution, even under the Obama administration and the new DHS Secretary, Janet Napolitano.

Problems of air safety persist. Periodic lapses in security still occur at all major airports, and smaller airports and private planes are not being watched carefully enough. There are concerns as well about the vulnerability of chemical plants, some of which are located in populated areas, with hazardous chemicals that could potentially kill ten of thousands of people. The corporate owners are loath to spend money on security or switch to less dangerous chemicals for their products because of the added expense. Congress, however, is unwilling to force safety standards on the chemical industry as it is a source of funds for many members. The transportation of hazardous substances through urban sites in tanker trucks or railroad cars is also not properly regulated. In fact, it would be easy for terrorists to hijack gasoline or chemical tanker trucks and use them as rolling bombs, much as the 9/11 terrorists did with aircraft. Air cargo is also not being rigorously screened for explosives or hazardous materials.

During his administration, President Bush declared in regard to possible attacks on the nation's infrastructure:

> The government should only address those activities that the market does not adequately provide—for example, national defense or border security. . . . For other aspects of homeland security, sufficient incentives exist in the private market to supply protection.[71]

Even before this era of fiscal austerity, Congress and President Bush were reluctant to commit the necessary funds to provide a high level of domestic security. In fiscal 2005, the DHS received just $2.6 billion to safeguard all of America's infrastructure and vital systems underpinning the economy and society.[72] In 2003, the Bush administration sought only 25 percent of required funding for first responders, and the formula employed gave Wyoming eight times more funds per capita than California.[73] Fortunately, there have been no successful terrorist incidents involving US civilians since 9/11, though a number of plots have been foiled within the country and on airplanes. The federal government also cut funds to dispose of nuclear materials that could be employed in making dirty bombs and did not provide adequate government oversight of dangerous biological materials.[74] There was and still is an emphasis on scrutiny of people who fly into America. Rather than terrorists, however, the obstacles to air travel discourage mainly tourists, students, and scientists, visitors the nation should be trying to attract.

The inability to monitor goods entering US ports also provokes anxiety.[75] Most foreign products are shipped to America in large metal containers, only a small percentage of which are examined before they reach the US. (A program in conjunction with a few foreign governments allows these containers to be inspected in the ports of origin, then sealed before they are shipped.) Coast Guard ships do intercept some incoming vessels to inspect while they are out at sea. It would still be simple for a terrorist group disguised as a legitimate business to ship weapons, explosives, or even WMD, including nuclear devices, to the United States, the odds being that random searches would not uncover them. Stephen Flynn, a senior fellow at the Council on Foreign Relations, noted in 2004, "The federal government is spending more every three days to finance the war in Iraq than it has provided over the past three years to prop up the security of all 361 US commercial seaports."[76]

America's national security problems are heightened by Congressmen who want pork for their districts and special considerations for their cronies and campaign contributors. As an example, the delay in having tamperproof ID cards for transportation personnel can be traced to a Republican Congressman from Kentucky, Harold Rogers, chairman of the House subcommittee overseeing the DHS budget,[77] who directed contracts for the identification cards to companies in his home district. DHS had previously chosen a "smart card" with embedded computer chips and a more advanced technology from another company. Millions of dollars were spent testing the two alternatives, much of it going to businesses in the Congressman's district, until it was acknowledged that the smart card was far better. Rogers's political war chest grew by about $100,000, contributed by people connected to the firms that received DHS work. Other corporations outside of Rogers's district, but with ties to the Congressman, also won substantial DHS contracts and gave large sums to his political campaigns. After the Republicans gained control of the House in the 2010 elections, Rogers was named by their leadership to head the House Appropriations Committee in charge of government spending.[78] He had previously been labeled by a Kentucky newspaper as "the Prince of Pork."

Americans live in an open society and it is impossible to protect the multiplicity of soft targets present everywhere. Al Qaeda, however, seems to be mainly interested in attacking high-visibility targets for propaganda purposes, where they can cause major damage and loss of life. Since Congress itself decides where much of the spending on national security goes, money is often distributed to cities and states on the basis of political clout rather than risk. But the Department of Homeland Security itself also seems to ignore risk in allocating funds. In 2006, Louisville, Kentucky and Omaha, Nebraska saw their funding increase while New York and Washington's funds were cut. On the DHS list of possible terrorist targets were petting zoos and flea markets in rural towns, while bridges and tunnels in urban areas were omitted. These decisions had to be approved by the hierarchy in the department, including Secretary Chertoff, who defended the process that assigned the grants.[79]

In addition to its role in combating terrorism, DHS is also responsible for the management of natural disasters through the Federal Emergency Management Agency. FEMA's bungling of help after Hurricane Katrina in 2005, directed by Bush's crony Michael Brown, was further evidence of incompetent leadership at the DHS. After Brown was fired, seven candidates to head FEMA or to take other important positions at the agency turned down the offers.[80] The extraordinary amounts of fraud and waste eventually uncovered in FEMA's handling of Katrina further demonstrated the inadequacy of the bureaucrats in that agency.[81] The government response to the BP oil spill in the Gulf of Mexico in 2010 was managed by the Department of the Interior and the EPA, as well as the DHS, with the Coast Guard directing the capping of the well.[82] It appears to have been better coordinated than the response to Katrina, but was still problematic.

Although terrorism remains a threat to America, it is startling how many senior officials at the Department of Homeland Security left their jobs after just a short stint to work as lobbyists or for corporations that have or seek contracts with DHS. As of 2006, at least ninety of their top personnel had become "executives, consultants, or lobbyists for companies that collectively do billions of dollars' worth of domestic security business."[83] This includes former Secretary Tom Ridge, former Deputy Secretary Admiral James Loy, and former Under Secretary Asa Hutchinson, as more than two-thirds of DHS's top officials followed this path. With ambiguous laws regarding conflict of interest, these individuals had no difficulty obtaining lucrative positions from private firms to shill for government contracts with DHS employees who were friends or acquaintances.

## Foreign Policy

A country's foreign policy is shaped by multiple considerations, among which are its ability to project power, the strength of its economy, its value system, and its perceived national interests. Its success or failure during a particular period should be determined not by what actions were taken or not taken, but by whether its relations with other nations were enhanced, whether peace and stability were fostered, and whether its position in the world vis-à-vis other countries was augmented or diminished. Robert Kaplan noted in *Warrior Politics*:

In a world in which democracy and technology are developing faster than are the institutions needed to sustain them—even as states themselves are eroding and being transformed beyond recognition by urbanization and the information age—foreign policy will be the art, rather than the science, of permanent crisis management.[84]

The citizens of many countries have negative perceptions of America, whether or not their leaders profess support for the US. From once being revered and emulated in much of the world, America has gone to being feared and in many instances hated, especially in Muslim nations. The lightning rod for much of this hostility was the Iraq War, though there were other factors at work even before America invaded Iraq. In addition to the American backing of Israel, the Bush administration rejected the Kyoto Protocol on global warming without offering alternative proposals, scrapped the antiballistic missile treaty, and rejected jurisdiction of the International Court over Americans for possible war crimes. Whether or not Washington had good reasons for these actions, they were executed in a high-handed way, without adequate explanation.

Although Bush had suggested the need for humility in America's foreign policy during one of the presidential debates in 2000 ("If we're an arrogant nation, they'll resent us; if we're a humble nation, but strong, they'll welcome us."[85]), his administration heightened international hostility toward the US by its hubris and disregard for public opinion in other countries. There was also the stated objective of "spreading democracy," with aspects reminiscent of colonialism, with its "white man's burden" bringing civilization/democracy to less fortunate peoples. Certain attributes of American life also reinforce the disdain other nations feel toward the United States, such as the death penalty, liberal gun laws, violence, pornography, and indifference to the environment. Immediately after 9/11, there was a torrent of sympathy and good will in much of the world toward the US that soon dissipated because of the words and actions of America's leaders. Nations were told they could either be for or against the US, as it fought the war on terrorism based on the concept of preemptive war. The citizens of most countries did not accept the rationale for the invasion of Iraq, and as pictures of the death and suffering of Iraqi civilians flashed across the world's TV screens, revulsion grew and opposition hardened. This was reinforced by Abu Ghraib, Guantanamo, rendition of suspected terrorists, and extra-legal kidnappings. Lecturing other countries on human rights, America was regarded as hypocritical. The United States projected an image of being above the law, doing whatever it wanted, and getting away with it because it was powerful. It was seen as a bully among nations, always wanting to get its way.

Since President Obama's election, the perception of the US has changed for the better, although the majority of citizens of most Muslim nations still view America suspiciously, if not with outright hostility. Obama has emphasized his willingness to speak with America's enemies, such as Iran, and pursue a multilateral approach to international problems, unlike President Bush. He is also more open to environmental issues and has a greater interest in controlling nuclear proliferation. Just the fact of Obama's ascension to the presidency has sent a message to the rest of the world about America's racial tolerance, class mobility, and the possibilities for merit-based advancement. The war in Iraq has also ended on his watch. And there have thus far not been any major negative repercussions from the WikiLeaks release of American diplomatic information. Still, diplomatic dilemmas for the US abound around the world.

Foreign policy challenges that have not been touched upon previously and America's relations with major players in various regions of the world bear scrutiny. A brief (and incomplete) analysis follows.

~~~

In terms of US objectives, Latin America can be considered a disappointment. Peter Hakim wrote in *Foreign Affairs* in 2006:

> After 9/11, Washington effectively lost interest in Latin America. Since then, the attention the United States has paid to the region has been sporadic and narrowly targeted. . . .

Few Latin Americans, in or out of government, consider the United States to be a dependable partner.[86]

America's focus on drugs and particularly security issues since 9/11 has kept it from engaging Latin American countries on the broad range of matters of importance to both sides.[87] Poverty and the marked inequality in the distribution of wealth remain major problems in Latin America, and trade issues with the US remain unresolved. With an abundance of natural resources waiting to be harvested in the region, China has made significant inroads in a number of countries.

The brothers Castro are still in power in Cuba, with Raul assuming the leadership from Fidel in 2006. The US embargo on trade with Cuba remains in place after fifty years despite disapproval from other Latin American countries and some American businesses. Hugo Chavez in Venezuela, a perpetual thorn in America's side, continues to suppress the democratic opposition in his country. He has an ally in Evo Morales, a populist elected in Bolivia by the indigenous population. Daniel Ortega, the Sandinista leader in Nicaragua and another friend of Chavez, has regained power through the ballot box. Chavez has also started a satellite news network, TeleSUR, available throughout Latin America, that presents the news with an anti-American slant.[88]Argentina's populist government under the Kirchners has been inclined to support Chavez rather than America, remembering the failure of the International Monetary Fund to offer help when Argentina was going through its fiscal crisis in the early years of the last decade. With Nestor Kirchner's recent death, the nation's future is uncertain, even though the president, Kirchner's widow, is in power.[89] Brazil under Lula da Silva and his successor Dilma Rousseff[90] has become a regional power emerging onto the world stage, with some areas of interest shared with the US and some that are in conflict. Given its great natural wealth and demographics, Brazil's star should rise dramatically in the next ten years making it incumbent upon the US to sustain an active dialogue with its leaders. That the nation is one of the world's largest democracies should be a common bond with America. Though Colombia has stabilized in the last eight years first with Alviro Uribe in control and now with his former defense minister Juan Manuel Santos as president[91], it remains the major source of cocaine and other drugs sold on American streets. It also has a sputtering leftist insurgency. However, it continues to be the strongest US ally in Latin America.

The drug trade and immigration are notable bones of contention between the US and Mexico. Drug cartels have terrorized much of the country, intimidating the populace and corrupting the police and politicians. President Calderón has focused his efforts on eliminating the drug cartels, but thus far the Mexican authorities have been unable to control them. Violence has only increased during Calderón's years in office as government forces and crime syndicates battle in the streets. The US is the major source of weapons for the drug gangs, sold in gun shops near the border. Americans are also the prime customers for Mexican drugs. With the Mexican economy remaining weak, immigration to the US is like an escape valve for the population, with remittances back home helping to support many families.

Canada, America's largest trading partner, was outspoken in its opposition to the war in Iraq, but has supported the US in Afghanistan, sending troops there as part of NATO and taking considerable casualties. There are minor economic disagreements between Canada and the US, but the overall relationship is strong.

Since Vladimir Putin was elected president, democracy in Russia has been under assault, with power increasingly concentrated in his hands and those of his associates. Little changed in 2008 when his handpicked successor, Dimitry Medvedev, assumed the presidency and Putin became prime minister.[92] With oil and gas wealth supporting its economy, Russia became more aggressive internationally, opposing a number of American initiatives. However, with Obama in the White House since 2009, there has been more cooperation between the two nations. Russia has been more willing to pressure Iran over its nuclear programs, and both America and Russia ratified the START treaty to reduce nuclear weapons. The Russian leadership has even allowed US military supplies to be shipped across the country to support the war in Afghanistan. The new attitude between the two nations began after the US abandoned its plans to place defensive missile systems in some of the Eastern European countries. Subsequently, there has been talk of Russia working with the US on the development of a different system to protect Europe from any Iranian threats. Although American leaders see the realpolitik necessity of cooperating with Russia, they are nonetheless aware of its suppression of opposition political parties and individuals, killings of journalists, lack of law in commercial dealings, and wholesale corruption throughout the country. Still, Russia is a player the US likes to have on its side, with the resulting necessity to overlook some of the nation's autocratic conduct.

The Middle East remains the world's tinderbox and America has been playing with matches, given its unconditional backing of Israel and the recent war in Iraq. In addition, America's oil dependency has forced it to support a number of dictatorial states and to ignore violations of human rights. Dealing with some of these nations, the US is in a double bind, for if it pushes for democracy, Islamic fundamentalist governments may emerge, unfriendly to America and the West. This was the case when Hamas won the Palestinian elections in Gaza. America's backing of the regimes in Saudi Arabia and Jordan while chastising Syria and Iran for their lack of democracy is inconsistent to many observers, showing that America is willing to surrender its principles to expediency. (Egypt under Hosni Mubarak was an autocratic state and yet was one of the largest recipients of American foreign aid.) The recent revolutions in Tunisia, Egypt, Yemen, and Libya have also affected the other regimes in the Middle East, with no clarity as to how they will play out.

The United States' uncritical support of Israel since its founding has earned America the enmity of much of the Muslim world. Domestic considerations, particularly the Jewish lobby and Christian conservative backing of Israel, have undoubtedly played a role in American policies. Although the US has rightly condemned Palestinian terrorism and violence, Washington has too often ignored Israeli failure to restrict its settlements in the West Bank and other violations of its agreements. This inaction reinforced the belief among the Arabs that America is biased in favor of the Israelis. The recent attempts by President Obama to restart direct peace talks between the Israelis and Palestinian Authority collapsed over Israel's refusal to halt settlement building, but trying for a peace deal remains a cornerstone of Obama's foreign policy. However, indirect talks, with former Senator George Mitchell as intermediary, went nowhere, with Netanyahu's right-wing Israeli government showing little willingness to make concessions.[93] On the other hand, Hamas's refusal to recognize Israel, its sponsoring of violence, and its control of Gaza appear to make the stalemate even more intractable. The Obama administration, as previous US administrations, has no other option but to keep trying for a solution.

Lebanon, the only putative Arab democracy, is currently a nation whose government is held together with baling wire. A series of assassinations of Lebanese leaders, including the Sunni Prime Minister Rafik Hariri in 2005 and the Christian government minister Pierre Gemayel, along with the war between Israel and Hezbollah in 2006 have undermined the stability of the country. The assassinations have been blamed on pro-Syrian elements within Lebanon, with the country split between those who supported an international investigation (the Sunnis, Christians, and Druse) and those who wanted it stopped (the Shiite parties, Hezbollah and Amal, and some Christians). Hezbollah, a proxy of Iran with a history of terrorist activity, has used its military power to obtain a veto over the government's actions and threatened violence if any of its members were implicated in the investigation by the UN-supported tribunal.[94] However, in June 2011, after the Special Tribunal for Lebanon indicted four men who were connected to Hezbollah for the assassination, there was no military response by the group. They did, however, refuse to hand over the men to the Tribunal for prosecution. Saad Hariri, Rafik's son, was forced out as prime Minister in January 2011 by Hezbollah, who installed Najib Miqati, a Sunni sympathetic to their interests. The Lebanese army appears incapable of controlling Hezbollah's sectarian militia.

Syria has been a fiefdom of the Assad family for over forty years, with Bashar succeeding his father Hafez al-Assad upon his death in 2000. The Assads are Alawites, a religious minority that is a Shiite offshoot, and they have put their co-religionists in positions of power in the country where they dominate the Sunni majority. They also controlled Lebanon, their next-door neighbor from 1976 until Syrian troops were forced out by the United Nations in 2006. Syrian support of Hezbollah helped this Shiite organization gain strength in Lebanon, to the point where they are now ascendant. Unlike other Sunni majority nations in the region, Syria under the Assads formed an alliance with Iran, which is able to ship weapons to Hezbollah across Syrian soil. The US for years has tried to split Syria away from Iran with various inducements, but its efforts have been unsuccessful. The Arab Spring also came to Syria in 2011, with large demonstrations against Bashar Assad's rule and demanding freedom. How this will all play out is uncertain. Afraid of an Islamist takeover, the US was initially unwilling to get involved in Syrian politics but did eventually support the calls for greater freedom and was critical of Assad and his coterie.

Saudi Arabia, purportedly a friend of America, also presents problems for US makers of foreign policy. The Wahhabist brand of Islam emanating from Saudi Arabia promotes religious fanaticism and hatred of non-Muslims, Western culture and values, with animosity toward Shiites as well. The seeds that produced suicide bombers and Islamic terrorism grew in the soil of Wahhabism, with the madrassas and schools teaching this religious philosophy, and the Imams who preach it, funded by the Saudis. These institutions use texts for instruction that are filled with anti-Western, anti-Christian and anti-Semitic diatribes, reinforcing hostility to other religions. Washington has repeatedly asked the Saudis to remove the offensive texts from all schools, to reform their curricula, and to stop funding institutions that espouse intolerance, but thus far progress on these requests has been minimal. King Abdullah, who appears to be a moderating force in the kingdom, is old and ill, and the policies of his successor cannot be predicted. Yet America remains dependent on Saudi oil.

Yemen, Saudi Arabia's southern neighbor, has been ruled by President Ali Abdullah Saleh for over thirty years. He has recently been challenged by street demonstrations inspired by Egypt and Tunisia calling for his removal. Wounded by insurgents, he went for treatment to Saudi Arabia, which has been supporting his regime. A tribal society plagued by corruption and poverty, Yemen has had several long-standing insurrections and a southern secessionist movement, the south and north having joined only in 1990. Al Qaeda and Islamists have been thriving in the mountainous lawless areas and the US has been using drone attacks to try to eliminate some of the militants. Whether or not the Saleh government will survive is uncertain, as is what might follow if he does not.

Aside from its nuclear policy, Iran's hard-line attitude toward Israel and the West make it difficult for the US to engage it diplomatically. The Iranian presidential election in 2009, supposedly won by Mahmoud Ahmadinejad, appears to have been stolen by the militants from the reform candidate Hossein Mousavi.[95] The Revolutionary Guards and other state forces violently suppressed the opposition afterwards, with Supreme Leader Khamenei vetting the election results. Since then, there have been arrests, beatings, and even executions of opposition members, with the state showing no concern for human rights. Sanctions passed by the UN Security Council in response to Iran's nuclear program and even greater restrictions on Iranian commerce by the US and the European Union have apparently affected the economy, but not enough for the Iranians to forgo further nuclear development. While the US, Israel, the European nations, and most Middle Eastern countries agree that Iran should not be allowed to develop nuclear weapons, it is unclear how this will be prevented.

American interests in sub-Saharan Africa involve promotion of freedom and human rights and prevention of hunger and disease. With an insatiable appetite for natural resources, China has been competing with the US for influence on the continent, bolstering a number of dictatorial states. Since the withdrawal of the colonial powers in the '60s and '70s, the new nations in Africa have been a cauldron of war, famine, and AIDS as a result of Cold War rivalry, tribal and religious animosities, corruption, and a failure of leadership. The humanitarian disasters playing out in Africa have required major food and economic assistance from the developed world and military intervention that has usually not been forthcoming to prevent genocide and ethnic cleansing. In the Sudan, the conflict in Darfur is still simmering, and President al-Bashir has been indicted by the International Court for genocide.[96] Southern Sudan recently seceded from the north through elections, but needs major assistance to become a functioning state. The unending civil war in Somalia continues, with radical Islamists seemingly dominant. In Nigeria, the most populous nation on the continent, clashes have been occurring between Christians and Muslims in the north, with an insurgency active in the delta, where much of the country's oil is produced. President Mugabe is still in control of Zimbabwe, though he apparently lost the last election, and there has been strife regarding election results in a number of so-called democratic sub-Saharan countries, including Kenya, Ivory Coast, and the Congo. In the Ivory Coast, a civil war raged when President Gbagbo refused to step down to allow the winner, Alassane Ouattara, to assume the presidency.

Until recently, Arab North Africa was controlled by autocratic regimes in Algeria, Libya, Egypt, and Morocco. However, in January 2011, the repressive President Ben Ali of Tunisia was overthrown in a populist revolution driven by rampant corruption and economic stagnation in the country.[97] The Egyptian people soon followed, removing Hosni Mubarak as president and moving toward democracy. Egypt under Mubarak had been the fulcrum of US policy in the Arab world and it is too early to tell what the new government's relations with America will be. As of August 2011 the revolt in Libya was still raging, with Qadaffi appearing to be on the defensive, but the outcome still in doubt. The US needs to bolster democracy in the Arab world even though governments may arise that are not supportive of American interests in the short term. In the long run, education of the populace, economic growth, reduced corruption, and democratic regimes are the best answer to radical Islam, America's bitter enemy.

Pakistan, one of America's apparent allies in the war against terrorism, is a volatile nation with endemic corruption, possessing a nuclear arsenal. Since gaining independence from Britain in 1947, the military has periodically replaced civilian governments, eventually re-establishing putative democratic rule. Most recently, in 2008, General Pervez Musharraf was replaced as president by Asif Ali Zaedari, the husband of the assassinated leader of the People's Party, Benazir Bhutto. Since then, the People's Party's coalition government under Prime Minister Gilani has been plagued by war in the northwest provinces, terrorism, and natural disasters. A coup by radical military elements or Muslim extremists could be extremely dangerous for the United States and the West. It was a Pakistani scientist, Dr. Abdul Qadeer Khan, who sold nuclear technology to North Korea, Iran, and Libya, possibly with approval of the military. The ISI, Pakistan's intelligence service, or some of its rogue elements, is thought be supporting the Taliban in Afghanistan to counteract any Indian attempts to establish a foothold there. They are also backing militant Islamic organizations within the country to use against India in the conflict over Kashmir, and may have aided these organizations in planning and executing acts of terrorism on Indian soil. Militant Sunnis and Al Qaeda have also perpetrated suicide bombings and assassinations against the Shiites, Sufis, and Christians in Pakistan, as well as secular leaders; moderate Muslims are fearful of speaking out against them. The head of the Pakistani military, General Kayani, is respected by Western analysts and has directed the army in its campaign against the Islamists in the tribal territories.[98] He has denied any desire to assume leadership of the country to restore stability. The US has tried to get Pakistan to move even more forcefully against Islamist elements in the northern tribal areas, but its military has so far resisted. However, they have tacitly supported drone attacks by the US in this region against Al Qaeda and the Taliban. Pakistan is currently one of the major recipients of American military and civilian aid, but this has not given the US much leverage in terms of its policy objectives.

American military analysts have raised questions about whether the war in Afghanistan can be won as long as the Taliban are allowed sanctuaries in Pakistan. The operation that killed bin Laden on Pakistani soil by American Special Forces without prewarning the Pakistani government has further inflamed relations between Pakistan and the US.

India, the largest democracy in the world, is an important ally for America, with an expanding economy, a thriving services and technology sector, and a newly emerging middle class. In spite of this, rural poverty and malnutrition remain major problems. Besides being a significant trading partner, India is also seen by the US as a potential counterweight to China and a force for stabilization in South Asia, as well as a generator of economic growth in the region.[99] It is also a partner in the war against terrorism, and a target of Muslim extremists. The nuclear agreement by the Bush administration and India in 2005 helped cement ties between the two countries. It eliminated some of the mutual suspicion that had previously existed when India had been one of the leaders of the non-aligned bloc, though the agreement wasn't ratified by the US Congress until 2008.[100] In recent years, having moved away from a stultifying socialist ideology, India has enjoyed surging economic growth under the political direction of the Congress Party. President Obama's visit to India in November 2010 further improved relations between the two nations and finalized a number of business deals.[101] Its major obstacles to even greater advancement are its pitiful infrastructure, paltry educational opportunities for much of the population, and a government bureaucracy that moves at a snail's pace to grant approval for new construction or businesses. The deep-seated hostility between India and Pakistan, two neighbors with nuclear arms, and the Islamic terrorists in Pakistan, who are unconcerned about setting off a conflagration, have kept US diplomats hard at work to help settle the outstanding issues between the two nations.

In the next several decades, relations between China and the US will be as critical to America and the rest of the world as the battle against terrorism. The trade issues and friction between the two countries can be expected to increase as China's economy continues to grow. The status of Taiwan is another source of potential conflict that will play out in the future. China's refusal to grant any small measure of autonomy to Tibet and Xinjiang, and its military suppression of the riots in both areas, raise questions about possible future ethnic unrest in the country.[102] One of China's answers to the separatist tendency among the Tibetans and Uighurs is to push economic development in these provinces, but also to encourage migration there by the nation's Han majority. China has also had confrontations with Japan over the rights to some small islands in the East China Sea that have possible lucrative oil and gas fields as well as fishing grounds.[103] There have also been conflicts with Vietnam over islands in the South China Sea with similar possibilities for oil and gas exploration.[104] China's military is currently in the process of modernizing, which might be expected given the country's economic prowess. Its goal is to be able to project power in the near regions of the Pacific, but its reach will likely be even further. While China asserts this buildup is for defensive purposes, it will challenge US dominance in the Pacific and back up China's claims to territory with military force. Some of China's neighbors are becoming wary and looking to the US for support.

Thus far, China has not been helpful in resolving the standoff with North Korea over its nuclear weapons, with China's assistance needed to try to reach a satisfactory conclusion. China seems to be satisfied with the status quo, afraid that too much pressure on Pyongyang could lead to a North Korean governmental breakdown and an exodus of refugees. There is also ambivalence about the possible unification of the two Koreas. While the opportunities for trade would increase, it might place American troops close to the Chinese border. Though the Chinese did support the June 2010 round of UN sanctions against Iran over its nuclear program (after it was watered down),[105] it continues to import a considerable amount of Iranian oil and in all likelihood is still trading with Iran either directly or through intermediaries. Human rights and rule of law also remain contentious issues between China and the US, but America's ability to effect change in these areas is limited. Whatever concerns might stand between China and the US, their economic interdependency makes an open break improbable.

Japan, the third largest economy in the world, is a staunch ally of the US. Its economic growth has been limited since the '90s because of a real estate bubble and an excess of nonperforming loans on the books of many Japanese banks. But its demographics may be its most critical problem, as the population is aging, the birth rate is low, and there will not be enough workers to support the elderly within a few decades. This dilemma is exacerbated by Japanese reluctance to build its work force with immigrants. Though the Japanese are troubled by North Korea's nuclear buildup and the conflict with China over the islands in the East China Sea, its constitution, instituted after World War II, restricts its military to "self-defense" forces.[106] Because of this, it is reliant on the US military and nuclear umbrella for protection. For decades, local citizens have protested the presence of American military bases on Okinawa, but the central government wants American troops to remain. Japan was essentially a one-party state for over fifty years after World War II, with the Liberal Democrats in control. In the 2009 election they were defeated by the Democratic Party but there have been few policy changes since then.

South Korea is also dependent on the US military in its ongoing "cold war" with the North that occasionally breaks out into overt skirmishes. After the Asian currency crisis in 1997, South Korea rebounded strongly and is now the fifteenth largest economy in the world,[107] a major producer of high-tech equipment. The recent trade agreement between the US and Korea has further cemented ties between the two nations. With North Korean heavy artillery within range of Seoul, the Korean population takes any rise in tension with the North seriously. Given the North's economic backwardness and its inability to produce enough food for its people, its long-term stability is uncertain. How change will come about and how it will affect South Korea is unknown.

America's relationships with the democratic countries of the European Union have been aided by the commonality of their belief systems that emphasize the importance of freedom and human rights. The divide that developed because of the Iraq War and its abuses was bridged for the most part when President Bush left office and was replaced by Obama. However, there are still differences between Europe and America on policy issues, particularly regarding trade and economic matters. France's relationship with America took a turn for the better when Nicolas Sarkozy was elected president. America and England remain very close in terms of their perceptions of how to deal with the rest of the world. Since the Conservative and Liberal coalition under David Cameron succeeded Labor in running the government, there has been no major change in the rapport between the two countries. Germany under Angela Merkel has been more understanding of US positions than when Gerhard Schröder and the Social Democrats were in power, but the country remains more aligned with Russia than America would like. There have also been some differences on post-recession economic policy. The Eastern European nations that were previously behind the Iron Curtain are mostly supportive of American initiatives, grateful for being freed from their Soviet bonds. In general, on most issues the US and Europe see the world through similar lenses and are able to work together to try to solve problems of mutual interest like Afghanistan or the Iranian nuclear program.

The major challenges confronting America are numerous and won't disappear spontaneously or with wishful thinking. America needs politicians with foresight and fortitude who are willing to work hard, compromise when necessary, and find solutions to the problems that are eating away at the foundation of the nation, threatening to bring about a collapse of the entire structure. America needs politicians willing to exert leadership, unafraid of the slings and arrows of the lobbyists and special interests, and willing to tell their constituents the painful truth about the way things are. Thus far, neither the Republicans nor Democrats have provided the sort of men and women American democracy requires, giving it instead politicians constrained by ideology and wedded to perks and pork. The doctrines of the Tea Party will only heighten partisanship. America needs a third party of the center to bring about the necessary changes in its political system.

# References

1 Thomas Paine, *Common Sense*, Penguin Books, New York, NY, 1986 (originally published in 1776), 63.

2 Niccolò Machiavelli, *The Prince*, trans. Daniel Dommo, Bantam Classics, New York, NY, 2003 (originally published in 1513), 42.

3 Paul Kennedy, *The Rise and Fall of the Great Powers*, Random House, New York, NY, 1987, xvi.

4 Ibid., 444.

5 "World Wide Military Expenditures," Global Security.org, www.globalsecuirty.org/military/world/spending.htm.

6 Joseph S. Nye, Jr., *Bound To Lead*, Basic Books, USA, New York, NY, 1991, preface to the paperback edition, xvi.

7 Richard A. Clarke, *Against All Enemies*, Free Press, New York, NY, 2004, 227.

8 Bob Woodward, *State of Denial*, Simon and Schuster, New York, NY, 2006, 51.

9 Clarke, 256.

10 Robert D. Kaplan, *Warrior Politics*, Vintage Books, New York, NY, 2003, 9.

11 Amy B. Zegart, "An Empirical Analysis of Failed Intelligence Reforms Before September 11," *Political Science Quarterly*, 2006, Vol. 121, No. 1, 33.

12 Ibid., 35.

13 Clarke, 215.

14 Clarke, 30–33.

15 Paul R. Pillar, "Intelligence Policy and the War in Iraq," *Foreign Affairs*, March/April 2006, Vol. 85, No. 2, 15–27.

16 Clarke, 268.

17 "US Intelligence and Security Agencies," FAS Intelligence Resource Program, www.fas.org/irp/official.html, updated January 7, 2006.

18 Scott Shane, "In New Job, Spymaster Draws Bipartisan Criticism," New York Times, April 20, 2006, A1.

19 Mark Mazzetti, "Spymaster Tells Secret of Size of Spy Force," *New York Times*, April 21, 2006, 21.

20 Pam Benson, "Director of National Intelligence names deputy to boost collaboration," CNN Politics, August 20, 2010. http://articles.cnn.com/2010-08-20/politics/intelligence.integration-of-intelligence-intelligence-community?_S=PM:Politics.

21 Patrick Radden Keefe, "Don't Privatize Our Spies," *New York Times*, June 25, 2007, OpEd, A19.

22 Mark Mazzetti and Scott Shane, "Director of C.I.A. Is Stepping Down Under Pressure," *New York Times*, May 6, 2006, A1.

23 Mark Mazzetti, "Career C.I.A. Figure Is at Eye of Scandal," *New York Times*, May 12, 2006, A30.

24 Charles Babington, "Hayden Confirmed as C.I.A. Chief," *Washington Post*, May 27, 2006, A02.

25 "CIA Leadership," February 13, 2009, www.cia.gov/about-cia/leadership/leon-e-panetta.html.

26 Selig S. Harrison, "Did North Korea Cheat?" *Foreign Affairs*, January/February 2005, Vol. 84, No. 1, 99–110.

27 Mitchell B. Reiss and Robert Gallucci, "Dead to Rights," *Foreign Affairs*, March/April 2005, Vol. 84, No. 2, 142–145.

28 David E. Sanger, "Nuclear Test Was Decades in the Making," *New York Times*, October 9, 2006, A9.

29 Norimitsu Onishi and David E. Sanger, "Missiles Fired by North Korea; Tests Protested," *New York Times*, July 5, 2006, A1.

30 John M. Glionna, "South Korea braces for surprise attack despite North's signs to contrary," *Chicago Tribune*, December 22, 2010, www.chicagotribune.com/news/nationworld/la-fg-korea-tension-20101222,0,1569495.story.

31 Kenneth Pollack and Ray Takeyh, "Taking on Teheran," *Foreign Affairs*, March/April 2005, Vol. 84, No. 2, 20–34.

32 "Nuclear Weapons," GlobalSecurity.org, 2006, www.globalsecurity.org/wmd/world/iran/nuke.htm.

33 David E. Sanger, "For Bush, Talks With Iran Were a Last Resort," *New York Times*, June 1, 2006, A18.

34 Jonathan Fildes, "Stuxnet worm targeted high-value Iranian assets," BBC News, September 23, 2010, www.bbc.co.uk/news/technology-11388018?print=true.

35 Jonathan Rauch, "Containing Iran," *The Atlantic*, July/August 2006, 33–34.

36 Kathy Gannon, "Afghanistan Unbound," *Foreign Affairs*, May/June 2004, Vol. 83, No. 3, 35–46.

37 Stephen Biddle, "Afghanistan and the Future of Warfare," *Foreign Affairs*, March/April 2003, Vol. 82, No. 2, 31–46.

38 Clarke, 245.

39 "U.S. Afghan troop buildup completed," UPI.com, September 13, 2010, www.upi.com/Top_news/US/2010/09/13/US-Afghan-troop-buildup-completed/UPI-75331284436563/.

40 Ewen MacAskill, "Afghanistan policy review expected to point to modest US troop withdrawal," Guardian.co.uk, December 15, 2010, www.guardian.co.uk/world/2010/dec/15/barack-obama-review-afghanistan-policy/.

41 Christi Parsons and Paul Richter, "NATO sets 2014 target for Afghan pullout," Chicagotribune.com, November 10, 2010, www.chicagotribune.com/news/nationworld/la-fgw-nato-afghanistan-20101121,0,7613802.story.

42 Gerald F. Seib, "Exit Plan Critical to Afghan Buildup," *The Wall Street Journal*, November 17, 2009, http://online.wsj.com/article/SB125840201623250945.html.

43 Carlotta Gall and Ruhullah Khapalwak, "An Election Gone Wrong Fuels Tension in Kabul," *New York Times*, December 29, 2010, A4.

44 "Al Qaeda Resurgent," *New York Times*, February 25, 2007, Editorial, Week in Review, 13.

45 Aryn Baker, "Pakistan: Behind the Waziristan Offensive," October 18, 2009, Time.com, www.time.com/time/printout/0,8816,1930909,00.html.

46 Ranj Alaaldin, "US exit from Iraq is a phoney withdrawal," *Guardian*, August 20, 2010, www.guardian.co.uk/commentisfree/2010/aug/20/us-iraq-exit-phoney-withdrawal/print.

[47] "New Iraqi government taking shape," UPI.com, December 10, 2010, www.upi.com/Top_News/Special/2010/12/10/New-Iraqi-government-taking-shape/UPI-265612006139/.

[48] "Infighting delays Iraqi government formation," Reurters.com, December 20, 2010, www.reuters.com/assets/print?aid=USTRE6BI12P20101220.

[49] "Iraq and the Kurds: The Struggle over Kirkuk," The Crisis Group, January 2010, www.crisisgroup.org/en/key-issues/iraq-and-the-kurds-the-struggle-over-kirkuk.aspx.

[50] Thomas Ricks, *Fiasco: The American Military Adventure in Iraq*, Penguin Press, New York, NY, 2006, 3.

[51] Paul Pillar, 20–21.

[52] Ricks, 42–43, and other sites.

[53] Michael R. Gordon and General Bernard E. Trainor, *Cobra II*, Pantheon Press, New York, NY, 2006, 26, 101–103.

[54] Ibid., 4.

[55] Ibid., 103.

[56] Larry Diamond, "What Went Wrong in Iraq," *Foreign Affairs*, 2004, Vol. 83, No. 5, 36.

[57] Gordon and Trainor, 475.

[58] Ricks, 158–159.

[59] Larry Diamond, 37.

[60] Lieutenant General Gregory Newbold (Ret), "Why Iraq Was a Mistake," *Time*, Viewpoint, April 17, 2006, 42.

[61] Thom Shanker, "Army Career Behind Him, General Speaks Out on Iraq," *New York Times*, May 13, 2007, 20.

[62] David S. Cloud, "Ex-Commander Says Iraq Effort Is a 'nightmare'," *New York Times*, October 13, 2007, A1.

[63] Sheryl Gay Stolberg and Carl Hulse, "Bush Rules Out Bid by Congress for Iraq Pullout," *New York Times*, March 21, 2007, A1.

[64] Carl Hulse and Jeff Zeleny, "Stymied by G.O.P., Democrats Stop Debate on Iraq," *New York Times*, July 19, 2007, A1.

[65] Robin Toner, "Who's This 'We,' Non-Soldier Boy?" *New York Times*, June 25, 2006, Week in Review, 3.

[66] David Leonhardt, "What $1.2 Trillion Can Buy," *New York Times*, January 17, 2007, Business, 1.

[67] Mark Mazzetti, "Spy Agencies Say Iraq War Worsens Terrorism Threat," *New York Times*, September 24, 2006, 9.

[68] "Summary of the Executive Order Establishing the Office of Homeland Security," October 8, 2001, www.whitehouse.gov/news/release/2001/10/20011.

[69] "Department of Homeland Security," http://en.wikipedia.org/Department_of_Homeland_Security.

[70] Associated Press, "Security Falls Short of Goals, Auditors Report," *New York Times*, September 6, 2007, A25.

[71] Quoted in Stephen Flynn, "The Neglected Home Front," *Foreign Affairs*, September/October 2004, Vol. 83, No. 5, 24.

[72] Ibid., 23.

[73] Clarke, 259.

[74] Flynn, 23.

[75] Eric Lipton, "Testers Slip Radioactive Materials Over Borders," *New York Times*, March 28, 2006, A14.

[76] Flynn, 22–23.

77 Eric Lipton, "In Kentucky Hills, a Homeland Security Bonanza," *New York Times*, May 14, 2006, 1.

[78] Brian Faler and Lisa Lerer, "Republicans Select Rogers to Head House Appropriations Committee," Bloomberg Businessweek, December 8, 2010, www.businessweek.com/news/2010-12-08/republicans-select-rogers-to-head-house-appropriations-committee.html.

[79] Mimi Hall, "Uproar unmuffled over anti-terror money," *USA Today*, June 8, 2006, 3A.

[80] Eric Lipton, "Nominations Made for Top Post at FEMA and Three Other Slots," *New York Times*, April 7, 2006, A10.

[81] Eric Lipton, "Breathtaking Waste and Fraud in Hurricane Aid," *New York Times*, June 27, 2006, A1.

[82] Janet Napolitano, "The Ongoing Response to the Deepwater BP Oil Spill," *DHS Journal*, http://journal.dhs.gov/2010/05/ongoing-response-to-deepwater-bp-oil.html.

[83] Eric Lipton, "Former Antiterror Officials Find Industry Pays Better," *New York Times*, June 18, 2006, 1.

[84] Kaplan, 14–15.

[85] Online News Hour, "Presidential Debate," October 12, 2000, www.pbs.org/newshour/bb/politics/july-dec00/for-policy_10-12.html.

[86] Peter Hakim, "Is Washington Losing Latin America?" *Foreign Affairs*, January/February 2006, Vol. 85, No. 1, 39.

[87] Jorge Castaneda, "The Forgotten Relationship," *Foreign Affairs*, May/June 2003, Vol. 82, No. 3, 67–81.

[88] Franklin Foer, "The Talented Mr. Chavez," *The Atlantic*, May 2006, 94–105.

[89] Mac Margolis, "Kirchner's Death Leaves Argentina in Political Disarray," *Newsweek*, October 28, 2010.

[90] Alexei Barrionuevo, "Brazil's New Leader Begins in Shadow of Predecessor," *New York Times*, December 31, 2010, www.nytimes.com/2011/01/01/world/americas/01brazil.html?_r=1&pagewanted=print.

[91] Juan Forero, "Juan Manuel Santos takes oath as Colombia's new president," *The Washington Post*, August 8, 2010, A11.

[92] Peter Finn, "Putin's Chosen Successor, Medvedev, Elected in Russia," *The Washington Post*, March 3, 2008.

[93] George S. Hishmeh, "What More Can Obama Do," *The Palestinian Chronicle*, January 5, 2011, http:/palestinianchronicle.com/print_article.php?id=16550.

[94] Heather Murdock, "Expected Hezbollah Indictments Have Lebanese on Edge," VOANews.com, November 2010, www.printthis.clickability.com/pt/cpt?expire=&title=VOA+7C+Expected-Hezbollah-Indictments-Have-Lebanese-on-Edge-109-880654.html.

[95] Casey L. Addis, "Iran's 2009 Presidential Elections," Congressional Research Service, July 6, 2009, www.fas.org/sgp/crs/mideast/R40653.pdf.

[96] Mike Corder, "Al-Bashir Arrest Warrant Issued By International Criminal Court," Huffington Post, March 4, 2009, www.huffingtonpost.com/2009/03/04/albashir-arrest-warrant-i_n_171703.html?view.

[97] David D. Kirkpatrick, "Tunisia Names Unity Government," *New York Times*, January 17, 2011, A1.

[98] Nahal Toosi, "Ashfaq Parvez Kayani, Pakistani General, Balances All Sides of Conflict," Huffington Post, 7/29/10, www.huffingtonpost.com/2010/07/29/ashfaq-parvez-kayani-paki_n_663282.html.

[99] C. Raja Mohan, "India and the Balance of Power," *Foreign Affairs*, July/August 2006, Vol. 85, No. 4, 22–23.

[100] Jayshree Bajoria, "The U.S.—India Nuclear Deal," Council on Foreign Relations, November 5, 2010, www.cfr.org/publicantion/9663/usindia_nuclear_deal.html.

[101] "Obama calls India a job-creating giant for U.S." msnbc news services, November 7, 2010, www.msnbc.msn.com/cleanprint/CleanPrintProxy.aspx?1294366241175.

[102] Christian Le Mière, "China's Western Front," *Foreign Affairs*, August 14, 2009, www.foreignaffairs.com/print/65213.

[103] Kevin Voigt, "China-Japan fight goes deeper than islands," cnn.com, September 22, 2010, www.cnn.com/2010/Business/09/22/china.japan.island.dispute/index.html?hpt=Sbin.

[104] Ishaan Tharoor, "China and Vietnam: Clashing Over an Island Archipelago," *Time*, January 14, 2010, www.time.com/time/printout/0,8816,1953039,00.html.

[105] Max Fisher, "Why Russia and China Joined Iran Sanctions," *The Atlantic*, May 2010, www.theatlantic.com/international/print/2010/05/why-russia-and-china-joined-on-iran-sanctions/56905/.

[106] Lee Hudson Teslik, "Japan and Its Military," Council on Foreign Relations, April 13, 2006, www.cfr.org/publication/10439/japan_and_its_military.html.

[107] Martin Fackler, "Lessons Learned, South Korea Makes Quick Economic Recovery," *New York Times*, January 7, 2011, A7.

## CHAPTER 6

# Laying the Foundation

Men who are governed by reason—that is, who seek what is useful to them in accordance with reason—desire for themselves nothing which they do not desire for the rest of mankind, and consequently, are just, faithful, and honorable in their conduct.
—Baruch Spinoza, *The Ethics of Spinoza*[1]

A long habit of not thinking a thing wrong, gives it a superficial appearance of being right.
—Tom Paine, *Common Sense*[2]

America has evolved into a state that would be unrecognizable to the Founding Fathers, its government unable to operate effectively as officeholders preen and posture for their partisan bases instead of trying to negotiate necessary legislation. Its two political parties have depreciated the value of the franchise to the point where a substantial proportion of its citizens (particularly the young) do not vote, believing the ballots they cast are worthless. Ideologues pick the candidates for public office in party primaries, forcing them upon the voters in the general elections, generating little popular enthusiasm. In addition, with state legislatures gerrymandering the congressional and legislative districts and officeholders able to raise huge sums of money to bolster their campaigns, incumbents on both the state and federal levels (notwithstanding the 2010 campaign) are overwhelmingly reelected, barring politically cataclysmic events. Once in office, the so-called representatives of the people attend more to the needs and wants of the special interests and the very affluent than their constituents, ordinary citizens having little power in determining how essential issues will be managed. Unless they are part of organized pressure groups willing to contribute money to politicians and able to use lobbyists to amplify what they have to say, their voices go unheard in Washington. While the growth of the Tea Party is testimony to citizens' unhappiness with politicians and government, the solutions they propose are not realistic for a modern state competing in a knowledge-based global economy and concerned with its security.

America needs new leaders who are honest and forthright, willing to handle problems expeditiously, omitting the spin, obfuscation, and procrastination characteristic of the current political hierarchy. The nation's dependence on foreign oil is intolerable, its unfunded liabilities vast and growing, its ballooning national debt and trade deficits unsustainable. To correct these imbalances, sacrifice and pain are inevitable, but none of America's leaders have been willing to say so. There cannot be unlimited spending on guns and butter combined with lower taxes indefinitely, no matter what the politicians say. Cutting spending alone will not only fail to do the job, but could possibly injure essential programs. The politicians are deluding themselves even as they try to delude their constituents, believing they can shape the world they want with smoke and mirrors. Though the war on terrorism and the war in Afghanistan have been in progress for some time now, with the war in Iraq just concluding, these conflicts have not touched the lives of the majority of Americans, aside from minor inconveniences at airports. While true patriots would be prepared to relinquish individual goals and change lifestyles for the good of the nation, elected officials have not asked citizens to modify the way they live to the smallest degree since these confrontations began. This is merely one indication of why the nation needs men and women who can be trusted to construct a government of truth and substance, who are willing to tell citizens things they do not wish to hear but are factual, who are willing to sacrifice because it is necessary, who do not want to lay the burden of their living well on their children and succeeding generations. A permanent centrist third party, such as the Civic Alliance, could provide the kind of reality-based, incorruptible, pragmatic leadership absent in the established parties.

Questions will arise about whether the Civic Alliance can produce a significant change in traditional American politics and whether the concept of a competitive third party is merely wishful thinking. But there are many reasons to believe that the elements for success are now present. These include the disgust and antipathy enveloping both the Republicans and Democrats, voters' disillusionment with the government and its policies, and the new capabilities of instant communication and networking provided by the Internet and social networks. Unlike previous attempts to reform the political system, a new party could easily spread its transformational message, keeping its supporters constantly engaged and the American public in the loop. Even early in its development it might be able to capture enough seats in Congress to make a political impact by controlling the balance of power. It might also be able to influence the behavior of the Republicans and Democrats with its renunciation of vitriol, its clean hands, and practical public persona.

Ted Halstead and Michael Lind observed in *The Radical Center*:

> Underlying the growing political disengagement and dealignment is a widespread, if largely unspoken, sense on the part of the American people that the parties, ideologies, and institutions that have defined our social and political order in the past are simply incapable of addressing the challenges and opportunities awaiting us in the Information Age. . . . our leading parties are now relics of a bygone era.[3]

The Civic Alliance will be a political party conceived and brought to fruition in the digital age, whose ideas, techniques, and platforms reflect innovative thinking, with a willingness to experiment to achieve its goals. But it will be grounded by its desire to improve the lives of America's citizens, never forgetting that a political party should be a servant of the people and not its master.

In order to reform its political system and accomplish the necessary metamorphosis, Americans must have a mindset receptive to the need for a centrist third party and the possibility of change. Part of this mindset has already been laid: the widespread negative perception of America's political institutions and the realization that they do not function adequately in an increasingly complex society. There is little question that most of America's citizens believe this to be true, given the consistently low marks the president, Congress, and the political parties receive in various polls. The modest percentage of Americans who vote in elections can be seen as additional affirmation of this judgment.

Another prerequisite for a reformist third party is the conviction that an organization capable of spearheading the required transformation would be welcome on the political scene. Again, polls seem to reinforce this belief, as well as the previous third-party presidential challenges by Ross Perot and John Anderson, which received substantial backing from the public. Currently, Americans seem even more unhappy with their government and the political parties than in the past, the Tea Party merely one manifestation, making this a prime time to build a permanent third party of the center. Thus, some elements appear to be in place to initiate this new movement. But others are required.

## Citizen Responsibility

The obligations and responsibilities of a nation's citizens depend on the nature of the government, the established traditions, and the cultural norms. Rousseau speaks of citizen participation in society in *The Social Contract*:

> The undertakings which bind us to the social body are obligatory only because they are mutual; and their nature is such that in fulfilling them we cannot work for others without working for ourselves.[4]

In other words, involvement in politics benefits each of us as well as society as a whole so it is in our own interest to be engaged. Different forms of democracy and different stages of development have different expectations of their citizens. Managed democracies and totalitarian states are likely to discourage citizens from participating in political decisions, instead demanding compliance with proclaimed statutes.

During the nineteenth century, democracy in both theory and practice generated considerable excitement among Americans, with much greater interest and connection to politics than is true today (with the exceptions of women and slaves). Freedom—the idea that men could rule themselves and determine their own fate—was a new and exhilarating concept. Many of the immigrants who settled in America were escaping oppression in Europe and were delighted to be included in the process of self-governing. Citizens were more knowledgeable about the issues of the day and the candidates for office, reading the newspapers avidly and discussing politics regularly with their friends and neighbors. There was also more interaction and debate among political candidates and voters, with the populace listening enthusiastically to lengthy speeches and asking pointed questions. Politics was a form of entertainment for many Americans and a respite from daily activities. People were more passionate about joining political parties and there was greater flux as new organizations were born and died. A higher percentage of the electorate went to the polls, enjoying the privilege of choosing their own leaders, a right that had recently been attained with the blood of their countrymen.

Today, with numerous sources of entertainment, Americans are deluged with choices, their time occupied with work or pleasurable activities. Many citizens have become indifferent to voting and the electoral process, having forgotten or never having learned how important their franchise is. As Stephen Schneck noted in his essay on *Political Parties and Democracy's Citizens*:

> Citizens in general are opting out of regular, organized and dutiful participation in politics—evidenced by low voter turnout, disgust with politics, diminished involvement in civic duties, and declining interest in public affairs.[5]

They are more attuned to making money or "having fun" than their responsibility as citizens, which entails some commitment of time. Perhaps because freedom has been a fact of life in the United States for so long, a large portion of the population has come to take it for granted and consequently neglect their civic obligations. The nation's young people appear to be even more disengaged and uninterested in politics than the rest of the populace. Citizenship should not be a passive function. Those who enjoy the advantages of democracy must realize it comes with responsibility: a duty to educate oneself about the important issues, discuss political matters with one's compatriots, and support the candidates for office who best reflect one's views.

Many citizens might reply in rebuttal that their votes are inconsequential since the choice of candidates is often unattractive or unacceptable, restricted to selecting the lesser of two evils, and that the established parties are both corrupt. These are valid points and the parties themselves along with the political system they developed are mostly to blame for this. But it is the fault of America's citizens as well who have abrogated their responsibilities and have not demanded better candidates along with a more transparent political process. Partisans pick ideologues as candidates for office in party primaries because moderates don't vote in large enough numbers to propel centrists to victory. As Marjorie Randon Hershey noted in *Party Politics in America*, "It is the strongest partisans who are most likely to vote, to pay attention to politics, and to take part in political activities."[6] Citizens also allow officeholders to enact measures that favor special interests because they do not examine the voting patterns of their representatives and drive those who are corrupt from office.

Ultimately, in a democratic system of government, it is the citizens who have the power to decide which men and women will represent them, what legislation will be passed by their agents, and how the nation will be governed. With the political process currently controlled by the two conjoined parties who use it to benefit themselves, it is new leaders who are needed to mobilize citizens and take back the government from the ideologues and special interests. The Civic Alliance can provide these leaders and will be dedicated to educating citizens about how they can participate and reform the system. Schneck again:

... good citizens do not spring full grown from their private lives and they do not emerge complete from that nonpolitical, quasi-public sphere we call "society." Instead ... they are "cultivated" in unique, public, political spaces wherein they acquire the virtues, knowledge and pragmatism necessary for good citizenship.[7]

## Political and Civic Education

Robert Shogan observed in *The Fate of the Union*:

The purpose of politics is to express the often conflicting concerns of the voters. The role of government is to resolve these concerns equitably. To put it in the simplest terms, politics defines what people want; government decides what they get. For democracy to work, government must respond to politics.... political parties ... are the best means available for connecting politics and government, by providing voters with meaningful choices between policies and candidates, and for holding government accountable to the electorate.[8]

The parties, the political system, and the government have not been providing meaningful choices or functioning to the satisfaction of the American people. For the required changes in the equation to occur, citizens must be attuned to politics, aware of the problems that exist and how to address them. This is particularly important since they will be called upon to make sacrifices in the near future and must understand the reasons this is necessary. A poll in 2007 to determine Americans' knowledge about political issues was disheartening. It revealed that only 69 percent of respondents could name the vice president, 66 percent the governor of their state, 36 percent the president of Russia, and 21 percent the secretary of defense.[9]

Educating the nation's citizens about politics and government and encouraging them to become involved to a much greater extent should be a major goal of the Civic Alliance or any centrist third party. Hershey again: "More education helps people understand the complexities of politics and gives them the tools to get the information they need to make political choices."[10] Educational programs for the public can be supported by the party's endowment if this is legal, or perhaps through a foundation, by general funds, or by an affiliated organization. This initiative should be continuous, rather than suddenly springing to life around election times, and should be aimed at every segment of the population. All the media should be used in this mission to reach the largest audience. It should not focus merely on bringing party members and likely supporters to the polls, but on providing information to all citizens that they are unlikely to find on the web, in the usual magazines and newspapers, or newscasts and politically-oriented programs, allowing them to know the true state of the union.

The challenge for the Civic Alliance will be to present this information in a stimulating way to capture people's attention and keep them watching, listening, or reading. Rather than just reiterating what is occurring in the political arena, the information should explore background data and the reasons behind these events, along with their possible impact on American citizens, the country, and the world. This needs to be accomplished without slant or bias, even if what is being presented paints the Civic Alliance in an unflattering light. It is more important to maintain the public's trust with unstinting honesty. Currently, political messages consist of sound bites that are "dumbed down" by political consultants for an audience that is obviously not respected for its attention span or acumen. Politicians and the political parties need to treat America's citizens as intelligent individuals who can handle both positive and negative news and understand issues with some degree of complexity.

The format may vary with the medium used, the funding on hand, and the significance of the particular issue. Certainly, the Internet, social networks, blogging, and/or a constantly renewed informational website are inexpensive, effective ways to communicate with people efficiently and to keep computer-savvy citizens on top of events. For party members and others who are interested, regular email could be employed to disseminate reports. Since transparency is one of the tenets of the Civic Alliance, information sent to party members should be accessible to the general public as well.

On television and radio, brief spots could be used repetitively to get messages across, or infomercial-type programs could be broadcast on cable TV channels. Perhaps presenting a political program on the same channel at the same time each week might build an audience, similar to a weekly sitcom or crime story, as the word spread to friends, family, and beyond. Interspersed with current politics would be interesting vignettes of American history and explanations of how the government is supposed to work, pointing out constitutional conflicts and how they were resolved. To hold people's interest, the content might be "spiced up" with personal facts about various politicians as long as they were known to be true, for nothing seems to get people's attention as much as gossip about celebrities and their foibles. Corruption and ethical misconduct by political figures would also be highlighted. (Hammering away at these lapses might drive the public to clamor for reform.) It should be kept in mind that presenting information in too dry a fashion could turn people away. Bright, perceptive media personnel and exceptional writers who believe in the Civic Alliance's objectives to help develop these programs would be critical. It would not be helpful if citizens regarded the programs as boring history lessons.

Frequent polling of party members and other citizens would monitor the educational efforts and determine which methods were most effective in reaching people and holding their interest. If presented properly, party membership would grow as a result of these programs. Even more important would be to move apathetic individuals to become activists, with increasing numbers of men and women joining in the political process. The Civic Alliance wants to educate Americans of every political persuasion about politics and government, but the party would specifically target those who might be deemed moderates, centrists, or independents, as these people hold the key to reform and good government.

As much as the Civic Alliance will try to educate the American public about politics, it is important for its members to remember that communication must flow in both directions and the party must constantly educate itself as well about the needs and desires of the citizenry. The party cannot impose its will on its fellow Americans, but must be responsive to their will, hoping that citizens will become informed about the issues and participate productively in decision making. Ultimately, as John Green asserts in *The Politics of Ideas*, "the success of any party policy depends on how well it resonates with the voters."[11]

Another important Civic Alliance function should be to train citizens to become politicians: to run for office, work as staff members for legislators or government executives, or become political party administrators. Founding and endowing an "American Political Institute" would provide a postgraduate center to teach legislative and administrative skills and ethics to people contemplating careers in politics, instructing them how to delegate authority, how to negotiate with other players, how to maintain oversight, and so on. Other political parties would be welcome to train their members at the Institute as well. There are a number of ways this could be effected. Several universities around the country with well-regarded political science faculties could deliver particular programs, either in conjunction with each other or separately, granting degrees or certificates upon completion of the course of study. Some of the classes could be given over the Internet in addition to lectures at the universities. A physical campus for the institute in the Washington area could also be created to offer onsite classes. In addition to academic personnel, active or former politicians could be used as instructors. It might also be possible to emulate some of the MBA programs and give courses on weekends to working politicians who wanted to take formal courses in politics on a graduate level. The faculty would determine the number of courses and the time period required for a degree. Holding this degree would signal a significant level of competence to the electorate.

## Social Ethics and Values

Integrity and uprightness in politics are cornerstones of Civic Alliance doctrine. Although it may seem utopian and unattainable, this new party might aspire to even loftier goals, aiming to bring about an ethical transformation and change in the values of American society, rather than just in the political sphere. While this concept is an ideal and could be seen as being beyond its scope, the new party at the very least should strive to keep ethics and values in the forefront of public consciousness. Social norms in America are set by its most prominent and respected members—political leaders, businessmen and women, and recently sports and entertainment celebrities. Unfortunately, none of these groups provide positive role models for the nation's citizens, with cheating, lying, stealing, and other tainted behavior considered acceptable by many major figures. This is reinforced by movies and TV shows in which successful characters cheat or are corrupt. The credibility of institutionalized religion in modeling high standards has also been compromised by pedophile priests who were protected by their superiors, and other prominent religious figures who committed adultery. Parents and teachers are failing as well to adequately impress on children the importance of ethical conduct.

As previously shown, corruption and disregard of ethics in the political sphere is extensive. The mortgage mess and the recent financial meltdown indicate that the corporate world may be even more corrupt and venal than the political arena. Illegal activities and infractions by business executives are a recurrent refrain, with new choruses being added every day. Among the publicly known offenses are backdating of stock options, insider trading, excessive compensation of corporate officers by hand-picked cronies, golden parachutes for executives, bonuses for short-term gains from inappropriate transactions, falsifying data on corporate reports, bribery to gain contracts, and on and on. Some of these actions have led to criminal indictments, convictions, and dismissal from office, but often there have been no penalties at all. The malefactors have been able to walk away with huge pay packages along with contempt for stockholders and the public. What kind of message does this send to children and ordinary citizens?

The sports world is rife with cheating and illegal behavior, as the players of the various games that transfix the nation's citizens will do anything to gain a competitive edge, vying for public adulation and increased monetary rewards. The use of various banned substances by athletes to enhance performance is the most common form of cheating, though other infractions occur when opportunities present themselves. And celebrities display a predilection for conspicuous consumption and material goods, presenting these as worthy goals. Many entertainment figures abuse drugs and flaunt infidelity, with rap stars lauding violence, the use of weapons, and the degradation of women. Yet these individuals remain in the public eye as role models, the people who seem to set the standards for behavior, especially for America's youngsters. Unsurprisingly, a survey involving over 5000 high school athletes in 2005 and 2006 revealed that 65 percent of them (as well as 60 percent of non-athletes) were likely to cheat on examinations.[12] This is a sad commentary on the prevailing mindset of young people, and how the need to succeed has subsumed ethical attitudes and actions even among teenagers. It does not bode well either for ordinary social interactions, or for political and corporate conduct in the future.

How can the Civic Alliance, a mere political party, hope to bring about a fundamental change in society? It cannot do it alone, but can certainly be part of the process. The transformation would begin with the political reforms that have been outlined, with more inclusive rules covering government ethics, stricter monitoring of personnel, more powerful enforcement panels, and effective campaign finance reform. This would reduce government corruption and encourage honest and ethical political leadership. Stricter laws and severe penalties for corrupt businessmen would also be required, with greater oversight here as well. Sports and entertainment stars might change their behavior if the punishment for infractions were ratcheted up significantly, whether through criminal penalties or banishment from their venues, making the risks for illicit behavior much greater.

The most important element to effect change, however, would be education of both adults and children. America's schools should be teaching ethics and the results of bad choices to the nation's youngsters, pointing out the mistakes and transgressions of public figures. Though this has been considered the territory of parents and religious institutions, it is obvious that they have not been effective and that additional help is necessary. Perhaps public figures who have strayed as well as those who are ethical paragons (if there are any) could discuss proper actions and behavior on television programs directed to school classrooms, followed by discussions in these classrooms. Reaching adults on issues such as ethics and values will be more difficult, but needs to be attempted. Here again, the Civic Alliance could run infomercials and advertisements with public figures reinforcing the importance of integrity and proper conduct for all citizens to try and improve society. What is needed is more sharing, more philanthropy, more involvement in communities, and less narcissism, materialism, and selfishness; more concern for fellow citizens and less for matters of self-interest. Above all, there should be an emphasis on living lives within ethical boundaries, and not overstepping the lines in attempts to gain advantages.

With a foundation in place, a centrist third party such as the Civic Alliance can be constructed. Though the need for political change is urgent, it may take a few election cycles to build the structure of this new entity to the point where it can compete effectively with the established organizations to bring about the necessary metamorphosis. Activists hungering for reform should not be demoralized by the time required. A sound edifice put together block by block with painstaking care will guarantee the party's endurance in the face of the political storms that are bound to buffet it in the years ahead.

## References

[1] Baruch Spinoza, *The Ethics of Spinoza*, Citadel Press, Secaucus, NJ, 1976 (first published in 1677), 90–91.
[2] Tom Paine, *Common Sense*, Penguin Books, New York, NY, 1976 (first published in 1776), 63.
[3] Ted Halstead and Michael Lind, *The Radical Center*, Anchor Books, New York, NY, 2001, 6–7.
[4] Jean-Jacques Rousseau, *The Social Contract and Discourses*, E.P. Dutton and Company, New York, NY, 1950 (originally published in French in 1762), 29.

[5] Stephen F. Schneck, "Political Parties and Democracy's Citizens," *The Politics of Ideas*, State University of New York Press, Albany, NY, 2001, 144.

[6] Marjorie Randon Hershey, *Party Politics in America*, 11th edition, Pearson/Longman, New York, NY, 2003, 113.

[7] Schneck, 133.

[8] Robert Shogun, *The Fate of the Union*, Westview Press, Boulder, CO, 1988, 7.

[9] "Public Knowledge of Current Affairs Little Changed by News and Information Revolution," Pew Research Center of the People and the Press, http://people-press.org/reports/display.php3?ReportID=319.

[10] Hershey, 146.

[11] John C. Green, "The Politics of Ideas: Introduction," *The Politics of Ideas*, State University of New York Press, Albany, NY, 8.

[12] Selena Roberts, "The Road to Success is Paved by Cheating," *New York Times*, April 8, 2007, 1.

CHAPTER 7

# Proposals For A Prospective Platform

> ... all things come about by change; accustom yourself
> to reflect that the nature of the universe loves nothing
> so much as changing things that are and making new
> things like them.
> —Marcus Aurelius, *Meditations*[1]

The campaign platforms composed by America's political parties
present idealized versions of how they would like the government
to function and the laws they would like to enact. The planks of
the platform are usually constructed by an insular group of activist
members supported by the party hierarchy. They contain some pie-
in-the-sky ideas unlikely to reach fruition, the party's core concepts
to satisfy the organization's base, and a few practical objectives that
may be successfully initiated if the party attains power. The percentage of the platform's planks that eventually become the law of the
land, however, is relatively small.

Some of the concepts in this chapter, which could be the basis
for planks in a Civic Alliance platform, are rough ideas, while others
could be approaches to achieving some of the party's goals.

## Reform of Political Ethics,
## Campaign Finance, and Lobbying

The political scientist Larry Sabato and reporter Glenn Simpson
stated in 1996:

> ... the most fundamental and compelling issue on the na-
> tional need-to-do agenda is political reform. Americans have
> lost faith in the system that sustains their democracy, believ-

ing that it serves special interests more than the general citizenry. . . . voters have been promised political reform repeatedly—and the promises have been repeatedly broken.[2]

Polls showed that in 1964, 76 percent of Americans trusted the government to do what was right most of the time, but in 1976, after Watergate, that had fallen to 19 percent[3] and remains low today. A prime objective of any third party must be to regain the trust of America's citizens. There must be a sundering of the connection between politicians and lobbyists to eliminate conflicts of interest, cutting off the flow of money and the allure of future jobs to officeholders.

In addition to its own internal rules for party members, the Civic Alliance will push for stringent reform of campaign financing and lobbying to remove temptation from all politicians. In various polls in the last decade, 73 percent of Americans favored legislation controlling political fundraising and spending, and a ban on the use of "soft money" in politics.[4] The McCain–Feingold Act of 2002 was a step in the right direction, but never went further. (Unfortunately, in 2010, the Supreme Court in *Citizens United vs. the Federal Election Commission* ruled that McCain–Feingold violated First Amendment rights to free speech for corporations and unions and overturned the law's prohibition on advertising by non-party organizations in Federal elections.[5]) Following the 2006 midterm elections, with a Democratic majority in Congress, minor reform measures were passed prohibiting favors and meals from lobbyists to congressmen, senators, and their staff members. But ways to get around the new laws were quickly devised.[6] The most blatant sources of conflict of interest remained intact, with funds from lobbyists and special interests going to campaign war chests and political action committees continuing unabated. Though bundling of contributions by lobbyists now has to be disclosed, the law does not pertain to non-lobbyists, including many of the most influential "bundlers."[7] In addition, congressmen, senators, and staffers can still go to work for lobbying firms after only a year's hiatus from government service, though there are ways to evade even this minor restriction.

Money may not be the root of all evil in elections, but it certainly undermines the fairness of the elective process. An essay by Wilson Carey McWilliams noted that to redress the political balance ... requires "rebuilding confidence that democratic institutions are more than shams: a first item, obviously, is policy effectively reducing the power of money in elections."[8]

Micah Sifry has asserted:

> ... because of the lack of public financing, even the good people in Congress are forced to spend most of their time chasing checks from the rich. Is it any wonder there's more interest on Capitol Hill in cutting tax rates for the wealthy, deregulating the financial sector, and making bankruptcy law friendlier to credit card companies than there is in ... rebuilding crumbling public schools?[9]

The ideal way to control the influence of lobbyists and special interests would be for the government to fund all campaigns for federal offices, limiting spending and abolishing political action committees and campaign contributions. Doing this would extirpate the major sources of political corruption in one fell swoop and would deprive wealthy individuals of an advantage. This is not likely to happen. Opponents would raise free speech arguments against it, in spite of the obvious fairness of having all candidates spending the same amount of money on their campaigns. The special interests would certainly fight it, since it would mean a loss of power for them. Incumbent congressmen and senators would be reluctant to support this kind of legislation, since they benefit from the funding pipelines they have developed that help them get reelected. Given the Supreme Court's recent actions, a Constitutional amendment would probably be necessary for any restrictive measures to become law, making its chances close to nil.

Other approaches could work. One might be to further limit the amount individuals could give to political campaigns and strengthen restrictions on bundling. Individuals, companies, or lobbying firms whose businesses were regulated by the federal government or that had government contracts could be prohibited from contributing to campaigns. These measures would not have the impact of obligatory public funding of campaigns for federal offices, but they might help to curtail the influence of the lobbyists and special interests. Restrictions on independent groups such as 527 or 501(c) organizations that can spend unlimited funds in support of candidates who favor specific issues must also be enacted. These organizations fall outside of current campaign laws and with their contributions are able to profoundly influence election results and afford wealthy individuals inordinate power.[10]

The move of congressmen, senators, and staffers to work for lobbying firms and special interests at lucrative salaries when they leave office has been part of the Washington culture for decades. As part of ethics reform, a gap of five years should be compulsory from the time an individual leaves the government to the time he or she can take a job as a lobbyist or work for a special interest in a capacity that involves dealing with federal officials. A five-year period would make officeholders less likely to do the bidding of lobbying firms in return for the promise of future employment. The hiatus would also give ex-congressmen, senators, and staffers less clout with their former colleagues and other government personnel, making them less attractive as shills for special interests.

Both Republicans and Democrats have been able to deceive their constituents about ethics reform, knowing they can double-talk their way out of any challenges over this issue and that their actions will have no consequences. Though a third party can press for changes to end political corruption, the final say on whether or not a transformation occurs lies with the voters, who must become engaged and knowledgeable enough to make it happen.

## Impartial Redistricting

Currently, congressional and state legislative election districts are usually redrawn after a census has demonstrated a shift in population, but this can also take place at a legislature's discretion. Though a few states employ impartial entities to do their redistricting, for the most part the legislatures perform this function, with politics driving their decisions. Although there are redistricting commissions

(RCs) in 22 states, they have differing degrees of authority over the actual process.[11] Often these bodies are composed of elected state officials or are appointed by state officials and are not politically independent. In general, the party in power controls redistricting and does it in ways that maximize that party's advantage.

The shapes of the districts that result are often outlandish, as politicians try to capture or exclude particular ethnic groups or economic classes in ways that will make the offices safe for their party, ignoring obvious boundaries like rivers, town lines, and the like. This gerrymandering is one of the reasons it is difficult to defeat incumbent candidates. It also helps ideologues attain office and neutralizes moderate candidates. To be truly fair to voters and candidates, redistricting should be accomplished by independent, impartial groups with no political agendas. Since it is unlikely the legislatures will relinquish this power freely, voters will have to take it from them, either through referenda or by electing candidates who support the change. To date, some attempts to do this have met with limited success, as politicians and special interests have fought vigorously to defeat these measures.

Various formats for independent panels can work. The most important part of the effort is to choose impartial members who pledge that their efforts will eliminate political bias and be fair. Nonpartisan redistricting is essential to the democratic process and will be one of the goals of the Civic Alliance.

## Fiscal Responsibility

As previously shown, America has been living beyond its means since World War II, with the imbalance between revenue and spending burgeoning during the Bush administrations and with the fiscal stimuli of the Obama years. Politicians ignored the consequences until the 2010 elections, when control of government spending and the budget deficits became important issues. The fiscal problems that must be addressed lie in three areas: the trade deficits, the budget deficits and national debt, and the unfunded liabilities of Social Security and Medicare.

## Trade Deficits

A discussion of the trade deficits and foreign debt by Brad Sets-er and Nouriel Roubini in *Foreign Affairs* in 2005 noted, "Looking ahead, the US debt position will only get worse. . . . sustained trade deficits will set off the kind of explosive debt dynamics that lead to financial crises."[12] Although there are short-term benefits for Americans, including cheaper goods and decreased inflation, Americans do not fully understand that the long-term impact of the trade imbalance, as economists have publicly debated, could have devastating consequences. It could lead to a diminished standard of living for future generations as well as loss of control over the nation's economic institutions.

If currency markets were free, trade imbalances would self-correct to some degree, as those countries that ran surpluses would see the value of their currencies rise, while those with large deficits would see their currencies fall. As it became more expensive to import various goods, less would be purchased and domestic production would be stimulated. The currency markets, however, are far from free and to help reduce its trade deficit, America must exert more pressure on China, Japan, and other nations to allow their currencies to float freely. America has made threats in the past to act against them with tariffs on their products and other punitive measures, but has not followed through aggressively enough.[13,14] If the renminbi and yen did rise in value, American products would also become cheaper in China and Japan, encouraging their citizens to purchase more. Washington also needs to press these trading partners to further open their markets to US goods. Their governments have to support domestic consumption as well as exports to drive their economies, increasing spending by individuals and families. Sherle Schwenninger describes this as "middle-class-oriented development."[15] Defending intellectual property rights is also vitally important in order for the US to reduce its trade imbalance with China.

The Civic Alliance will see to it that the nation's interests are better protected in all these areas in dealing with countries that consistently run trade surpluses with the US. The party will also use tax policies and whatever other incentives are available to strengthen America's domestic industries as an antidote to the trade deficit. Buying local products also creates American jobs and reduces carbon emissions from transportation, which should translate to support across the political spectrum.

## Budget Deficits and the National Debt

The chairman of the Federal Reserve, Ben Bernanke, as well as many others, have warned about the difficulties America faces because of its budget deficits and spending on entitlement programs.[16] A past comptroller general, David M. Walker, declared on the television program *60 Minutes* as far back as 2007 that "the government's fiscal crisis is so great that it threatens the future of the Republic."[17] Walker claimed that the most serious threat to the nation was not from terrorists but from "our own fiscal irresponsibility." Though polls have shown that a majority of Americans see the nation's persistent budget deficits as a crisis or major problem, the solutions and willingness to sacrifice have varied.[18] A poll in November of 2010 reported that Americans favored reducing federal services over raising taxes to constrain budget deficits.[19] Another poll in January of 2011 suggested that taxing the rich should be the first step in controlling the deficit.[20]

The hundreds of billions of dollars consumed by interest payments on America's debt is money thrown away that is vitally needed in other areas. The Department of Education budget was $46.8 billion for fiscal year 2010;[21] Health and Human Services was $79.6 billion, of which $32.1 went to the NIH for medical research.[22] In contrast, the budgeted expenditure in fiscal 2010 for the Department of Defense was $660.4 billion with a supplemental allocation of $33 billion.[23] The national debt is a burden that will be borne by the nation's children and grandchildren if a way is not found to lighten the load.

Changing the pattern of spending in Washington and instilling budgetary discipline will not be easy. As Gordon Black and Benjamin Black have described:

. . . today in America we are faced with a political system where officeholders find it extremely difficult, and at most times impossible, to say no to the large, highly organized, and well-financed coalitions that pursue their own financial self-interest through the political structure. . . . Rather than compete for federal funds, almost every interest becomes insulated from competition, leading inexorably to a budget process where the pressure to spend excessively is overwhelming. The establishment of a priority of claims, which is vital to rational public administration, never occurs. The entire political system is "biased" in favor of greater and greater expenditures.[24]

This addiction to spending that plagues the nation's congressmen and senators, who try to placate the special interests as well as their constituents with funds for various projects, must be eliminated.

To attack the national debt, America has to generate a budget surplus again, as occurred during the Clinton administration. In order to create a surplus, either revenues would have to be increased or spending reduced. Most likely, both will be required. A start would be adherence to the so-called "pay-go rule" for Congress that the Republicans permitted to lapse in 2002.[25] This obliged legislators to balance spending on entitlement programs by cutting other expenditures or raising taxes. It also necessitated equalizing the revenue lost from any new tax cuts by reducing spending or increasing other taxes. Cutting the deficit by reducing discretionary spending, aside from defense and national security, would do little to lower the deficit or national debt, since this encompasses only a small percentage of the total budget. Former Secretary of Defense Gates suggested cutting military expenditures on unnecessary hardware programs,[26] but met resistance from Congressional members whose districts might lose some jobs. It will be up to the Civic Alliance to educate the public about this challenge and devise strategies to address it. Any possible way to manage the deficit and national debt will be on the table, including less spending, reducing waste, and increasing taxes if necessary. If taxes are raised, however, they must be structured to have the least effect upon the middle class, as the financial situation for many of them is already precarious.

In November 2010, the so-called "deficit reduction commission" established by President Obama with bipartisan representation came up with a plan to slash the deficit and national debt.[27] Their recommendations included significant cuts in discretionary and military spending, changes in the tax code that would boost revenue, increased charges for Medicare patients, raising the retirement age for Social Security benefits to sixty-eight, and higher gas taxes.[28] These suggestions were immediately opposed by legislators on both the left and right, unwilling to consider the spending cuts or increase in taxes, and unwilling to tell their constituents that pain and sacrifice were going to be necessary. Politicians may talk about the critical importance of reducing the budget deficits and national debt, but their ideologies prevent them from admitting that comprehensive action is required that incorporates both spending cuts and increased taxes.

(Under pressure to raise the debt ceiling in July of 2011, Congress did come to an agreement to cut spending in a number of areas, but it was insufficient to affect the national debt in a meaningful way. No increase in revenues was included. Standard and Poor's subsequently cut the credit rating of the US from AAA to AA+.)

## Social Security

Unfunded liabilities of the Social Security and Medicare programs are thought by most economists to run in the trillions of dollars. One estimate put the total unfunded liabilities for pensions, health care, Social Security, and other benefits at $44.2 trillion, with 80 percent of that from Medicare.[29] The Concord Coalition placed the unfunded liabilities of Social Security and Medicare at $39 trillion in January of 2007.[30] To date, neither political party has offered serious proposals to rein in these programs. In fact, the Medicare Drug Plan of 2003 only made the situation worse. As Ted Halstead noted in the preface to *The Real State of the Union*:

Instead of facing this challenge honestly, both parties colluded to make it worse by supporting a large-scale expansion of Medicare, the most insolvent of the entitlement programs. It is as if a fire truck pulled up to a burning house, only to spray gasoline on the flames instead of water. Their rationale is to pander to the elderly voting bloc while avoiding for as long as possible the unpleasantness of stating the obvious: The coming entitlement crunch will force us to cut benefits, raise taxes, or both.[31]

In addition to demographics, Social Security's financial problems can be traced to irresponsibility by the nation's politicians, squandering past surpluses to pay for tax cuts and government spending outside the program. But that is now water under the bridge. To attack the portion of unfunded liabilities represented by Social Security, there are three possible approaches: increase Social Security taxes, decrease benefits to recipients, or raise the retirement age. Payment of these obligations out of general revenues is not a viable long-term answer. Increasing Social Security taxes would put an onerous burden on the reduced number of active workers who must support the program and does not appear to be reasonable. Lowering benefits to the elderly would also not be acceptable, as many vulnerable retirees would be affected, diminishing their quality of life. However, expanding the amount of income subject to the tax would heighten revenue and affect only the highest earners. This might be a partial answer.

Raising the Social Security retirement age to seventy, with early retirement benefits available at sixty-seven, would be a logical way to give the program a firmer financial footing. Though this strategy would present some hardships for those who were unprepared, it could be introduced gradually to alleviate any difficulties. People are now living longer and should be working longer as well, but instead spend many more years in retirement than was envisioned when Social Security was enacted in the 1930s. Increasing the retirement age would also help meet the needs of American businesses faced with the prospect of a declining pool of skilled workers as baby boomers retire.

Thus far, neither political party has shown the courage to offer meaningful proposals to balance the budget, reduce the trade deficit, or attack the nation's unfunded liabilities. These financial imbalances must be controlled before irreparable harm is visited on the economy and the nation. The recommendations of the deficit reduction commission are a fine starting point. Similar proposals could be included in a Civic Alliance platform.

(The exploding costs of Medicare and its unfunded liabilities can only be addressed in the context of total health care reform. This will be discussed in another section.)

## Reducing Government Waste and Inefficiency

Addressing the federal budget deficits and national debt also requires a reduction in government waste and inefficiency. First in line for curtailment should be pork and earmarks, which have become iconic examples of waste while sullying the reputations of elected officials. House Majority Leader John Boehner and the 112th Congress have vowed to eliminate earmarks, but it remains to be seen how effective their efforts will be. Both parties are equally at fault for this shameful state of affairs, with senators and congressmen anxious to feed at the public trough and dispense money to constituents, friends, and special interests. This tradition must be changed. (Though members of Congress affiliated with the Tea Party movement have decried pork and earmarks, many of them still attempt to have Congress appropriate funds for projects in their districts, whether or not they make economic sense for the nation.)

Non-competitive and cost-plus government contracts should also be abolished to produce savings. Bidding on government projects should be the accepted way of doing business, with low bidders getting the work as long as they are believed able to perform the jobs. Corporations should be held to the letter of their agreements as well. If there are cost overruns, the companies should assume the excess costs. If they are late with the work, or unable to deliver what they have promised, they should be penalized. The government should not lend financial assistance or excuse corporate entities that have failed to meet their responsibilities. Billions of taxpayer dollars have been lost because businesses have not performed according to their contracts, which government personnel then revised to favor the offending firms. (Many of these government agents and top military officers later go to work for the same companies they are supervising, after letting them off the hook for broken contracts.)

Norman Ornstein and Thomas E. Mann noted, "One of Congress' key roles is oversight: . . . Good oversight cuts waste, punishes fraud and scandal, and keeps policymakers on their toes."[32] Tens of billions of dollars were lost or stolen in Iraq because of lax practices by the military and the Civilian Provisional Authority, resulting in waste and criminal activity.[33] Similar waste and inefficiency occurred in reconstruction after Hurricane Katrina, with Congress disregarding its oversight responsibilities. Oversight and accountability must be present at every level of government so that this squandering of public funds will never be allowed to happen again.

The tendency to use private companies to provide services for the government must also be scrutinized carefully to see if it benefits the agencies that use them as well as taxpayers. While it may reduce the number of full-time government employees, does it save money and is the work performed as well? Are the contracts subject to competitive bidding?[34] Spending on private contractors by the federal government almost doubled during the Bush presidency, from $207 billion in 2000 to almost $400 billion in 2006. (CACI International, a company hired to examine possible instances of fraud and incompetence by other federal contractors, billed the government an average of $104 per person per hour, about double the pay and benefits of federal employees that did the same job.) Private contractors are now being used in virtually every sector of government, from secretarial work, flying pilotless drones, budgetary tasks, intelligence gathering, tax collection, and so forth.[35] Thousands of them are working for various government agencies in Iraq and Afghanistan, providing security and performing military and intelligence tasks, with little or no oversight. Outsourcing of tax collection by the IRS has led to privacy and security concerns as well as questions about cost.[36] Hiring more IRS officers would have allowed the agency to bring in more than $9 billion in additional revenue each year, at a cost of $296 million, or about three cents on the dollar. Private debt collectors were projected to help the IRS realize about $1.4 billion over ten years at a cost of $330 million, or 22 to 24 cents for each dollar collected, with less total revenue generated. The choice of private debt collectors does not make economic sense, but from 2000 to 2006, twenty of these contractors contributed $23 million in campaign funds to politicians and spent additional millions on lobbying. The overall growth of private contracting for government work was driven by the ideology of the Bush administration and needs stringent analysis of performance and cost effectiveness to determine its proper role.

Poorly planned and unnecessary projects are also responsible for large amounts of wasteful spending. The Pentagon bureaucracy has had particular problems in allocating funds in ways that fit with the evolving functions of the military, seemingly frozen in a cold war vision of their adversaries. They have consistently asked for funding for big-ticket items like new jet fighters costing tens of billions of dollars, heavy artillery pieces that cannot be moved easily, advanced destroyers and cruisers and so forth, though there are currently no enemies that would require these weapon systems. Though former Secretary of Defense Gates moved to cut some of these programs, there was resistance from defense industries, their lobbyists, the military, and Congress. Given the US budget deficits, prioritizing in defense spending is urgent, as America cannot afford to have every piece of equipment regardless of cost.

Agricultural subsidies running billions of dollars a year is another area that must be reexamined. They also put America at odds with the World Trade Organization and are seen as hypocritical for a country that proselytizes for free trade. Particularly abusive is the support given by the government to wealthy corporate farmers that bleed the country of huge sums.[37] (Small family farms may be another matter, as they do not have the same economy of scale and may need some help to keep operating.) Though farm-state congressmen of both parties will fight any attempt at reduction, significant savings could be realized.

Another opportunity to constrain government spending and increase efficiency could come through the use of specific metrics of productivity for government workers and government programs. These would be used to evaluate which employees were performing at a high level and which programs were truly effective. Pay for government workers should be based on merit as well as seniority and if a person is not performing, he or she should either be demoted or fired. Similarly, there should be analysis of those programs that are open to competition to see how well they are working.[38] (There is a Coalition for Evidenced-Based Policy in Washington that has been promoting evaluation of social programs to determine their level of performance.) Some programs continue to be funded indefinitely, even if they are not meeting their original objectives and similar programs are performing better. Eliminating those that are not meeting appropriate benchmarks would save money and improve government operations.

The amount of waste, inefficiency, and unnecessary spending in the federal budget appears to total hundreds of billions of dollars, while spending in vital areas like education and scientific research is inadequate and the budget deficit soars. The goal must be more intelligent allocation of funds and ferreting out waste and inefficiencies.

## Forcing Oversight

A centrist third party will be able to force oversight and monitoring of government activities. Its representatives on the congressional ethics committees will make certain that ethics rules are enforced, and that congressional investigating committees maintain oversight of executive branch personnel. However, a permanent independent ethics commission should also be established to examine corruption and ethical transgressions in all three branches of the government. The members would be essentially non-political, similar to the current independent counsels, appointed to long terms by Congress (six, eight or ten years) with full investigative capability. They would have the power to recommend pursuit of criminal charges, lesser administrative punishments, or fines. The creation of this commission with appropriate authority could end the charade of congressional ethics committees performing these roles, with congressmen who may have been compromised themselves investigating tainted colleagues.

Congressional oversight (or special commission oversight) should also extend to government contracts to be sure work is being done properly and taxpayers are not being cheated. With far too many no-bid and cost-plus contracts awarded to businesses on the basis of connections rather than expertise or price, and with over-billing and cost overruns by these companies rampant, it is imperative that these activities be more closely watched. The Inspector Generals of the various federal agencies and departments should also be strengthened along with stronger shield laws for whistle-blowers to provide further assistance in the battle against waste and corruption.

## Health Care Reform

Realistic health care reform is critical to America's long-term economic well being. Costs per capita are by far the highest in the world, yet longevity and infant mortality, the indicators of the effectiveness of health care, are among the worst for developed nations. At over 17 percent of the nation's GDP and rising, the increase in health care spending consistently outpaces inflation and will have dire economic consequences if left unchecked. Federal health care expenditures are skyrocketing as well through the growth of Medicare, Medicaid, and various other programs. The 2010 health care reform bill (Affordable Care Act) passed by Congress and signed into law by President Obama does not adequately constrain spending and is inordinately complex.[39] Though Congressional Republicans have vowed to overturn this bill, they have not presented an alternative that will control costs, be simpler to understand, and will provide care for those who are currently uninsured or underinsured. Any future health care program proposed must consider all three of these issues—cost containment, simplicity, and universal coverage, as well as improving the quality of care.

The areas of health care where major savings can be found are unnecessary care, administrative expenditures, and overhead. Unnecessary care is driven by the fee-for-service method of payment, where the more a physician does, the more he or she is paid. This has to be changed. High administrative costs and overhead are the result of the complexity of the health care system, with multiple insurance companies having multiple plans with multiple levels of coverage. Though controlling costs is paramount in terms of America's economic health, the Civic Alliance will generate a reform program that simplifies the system, provides universal coverage, and improves quality. It can be done if the nation's politicians are willing to confront health care's special interests, who have been obstacles to change for the past century. The proposals offered below describe paths that could be followed, but are far from mandatory and any other plans that accomplish the same ends would be welcome.

A two-tier system of health coverage could be a starting point for health care reform. Tier One, or New Medicare, would include universal coverage providing basic care for everyone, with a single-payer system similar to current Medicare, eliminating most overhead. The money this strategy would save would be used to cover those who are now uninsured. As in current Medicare, premiums would be paid by those being insured, but would be low enough for most recipients to afford them. Those on Medicaid and others who could not pay the premiums would be absorbed into the system and subsidized by the government. There would be substantial deductibles and co-pay provisions to make the system more efficient and lessen overuse.

To supplement individual premiums and support the costs of Tier One coverage, all businesses would be required to pay health care fees to the government (instead of to insurance companies), linked to the number of people they employed. Most businesses would save money under this plan since the expense of health care would be spread more evenly and there would be minimal administrative costs. Hospitals and other providers burdened with the costs of emergency care for the uninsured would be reimbursed by patients now having Tier One coverage. The role of private insurance companies in this system would have to be determined. Medicare might have these entities bid to run its programs for defined periods, awarding franchises to companies for states or smaller districts. Benefits would be uniform and easy to understand.

Tier Two insurance would cover deluxe rather than basic care, a Cadillac rather than a stripped-down Ford. It would be offered by private insurance companies and function in a similar manner to the current Medigap or supplementary plans, augmenting Tier One coverage. To simplify matters, there would be a limit on the number of plans insurance companies could provide, perhaps ten to twenty categories, with coverage spelled out. This would allow consumers to compare oranges to oranges in pricing and benefits, instead of the confusing array of thousands of plans now offered. Those who wanted everything possible in terms of care available would pay for that privilege, as this coverage would likely be costly.

Health care reform would also include an independent Medicare Board to assess what treatments and diagnostic testing were beneficial. This board would be an independent entity resembling the Federal Reserve Board, its members nominated by the president for lengthy terms and confirmed by Congress. They would set policy for health care providers regarding the use of expensive diagnostic and treatment options, their decisions guided by panels of experts from each specialty. The board would also determine reasonable reimbursement for medical providers like hospitals and physicians, which is already being done for current Medicare patients. The board would monitor treatments and procedures as well to be sure they were being properly used, reducing excessive and unnecessary care. Physicians would be encouraged to be members of Accountable Care Organizations (groups of providers) or on salaries, as over 30 percent already are. But providers could opt out of the system and receive direct payment from patients or transact mutually agreeable fees with Tier Two insurance companies.

If Congress allowed the Medicare Board to negotiate with

drug companies and medical device companies, additional savings could be generated. Americans pay 30 to 50 percent more for medications than patients in other industrialized nations, in effect subsidizing the cost of drugs for their citizens. This differential could be eliminated if the restrictions on Medicare's interactions with the pharmaceutical companies were ended, lowering costs significantly.

Preventive medicine, which has the potential to extend life as well as improve its quality and reduce costs, is an area of American health care that has not received enough attention. At present, reimbursement is structured to pay more for the treatment of illnesses than to try to prevent them, which often entails one-on-one discussions between physicians and patients that can be time-consuming. Physicians are loath to engage in this kind of labor-intensive counseling because they are not compensated for it. Any new program of health care coverage should take this into account, as fending off chronic illnesses like diabetes, hypertension, and atherosclerotic vascular disease could result in major savings.

Many Americans strongly believe that the federal government is incapable of running a national health care program, that any plan instituted by Washington will be more expensive and more inefficient than the current system controlled by the health insurance companies. This idea has been promulgated by the insurance companies, pharmaceutical firms, and organized medicine, all of which have a strong interest in maintaining the status quo. To mobilize opposition, this group labels any proposals for universal health care backed by the government as "socialized medicine." However, both the Medicare and VA programs are managed by the federal government. They are much less complex and more efficient than private insurance coverage with significantly less overhead (and VA physicians on salary), making them less expensive to run and with a greater proportion of their spending devoted to patient services.

Notwithstanding the recent reform bill, health care overhaul is needed containing the three elements noted to be essential, with stringent control of costs critical. Basic health care should be viewed as a right of all citizens and not a privilege dependent on employment or financial status.

# Changing the Electoral College System

Two aspects of presidential elections are contrary to democratic principles and need to be re-thought. One is the winner-take-all allocation of the electoral votes in each state. The second is control of the process by the state legislatures, able to supersede the state's popular vote. Article 2 of the Constitution declares that to elect the president, "[e]ach State shall appoint, in such Manner as the *Legislature* [author's emphasis] thereof may direct, a Number of Electors, equal to the whole Number of Senators and Representatives to which the State may be entitled in the Congress."[40] Thus the Constitution gives the right to the state legislatures and not to the citizenry to pick the electors who will vote for the president.

By 1830, to increase the power of the established political parties, state legislatures decreed that whoever won the popular vote for president in that state would receive all of its electoral votes,[41]a winner-take-all system *not* mandated by the Constitution. (The electors chosen were under no obligation to vote for specific candidates.) This method of selecting a president has resulted in three candidates assuming the office who had lost the popular vote—Rutherford B. Hayes in 1876, Benjamin Harrison in 1888, and George W. Bush in 2000. (In 1824, before the winner-take-all requirement was established, John Quincy Adams won after losing the popular vote.) The Supreme Court when deciding *Bush v. Gore* in 2000 emphasized that under the Constitution, voters do not have the right to select the presidential electors and that the power to decide how electors were chosen resides with the state legislators.[42,43] The Court's ruling indicated that the legislatures could change the method of choosing presidential electors even after the popular vote had taken place and that they could designate the electors themselves.[44] As described by Professor Demetrios James Caraley, this means "that in the leading democracy of the world, its citizens still do not have a constitutional right to vote directly or even indirectly for the president."[45]

The winner-take-all aspect of the electoral system has led presidential candidates to write off certain states and abandon campaigning there if they feel their chances of carrying the state are small. Because of this, the three most populous states, generally liberal New York and California, and conservative Texas, along with a number of other states, may receive little attention in the presidential races if they do not seem to be in play. However, since the winner-take-all allocation of electoral votes was formulated by the state legislatures and was not written in constitutional stone, it could be changed relatively easily in each state by a legislative measure.

For the popular vote not to determine the presidency is archaic as well as unfair. Ideally, the Electoral College should be abolished, though a constitutional amendment would be necessary for this to happen. The smaller states, who have disproportionate votes under this system, would likely oppose it and states' rights advocates would object to power being taken from the state legislatures (as delineated in the Constitution) and given to the nation's citizens. (However, under the Constitution, senators were originally chosen by state legislators and not directly elected by the people until the Seventeenth Amendment was ratified in 1913.) As Alexander Keyssar noted in an article in the *Political Science Quarterly*, "Election 2000 and *Bush vs. Gore* made clear that a partisan state legislature could hijack a presidential election."[46] A constitutional amendment that removes the state legislatures and Electoral College from the mix of the presidential elections would be an affirmation of democracy.

Even without a constitutional amendment, however, the states themselves can guarantee that victory goes to the presidential candidate with the most popular votes. A move in this direction is already under way called the "National Popular Vote" initiative.[47] This obligates presidential electors in the states that enact these laws to vote for the candidate who has amassed the most popular votes nationally. As of the end of 2010, six states had passed this bill, along with the District of Columbia.[48] It goes into effect once states with 270 Electoral College votes (a majority) make it the law, assuring that the president will always be elected by popular vote. When this happens, candidates will no longer be able to concentrate their efforts in so-called "battleground states," but will have to campaign nationally to win the popular vote.

# Judicial Reform

Most judges are or have been active members of political parties and are either elected or appointed to their positions. To be elected, they usually run on party tickets and must raise large sums of money to conduct their campaigns. Subsequent decisions from the bench have been shown to favor the judges' financial sources, no matter how much they insist they are free of bias. Many of these judges are also ideologues, with views that have been forged in the furnace of party politics. If they are elected to their positions, they must be nominated first in party primaries, which tend to choose avid partisans.

The process of judicial appointments is also highly politicized. Whether picked by governors, legislative panels, or the president, judicial nominees often hew to particular lines of thought. This is evident on the Supreme Court, where there are conservative and liberal blocs, each voting the same way on almost all issues, with one or two centrist judges as swing votes that determine the panel's stand in individual cases. Unfortunately, justices on the Supreme Court and Federal Court of Appeals are appointed for life, giving them the ability to influence government policy for decades, regardless of physical or cognitive infirmities.

Judicial reform, to make the justice system fairer and more responsive, should encompass a number of measures.

First of all, lifetime tenure on the highest courts should be eliminated and replaced with a lengthy term of fifteen to twenty years. With average life expectancy having increased from less than fifty years at the time the Constitution was written to nearly eighty years, Justices are now able to sit on the Court for forty or fifty years or longer, even with faltering mental acuity. (From 1789 to 1970, Supreme Court justices served on average less than fifteen years.[49] Since then, the average term has increased to more than 26 years.)

Second, candidates for judgeships at all levels should be evaluated by independent bodies like the American Bar Association. This group currently submits an analysis of candidates for the highest courts to determine their qualifications in terms of knowledge, temperament, and character. Only those felt to be highly qualified should be considered for appointment to the bench in the future.

Third, judges who stand for election to attain their positions should receive public financing for their campaigns, adhering to strict spending limits for both the primaries and general elections. This would end judges' dependency on special interests for funding.

Fourth, judges' salaries should be increased to make them more competitive with the private sector. While compensation for public officeholders can never match the going rate in the general economy, judges should be able to live comfortably on what they are paid. Higher salaries will allow the recruitment of more competent, experienced people, improving the legal system.

Ultimately, it would be worthwhile having all judges appointed to the bench from a pool of individuals who are rated highly qualified by other judges and lawyers, as competency cannot be decided on the basis of a popularity contest.

## Tax Reform and Income Inequality

The vast majority of Americans and politicians agree that the tax system needs an overhaul, though there is a wide spectrum of opinion on what should be done. In this time of budget deficits and climbing national debt, should the new schedule be revenue-neutral or be used to reduce the burden of indebtedness? The explosion of income inequality since 1980 also needs to be considered before tax reform measures are enacted, since past changes in tax policy are a prime reason that the assets of the most affluent have soared. It must be kept in mind that when government policy increases after-tax income of the affluent, the extra money they receive is put to work to generate income. (This may be temporarily good for the economy as it provides funds that can be invested productively, but it is especially good for affluent individuals and families, as that money can compound wealth.) For example, if a family earns $100,000 yearly and has $70,000 in after tax-income, there may be little left to invest after living expenses. But a family that earns $1 million and pays

$300,000 in taxes with $200,000 in living expenses has $500,000 to invest. If this continues for a number of years at a seven to ten percent compounded rate of return, it does not take long for this family to accumulate significant wealth. Imagine someone who makes $10 million and has $6 million to invest each year, or $100 million and $60 million to invest. People can spend just so much to live, which means the higher the income, the more that can be invested and the more capital that will be accumulated. With this pattern over time, greater wealth will be concentrated in the hands of already affluent families unless new tax policy changes the formula.

While social engineering should not be an objective of tax policy, Americans have to ask themselves whether they want to see the nation dominated by an aristocracy of the affluent, a plutocracy, as is currently happening. The more a small percentage of the population sequesters great wealth and passes it on to their children, the more they will evolve into a hereditary privileged class and be separated from other citizens. The alternative is for people to succeed because of their own intelligence and hard work in the meritocracy the Founding Fathers envisioned.

A commentary by Clive Crook in *The Atlantic* noted:

> America stands lower in the ranking of income mobility than most of the countries whose data allow the comparison. . . . In America, more than in other advanced economies, poor children stay poor . . . rich children stay rich as well.[50]

Contradicting the nation's historical mythology, much of this restricted mobility is the result of America's tax policies over the last several decades. Do citizens want it to continue?

The government strategy for obtaining revenue through taxes is a hodge-podge of laws and regulations of great complexity that have been written and revised many times. There have been attempts to favor certain individuals and classes of taxpayers at various points, with loopholes, shelters, and incentives inserted into the laws, adding to their labyrinthine intricacy. That said, the types of taxes Americans now pay are very different than in the early days of the Republic, the initial sources of government income being excise taxes on alcohol, sugar, and spirits.[51] Then, for most of the nineteenth century, tariffs on manufactured goods provided the bulk of revenue. During the Civil War, an income tax was levied for the first time, with the Sixteenth Amendment in 1913 making it a permanent fixture.[52] However, only the richest Americans were subjected to this tax until World War II transformed it into a mass tax, encompassing the middle class.[53] But it did remain progressive with those having the highest incomes paying the highest percentage. (Currently, the total tax collected by America's federal, state, and local governments is 28.2 percent of GDP, one of the lowest rates among affluent nations.[54])

To determine fairness regarding the type of taxes and the rates that should be instituted under reform, one might look at previous policies. (It should be remembered, however, that fairness is in the eye of the beholder, with one's income perhaps influencing perception.) Though income taxes are still progressive, they are much less so than in the past, the top marginal rate having dropped from 91 percent in 1960 to 35 percent recently.[55] In addition, the corporate income tax, which was once responsible for nearly 50 percent of federal revenues, has declined dramatically as Congress provided various corporate shelters. On the other hand, regressive taxes, such as Social Security and Medicare payroll taxes, have gone up considerably, placing a greater burden on the middle class. In 2011, the Social Security tax rate was 4.2 percent for employees and 6.2 percent for employers, for up to $106,800 of income.[56] Because of this cap, those earning $106,800 and below paid a higher percentage of their income for this tax than those earning more, the difference increasing as income rose. There is also a Medicare tax of 2.9 percent.

Claims have been made that higher marginal tax rates decrease the incentive for people to work harder and earn more. However, studies have questioned this assertion.[57] In 1981, Congress cut marginal rates significantly, then raised them on the affluent again in 1990 and 1993. During the '80s and '90s, notwithstanding the dissimilar tax policies, there was little divergence in real per-person economic growth. Yet "real per-person revenues grew about twice as quickly in the 1990s, when taxes were increased, as in the 1980s, when taxes were decreased."[58] In the 1950s, tax rates were much higher than today, yet Americans worked just as hard to get ahead.[59] It is possible in fact that higher taxes could serve as a stimulus, causing people to strive to earn more by making them feel poorer.

Another question that should be asked is whether earned income (wages) should be taxed at a higher rate than capital gains and dividend income, as is the case currently. The top marginal tax rate on wages is 35 percent and 15 percent on long-term capital gains and dividends. While it may encourage investment and the productive use of capital, should the most affluent, who have the most investment income, be taxed less on that passive income than hard-working wage earners? There is also the matter of sheltered income in hedge funds and private equity funds, which tax laws allow to compound tax-free for wealthy managers in offshore accounts.[60] The huge fees private equity fund managers receive on the deals they arrange are taxed as capital gains, 15 percent, rather than as income, 35 percent.[61] In addition to the reduction in income tax rates since 1981, lowering of the tax on dividends and the availability of various shelters have allowed many individuals and families to accumulate huge fortunes.

Tax reform needs to address simplification, fairness, and generation of revenue, as well as the problem of the alternative minimum tax (AMT). With all the contrasting views on how it should be done, reforming the tax code is a gargantuan task. There has been talk of changing the progressive nature of the income tax into a flat rate; that is, everyone who was taxed would pay the same percentage of their income, probably at a rate of 15 to 20%. Depending on the rate chosen, this could be revenue-neutral, or lower or increase revenue, but those individuals with the highest income would pay the same percentage as those earning much less. There has also been consideration given to lowering income tax rates and making up the revenue loss with a consumption tax of some sort, like a national sales tax, or value-added tax (VAT). These would be regressive, hitting the lower and middle classes hardest, unless focused on luxury goods. (There have also been proposals for a steeply progressive consumption tax that would affect the most affluent individuals who spend the most.)[62]

Ultimately, true tax reform will involve a pragmatic approach and spirit of compromise, perhaps requiring a multi-faceted plan. Lower tax rates for the middle class combined with higher marginal rates for the affluent should be contemplated. Eliminating corporate tax shelters and lowering the corporate tax rate would probably increase revenue and shift some of the tax burden back to businesses. Perhaps these could be combined with a consumption tax of some sort to further bolster revenue and attack the national debt. Though it will reduce government revenue to some degree, another idea that deserves consideration are tax preferences (lower taxes) for individuals who choose to work in areas of strategic need to provide them with an added incentive. The professions chosen might include teachers, mathematicians, scientists, and the like.

The estate tax also has to be revisited if the accumulation of dynastic wealth is to be lessened. Minimal taxes should be imposed on those with moderate estates, which will allow generational transfer of capital. However, a highly progressive tax rate should be required for the very wealthy, with provisions to protect homes, family businesses, and farms. There is no reason why hundreds of millions or billions of dollars should be passed down from parents to children in perpetuity, concentrating the country's wealth in a relatively few hands. In actuality, only a small percentage of families are now affected by the estate tax and this will continue if only the most affluent are targeted. In 2003, 2,448,288 Americans died, but federal taxes were required from only 30,276 of these decedents, a paltry 1.24 percent.[63] Interestingly, the largest estates, those over $20 million, paid only 14 percent of their net worth in federal taxes. Billionaire Warren Buffett, an avowed capitalist and free-marketer, has spoken in favor of the estate tax, saying that "[a] meaningful estate tax is needed to prevent our democracy from becoming a dynastic plutocracy."[64] Though Buffett's estate would wind up paying a hefty tax, he believes it is fair and better for the country.

Other sources of government revenue should also be scrutinized carefully to be certain the American people are being adequately compensated for rights leased to private interests. These include royalties for mining and drilling rights on public lands and coastal waters, where some sweetheart deals have been consummated. The right of lumber companies to harvest trees, and grazing rights for ranchers on federal land should be reviewed as well. Also of concern are auctions by the FCC of the wireless spectrum to cell phone providers and other communications companies (such as radio and TV stations) that allow them to operate by paying the government for that right, generating federal revenue. (An increase in the gasoline tax will be mentioned in another section.)

In addition to new tax policies, thought should be given to collecting the hundreds of billions of dollars retained by tax cheats. An estimated $300 billion owed to the government goes unpaid each year, increasing the load on responsible taxpayers.[65] Besides unreported income, funds are lost to offshore havens for corporations and wealthy individuals, and abusive shelters and loopholes are overlooked on returns that are not audited. Both the IRS and Treasury Department have reported to Congress "that cheating among the highest-income Americans is a major and growing problem."[66] As mentioned previously, the IRS has cut back on personnel and contracted out some of its tax collection to private companies, who have not been very successful in recovering revenue.[67] Notwithstanding the antipathy to the IRS in certain congressional corners, the agency needs more agents and more audits of tax returns, rather than increased privatization. In fact, pay for agents should be increased to attract high-caliber employees who can uncover shelters and contest those well-paid attorneys in the private sector.

America has to find some way to eliminate her budget deficits and pay down the debt, increase education funding, and pay for military modernization. National security measures need to be enhanced. The infrastructure needs repairs. These measures require federal revenue which comes through taxes. Proper reform can make the process simpler and fairer.

# Jobs, Wages, and Manufacturing

Although the stock market rose again after the financial meltdown and the economy stabilized, this tide of good fortune did not lift all boats. Once more, the benefits flowed mainly to the very affluent, leaving many citizens stranded on the shore. Given the vast number of Americans who have lost well-paying manufacturing jobs and the white-collar positions that have disappeared, job retraining is essential. The emphasis should be on new skills in fields where there are shortages of workers, such as nursing and other health care positions, data entry work, computer programming, and teaching, to mention just a few. Whether retraining takes months or years of education, government support should be available. Either expanding wage insurance or extending unemployment compensation for laid-off workers could provide assistance while they were developing the skills to compete in the new economy. Low-interest loans should also be accessible for entrepreneurial types who have lost their jobs and want to start businesses. (Perhaps a corps of successful entrepreneurs could be enlisted as well to help these budding businessmen). But in addition to aiding those who are currently displaced, the future must also be considered. Alan Blinder, in an essay in 2006 on outsourcing remarked, "Perhaps the most acute need, given the long lead-times, is to figure out how to educate children now for the jobs that will actually be available to them 10 and 20 years from now."[68]

Poverty remains a tough nut for American capitalism to crack. Though the economy apparently bounced back from the recent recession before retreating again in 2011, the poverty rate reached 14.3 percent in 2009, a fifteen-year high.[69] While unemployment may be the prime factor, a decent minimum wage is also needed to fight poverty. The last legislation that addressed this issue passed in May 2007, mandating a raise from $5.15 to $7.25 an hour over two years.[70] Though many employers are against any increase, the current level is not a living wage. To avoid having new bills constantly coming before Congress and provoking battles, a reasonable base should be established at a particular point, then indexed for inflation from that time forward the way Social Security benefits are calculated each year. Opponents claim that a jump in the minimum wage will increase unemployment, as businesses will be more reluctant to hire people. But, as long their labor costs make economic sense, businesses will hire whatever employees are needed.

As we have previously shown, industrial policies have been successful in numerous countries, with governments supporting and protecting industries from foreign competition until they were mature enough to compete on their own. This strategy has allowed China, Japan, and Korea, among others, to join the ranks of premier economies, luring American manufacturing and destroying American jobs. There is no reason this strategy could not be followed in the US, though it is antithetical to the market-based economic theories favored by Washington. Predicting winners and losers may be difficult, but there are nascent industries with huge future markets that could be given more solid footing, among them nanotechnology, fuel cells, and solar panels. An expert board of scientists, businessmen, and government officials would choose those industries that were most promising and deserving of help. With the right support and more efficient factories, it is also possible that some of the nation's old-line manufacturing could be revived.

In April 2007, a number of American industrial companies, including US Steel, Alcoa, and Goodyear collaborated with the United Steelworkers to "preserve and promote manufacturing in the United States."[71] This Alliance for American Manufacturing noted that one-sixth of American factory jobs were lost over the previous six years and felt that it was critical to reverse this trend, as manufacturing and economic diversity are vital for prosperity. They wanted Washington to be more aggressive regarding unfair trade practices and currency manipulation, fearful that all of America's manufacturing base could be gone within a decade if nothing was done. Not only were they concerned about the loss of jobs, but felt that manufacturing industries are important for national security. The organization believes that the National Association of Manufacturers is part of the problem, advocating for the multinational corporations who are transferring factories and jobs overseas. Domestic steel companies and the United Steel Workers have also filed anti-dumping suits against Chinese companies, charging they were sending subsidized steel to the US below cost.[72] The Civic Alliance would pursue whatever measures were legally available to stop unfair trade practices and encourage the rebirth of American manufacturing.

## Immigration Reform

Dealing with the tide of illegal aliens who have flooded America would not be difficult if logic and common sense were employed to address the problem. Instead, a fog of emotion has blinded many Americans to realistic solutions, with hard-line conservatives calling for a forced exodus of 13 million undocumented immigrants back to their countries of origin. Those who rail against "amnesty" and refuse to consider any type of compromise need to take a hard look at what they are asking and start thinking in practical terms of what can be done. They also have to stop playing the issue for political advantage and explain to their supporters why the expulsion of all illegal aliens can not be accomplished. However, measures can be taken to partially satisfy partisans on both sides of the debate.

First and foremost, America's borders must be secure. Accomplishing this objective has already been attempted on the Mexican border,[73] but was abandoned because of significant problems and cost.[74] With thousands of miles on the nation's perimeter, it will entail considerable funding and manpower. The southern border with Mexico appears to be most vulnerable, but every boundary must be covered. While this will require a multi-pronged approach including sensors of various sorts, aerial and satellite surveillance, more border patrolmen, and fences in some areas, it must be done in an intelligent, cost-effective manner. When fully realized, this strategy should markedly reduce attempts at border crossing, but additional action is required. Every person caught trying to enter illegally should be fingerprinted and photographed, with these records digitized and stored in an accessible data bank, then he or she should be sent back across the border. If an individual is subsequently encountered by the border patrol, harsher penalties should be imposed.

With the borders protected, the problem of illegal immigrants already within America can be approached. Since deportation is not a serious option, what alternatives are open? As an initial step, Congress should mandate registration for all illegal immigrants, threatening onerous penalties for those who do not step forward. Each one should be photographed, given an identification number, and asked to fill out documents, so it is known who is in America, how long they have been here, what their work history is, and what future they envision for themselves. As part of this process, each immigrant would also be fingerprinted and given a photo ID card with his or her thumb print. (The need for a national ID card will be discussed in another section.) Because these immigrants violated the law, they would also have to pay a financial penalty determined by Congress. When these measures were complete, they would be known as "guest workers" and would have legal status.

As registration moved forward, businesses would have no excuse for employing people without verifiable documentation, either proof of citizenship or an immigrant photo ID card. Anyone apprehended by the police or government agents who did not have these documents could be deported or imprisoned. Having a database of registered immigrants, the government could proceed to the next step: separating guest workers who wanted to stay permanently and eventually apply for citizenship from those who were in America temporarily for employment opportunities. Both groups would be required to pay appropriate taxes and could travel back and forth between the United States and their countries of origin. However, the temporary workers would be able to re-enter America to work only for a fixed period (3,5,7 years) after which they would have to reapply for temporary or permanent status.

The permanent guest workers could either remain as resident aliens, or try to become American citizens, the latter path most likely for the majority. Because they had come to the US illegally, there would have to be a waiting period before they could apply for citizenship, so they would not gain an advantage and bypass those who had observed the law. Applicants would also have to speak English and pass tests in American history and civics. All current and back taxes would have to be paid and there would be an extra citizenship fee in addition to the previous financial penalty because of their original illegal entry.

With the borders secure and an immigrant ID card system in place, a certain number of guest workers would be given visas each year to fill open agricultural and business jobs. All new workers would have to obtain photo ID cards at American consulates or embassies specifying the period they could be employed in the US and they would have carry the cards on their persons at all times. Men and women hoping to immigrate and attain citizenship at some point would have to become part of the pool of applicants. With these proposals enacted as law by Congress and signed by the president, the number of illegal aliens in the US would plummet.

Tamar Jacoby in a *Foreign Affairs* essay on immigration reform noted:

> The only practical solution is to give these unauthorized workers and their families a way to earn their way onto the right side of the law. This should be done not just for their sake but also because it is the only way to restore the integrity of the immigration code, bring the underground economy onto the tax rolls, and eliminate the potential security threat posed by millions of illegal immigrants whose real names no one knows and who have never undergone security checks.[75]

A USA Today/Gallop Poll in April 2007 revealed that 78 percent of Americans were in favor of earned citizenship for illegal immigrants.[76] The compromise immigration bill that made its way through Congress in May and June 2007 had a number of reasonable elements, but was far from a perfect bill.[77] It was not able to overcome the opposition of the virulent anti-immigration forces. In 2010, leaders in business, politics, law-enforcement and religion came together in Utah to fashion what is called the Utah Compact.[78] This moderate statement of principles said that states should not play a role in immigration policies and that it should be left to the federal government. An immigration bill with the measures described above is important for national security and economic stability and should be supported by the Civic Alliance. (H1-B visas for students and scientists will be discussed separately.)

## Education Reform

America will lose its economic preeminence if education does not become a priority. Children must be prepared to function at a higher level in an information-based world. To do this, major reforms of the "education industry" are needed. The No Child Left Behind law was of minimal assistance, with inadequate funding and reliance on state testing to determine school and student progress. The Obama administration with Arne Duncan as education secretary has used "Race to the Top" and other innovations to try to raise student performance, but the jury is still out on their utility. There has also been no conclusive data by proponents of school vouchers, charter schools, and other alternative methods of education as to whether any of them boost achievement. In fact, studies have shown that education and student proficiency vary greatly in public schools, charter schools, private and religious schools, indicating that none of these paths is inherently superior.[79]

To assure the quality of America's schools and teachers, the federal government should mandate national standards of proficiency for all grades in reading, math, science, and social studies. And to evaluate students' and schools' accomplishments, uniform national tests should be given at least every three grades. This way, a true picture of progress can be obtained to see whether various educational initiatives are succeeding, as state testing has not been stringent enough to yield useful metrics. School boards, administrators, and teachers may not be happy with national standards and testing, but their protestations must be overruled if America's children are to be provided with a first-rate education. Though education has traditionally been a local and state affair, in today's world this is inadequate. Some uniformity in the texts used for teaching, instead of diverse local favorites, would also be beneficial. But if national standards of achievement are not established, any educational efforts will be doomed to failure.

Teacher competency must be dramatically improved as well, raising the skills of many of the current instructors so they are more knowledgeable in their subjects and better able to inspire students to learn. This should start with an overhaul of the institutions that train teachers, which have been found to have "low admission and graduation standards."[80] To prove their qualifications, teachers should also be required to undergo national testing, with those who fail the tests allowed to retake them after a period of additional schooling or self-study. A second failure would cost them their jobs. Frequent classroom assessments of teachers should also be automatic with dismissals of those who are not up to snuff. Though teachers' unions would balk, firing teachers, even those with tenure, should not be a laborious process, with classroom inadequacies or deficiencies in knowledge reasons enough. Continuing education in their fields with retesting at fixed periods should also be required. However, good teachers are not necessarily those who have taken pedagogy courses as much as individuals who are enthusiastic and know their material. Teachers do not necessarily have to come out of education programs and should be sought among disparate groups, such as professionals considering career changes, artists, writers, salesmen, and so forth, who are looking for new challenges.

In addition, teaching careers must be made more attractive to top college graduates, persuaded that the excitement of shaping young minds outweigh any negatives. A Teaching Corps (similar to the current Teach For America program[81]), in which college graduates are willing to commit themselves to three to five years of teaching, would augment career teachers with motivated young people. But in order to recruit and retain quality teachers, compensation must be higher, as salaries are far too low for a comfortable middle-class life. Many bright women and minorities chose teaching as a career forty years ago because other avenues were not open to them. And back in 1970, an attorney starting at a top firm and a beginning public school teacher had a difference in salary of about $2000.[82] By the turn of the century, that lawyer earned more than three-and-a-half times as much as the teacher—$145,000 versus about $40,000. Common sense tells us that this crucial profession should be paid more and enjoy respect commensurate with their importance to society. Besides raising base pay, the best teachers should also receive merit pay in recognition of their performance and to inspire their peers.

School districts scrimp and save on physical plants and teachers' salaries to keep local property taxes low. If America continues to fund and direct education through local school districts, it will never achieve a twenty-first-century educational system. While some wealthy districts perform quite well, others fail miserably in terms of graduation rates and student proficiency. The nation cannot allow this disparity between districts to persist, with so many students lacking the skills to function in today's world. In an essay on education several years ago, James P. Pinkerton observed that 45 percent of school funding was generated from local sources, such as property taxes.[83] The difference in per-pupil spending among large school districts was enormous, from under $4000 in De Soto County, Mississippi to over $14,000 in Elizabeth, New Jersey. Not surprisingly, testing has shown a relationship between overall student proficiency and spending per pupil.

Increasing the length of the school day and the length of the school year are ways to give students more instruction, but would cost money to implement. There is nothing sacrosanct about a school day of six to six and a half hours, or a school year of nine to ten months. Having school run eight hours and the school year ten and a half months could add forty percent more hours of instruction for each grade and would surely increase proficiency. In addition, the nation must restore physically deteriorating school buildings and erect new ones to make schools more welcoming places to learn, with enough computers and learning aides available.

Attitudes must also change among students, parents, and society at large if education is going to improve significantly. Recognition and glory must no longer go mainly to the athletes, cheerleaders, and "cool kids" who get by without studying, but to the "nerds" and good students who work hard and are accomplished academically. Starting in elementary school, high achievers should be lauded by school authorities. And programs for the gifted should be expanded. The nation's children must regard being smart and knowledgeable in a positive way. Perhaps these messages can even be transmitted before formal schooling starts, with targeted advertisements on children's television programs, cartoons, and DVDs that promote learning. In addition, there should be more of a social onus on cheating in school focused on those who are not studying. Students also have to realize that peoples' capabilities are different and that even with hard work, not everyone will achieve equally. The effort is really what is most important, as it can lead to a solid work ethic and possible success later in life.

In December 2006, a blue-ribbon bipartisan panel of education experts proposed a major overhaul of the entire American education system.[84] Among their recommendations were beginning school at age three and having high school end at the tenth grade, with students having to pass proficiency exams to graduate. After the tenth grade, students would enroll in community or technical colleges, or take preparatory courses for selective universities and colleges. With the National Education Association and American Federation of Teachers apprehensive about many of the suggested changes, little further has been heard about these proposals.

College and graduate education also needs to be revamped, though not to the same degree as lower education. Acquiring a college degree has become so costly that lower-income and middle-class students cannot afford the tuition and fees, and better access for them is necessary. Children from the wealthiest quarter of the population were four times more likely to go to college than those from the poorest quarter in 1979.[85] That had increased to ten times as likely in 1994. The number and amount of federal Pell Grants to cover the costs of higher education for low-income students must increase and other types of innovative loans and grants must be devised. The direct loan program administered by the Department of Education and guaranteed by the government[86] is simpler and less costly than loans made by banks and other financial entities and should be expanded. Every person with the qualifications and desire should be able to go to college.

The federal government should also certify that the level of instruction at all institutions is adequate and that students are acquiring the necessary knowledge in their fields. Too many for-profit institutions are designed to harvest student tuition rather than to teach remedial and college-level courses, and graduation rates may be poor. Educational experts should determine whether national testing of students is necessary or frequent inspections of colleges and universities by panels of academics could do the job. Currently, private regional bodies are responsible for accreditation, but there have been proposals for a National Accreditation Foundation to be legislated by Congress.[87] A special committee on higher education in August 2006 suggested that urgent reform was needed, including holding colleges and universities more accountable for students' performance.[88]

## Bolstering Science and Technology

To maintain a productive economy and be competitive in the new global world, the US needs more scientists, mathematicians, and engineers. Just as the nation's general education has to improve, training in science and mathematics must be upgraded to attract more students to careers in these fields. And scientists need to be viewed as heroes and role models in the schools.

Financial incentives would also induce more top students to choose scientific careers. While there is always the hope of hitting the financial jackpot with some remarkable discovery, most scientists, engineers, and mathematicians need help funding the long years of study and the bills that pile up. More federal grants and forgiveness of loans for students in these fields to subsidize their educations should be available and salaries for academics should be supplemented, particularly for those just starting out. (Current levels of compensation in industry are generally sufficient.) While most scientists and mathematicians select their disciplines because of intellectual curiosity and excitement about their work, monetary rewards can only make the fields more alluring. Greater societal recognition of scientific achievement should be forthcoming as well, with more awards, medals, and bonuses.

There should also be more federal support for basic research, which has been lagging in recent years because of policy decisions by the government favoring a market approach to science (and everything else). The government had hoped that industry would pick up the slack, but businesses tend to be more focused on immediate returns. Basic research results in long-term payoffs for society and it is shortsighted to be cutting back in this area.

US immigration policy also has to be modified to allow scientists and engineers as well as aspiring students to be welcomed into the country. Barriers to immigrant scientists since 9/11 have resulted in a loss of brainpower that will affect the nation over time. H1-B visas for scientists and students have to be easier to obtain and ways are needed to retain scientists and engineers in America after their education is completed. If these men and women are being trained in advanced scientific and technological fields, it is important to try to keep them as productive contributors to the nation's economy. American scientists themselves believe that visa issues for foreign scientists and students are a major hurdle for scientific progress and research in this country.[89]

## Energy Independence, Global Warming, and the Environment

Because America's energy policy has been shortsighted for decades, it is necessary for Washington to move aggressively toward energy independence. This will require several strategies. To encourage the use of less gasoline and more energy-efficient cars, some analysts have suggested a hefty gasoline tax[90] that might fluctuate inversely with the price of oil, maintaining the total cost of gasoline at a fixed level, perhaps in the range of $4 to $5 per gallon. Washington should also mandate even higher CAFÉ standards for all vehicles, with better gas mileage across the board. (The move in 2011 by the Obama administration to raise average CAFÉ standards to 54.5 miles per gallon by 2025 is a giant step in the right direction and was received positively by the automobile companies.) Providing government money for research on fuel-saving engines, fuel cells, and alternative fuels would all be helpful, with the market ultimately determining which technology was used. Ethanol has been pushed by a number of politicians as the fuel of choice, but the effectiveness of this compound, though favored by the farm lobby, is questionable. (It is also beginning to drive up the cost of many foods.) Currently, hybrids and electric cars appear to be leading the pack of fuel-efficient vehicles, but natural gas is another possibility.

Government subsidies will have to support production of alternative sources of energy for a while if they are to run American industries and heat the nation's homes. Without subsidies, wind and solar power are simply too costly to compete with oil and coal, but may be more reasonable in the future. Coal gasification and coal burning with carbon dioxide capture and sequestration are also too expensive at this point, but may come down in price over time. Nuclear power is competitive cost-wise and does not release carbon dioxide, but proponents have to deal with safety issues and the disposal of spent nuclear fuel. In the last decade, natural gas has been found to be abundant in America and can provide a clean, relatively inexpensive source of energy. However, environmental problems involving extraction have to be managed.

It is not clear which technology or technologies will provide the best long-term answers for America. Though there have been calls for a Manhattan-type project to solve the nation's energy needs, thus far the politicians don't seem to have a sense of urgency. Venture capitalists have stepped into the breach to some degree, with alternative energy now a hot area in which to invest. Creating efficient storage batteries is also receiving attention. The Civic Alliance would push for an all-out drive to develop alternative energy, with a cooperative effort between government and the private sector.

There is also the issue of educating the public about energy conservation, which has been neglected by the government. An emphasis should be placed on buying energy-efficient appliances and bulbs, keeping thermostats down, installing energy-efficient windows, adequately insulating houses, cutting down on unnecessary driving, using mass transit when possible, and so forth. The

Civic Alliance would make education about energy conservation a legislative goal.

The problem of global warming ties in closely with cutting back energy use and lessening the nation's dependence on foreign oil. Reducing emissions of carbon dioxide to halt global warming has become imperative and America should assume a leadership role in this quest. Unfortunately, whatever steps the US takes will not be enough to stem the tide, as the growth of developing nations like China and India will overwhelm any conservation measures. A unified approach more far-reaching and comprehensive than the Kyoto Protocol is required, involving all of the world's nations, as everyone will suffer the consequences of failure. However, America can set an example. Much of what it should do is simply what is necessary for energy independence. One approach to the problem being used in Europe is a cap and trade system in a worldwide market for carbon offsets and credits to counterbalance the use of carbon elsewhere. However, this type of system has been subject to fraud; a carbon tax would be more effective. And given the astronomical profits of the oil companies and the way they have been evading taxes and royalties,[91] it would make sense to increase their taxes and direct the money generated into research programs on alternative fuels and ways to reduce carbon emissions.

In addition to efforts to limit global warming, America must be protective of the environment in general, since it has to live with the consequences if it degrades or pollutes the land, water, or air. The Federal Clean Air Act and other environmental laws must be strengthened, and agencies like the EPA, the Interior Department, and the Energy Department must be given directives (and funding) by Congress on actions that should be taken. (However, before any regulations are issued to protect the environment and slow global warming, the impact on jobs and the economy must be taken into consideration.)

# Foreign Policy

America's physical and economic security should be the number one priority in crafting foreign policy, with the protection and security of its allies of great importance as well. In this context, nuclear nonproliferation should continue to be one of the drivers of policy, particularly keeping these devices out of the hands of rogue nations and terrorists, and monitoring and controlling nuclear materials. Strategic planning must take into account the nation's dependence on foreign oil, as a curtailed supply or price spike could have a devastating effect on the economy. The trade deficit and American reliance on certain nations for manufactured products must also be considered. In terms of conflicts, future actions must recognize that the US has limited resources and is dependent on creditor nations for financing. America cannot afford to throw hundreds of billions of dollars away each year on what seem to be endless wars; in fact, the nation does not have adequate military manpower to fight them. It will be essential to craft explicit plans for the fallout from any hostilities engaged in, along with a defined exit strategy.

In spite of its advocacy role in matters of human rights, America's actions in the Iraq war, Guantanamo, Abu Graeb, and its rendition and torture of terror suspects tarnished its moral stature. The US has stood against genocide and the slaughter of civilians for political ends (though perhaps not as strongly as it might have) and has backed programs to reduce disease and poverty in third world countries (though with a smaller percentage of its GDP than other developed nations). Given its recent behavior, it may be more difficult for America to use its moral authority to pressure other countries to act in ways it perceives as righteous. Nevertheless, it should continue to hew to this line. It is possible that at some point in the future America will regain its lost stature and its voice will resonate.

In addition to extricating itself from Iraq, one of the first items on the nation's to-do list should be a more vigorous effort to close the open wound of the Israeli-Palestinian conflict. With US actions seen by the Arabs as strongly favoring the Israelis, it is in America's best interest to take a more even-handed approach, forcing the Israelis to adhere to the commitments they make. With the reservoir of hatred that now exists on both sides and the unwillingness of Hamas and other groups to recognize Israel, it may not be possible to bring about a lasting peace. But America has tremendous leverage with the Israelis it has not used that might make a difference in peace talks.

As a lesson from the debacle of Iraq, preemptive war should no longer be at the forefront of American policy unless the government is certain of an acute threat. Containment of America's enemies in conjunction with its allies has worked in the past and might work in the future in many situations. And negotiations with nations considered enemies may yield results and are always worth trying. On the other hand, the US cannot allow terrorists free rein to train and plan attacks. But if war is necessary, true multilateralism is important to share the burdens and give the nation's ventures more credibility. America has not been handed a mission to forcefully spread democracy throughout the world. That said, there is nothing wrong with lending support to fledgling democracies and democratic institutions in other countries. And trade relations with other nations should be based on equal access to markets, protection of intellectual property, and no currency manipulation.

In fighting terrorism, part of America's efforts must be directed to eliminating conditions conducive to its growth. The seed will not sprout if the ground is dry and unfertile. This means attempting to reduce poverty and unemployment in countries where terrorism is endemic. Having young men sitting around with no future and nothing to do makes recruitment easy for jihadists. Supporting public schools that encourage a broad education in at-risk nations will also help students question fundamentalist ideology. The US should also favor responsive leaders who promote options for their citizens other than violent struggle. This is particularly a problem in the Middle East where there are populist uprisings against autocratic leaders whom America has previously backed.

Foreign policy, as all of the government's endeavors, should be based on pragmatism and common sense, with no place for knee-jerk reactions. Though America is powerful militarily and economically, it is not omnipotent and needs to work with other countries to bring its visions to fruition. This entails the US heeding advice and feedback from these countries. Humility instead of arrogance should be its *modus operandi* as it tries to get things done. America can always become hard-nosed if its national interests are threatened and conciliation is not producing an acceptable resolution. And in its dealings with the rest of the world, it should keep in mind that perception counts almost as much as the truth in this era of instantaneous communication. Statesmen are needed who can wipe away the layers of grit and calumny that have tarnished the image of America and present a fresh picture of the nation to the world.

## National Security

The most effective way to enhance America's national security is to remove politics from the equation. Unfortunately, this may be difficult with a Congress responsible for funding and not disbursing enough, often specifying where and how funds should be used, and failing to provide proper oversight. Intelligence estimates and risk assessment should be the basis of measures taken in regard to national security by any government body.

In considering national security needs, both domestic requirements (protecting the homeland) and the use of military power overseas are important. Protecting America at home falls under the aegis of the Department of Homeland Security, the Department of Justice and the FBI, various other law enforcement organizations, the CIA, and other intelligence agencies. These federal agencies and departments work with state and local officials to safeguard the lives of American citizens, important landmarks, crucial infrastructure, plants, and equipment. It is obvious, however, that the nation has neither the manpower nor resources to adequately protect everyone and everything at every moment. Therefore, decisions about how and where to distribute funds and personnel are crucial.

For effective domestic national security, three areas need focused attention. The first is supplying biometric identification cards for workers in sensitive industries, including chemical and nuclear personnel, airport and other transportation workers, truckers of hazardous chemicals, and infrastructure workers. The second is to continuously upgrade the computer systems of the nation's intelligence agencies, particularly those of the FBI, which are apparently still lagging. The third is improvement in human intelligence capabilities. This means having enough operatives and translators who speak Arabic, Pashto, and Farsi to work with US agencies domestically and internationally. It may also require hiring operatives with repugnant backgrounds or objectionable characteristics because they are able to infiltrate terrorist organizations and supply information. In addition, the best and the brightest from American universities should be recruited to join the nation's intelligence team. The US must do whatever can be done to increase the flow of HUMINT—human intelligence—to keep America a step ahead of its terrorist adversaries.

Maintaining national security also entails the ability to project power abroad to keep enemies at bay and fight terrorists wherever they might be. Unfortunately, the wars in Iraq and Afghanistan have degraded the nation's military personnel and equipment, making another major conflict difficult to fight if the need arises. This situation must be corrected. The military is also having trouble retaining junior officers and NCOs because of the hardships they have had to endure in repeated deployments out of country. This has generated problems as well for National Guard troops and reserve forces, whose families and careers have been disrupted. If America is going to depend on voluntary enlistment to maintain a professional military to fight its wars, it must make service more enticing, not only from a financial standpoint but in terms of tours abroad and family relationships.

Because of the overall costs of the military, funding weapons systems and initiatives of the different services that often seem in competition with each other must be done judiciously. Some equipment in the pipeline seems more appropriate to fighting the Cold War than guerillas and insurgents. To win the kinds of wars that seem most likely in the next decade, America needs to provide the types of weapons that would be most useful and to increase the number of special forces, infantry, and marines. In 2006, President Bush acknowledged that the wars had overstretched the armed forces and that providing enough men for the missions at hand was difficult.[92] (There were 507,000 soldiers and 180,000 marines on active duty. In the 1970s and '80s, the army alone had about 800,000.) A reevaluation of the military budget could lead to substantial savings in addition to providing strength in the proper areas. In this dangerous age, America needs the most sophisticated, capable military in the world, large enough yet agile enough to engage enemies on multiple fronts.

## National Identification Card

When considering security and immigration issues, biometric identification cards are an essential element. However, libertarians on the right and civil liberties advocates on the left oppose national ID cards, fearing increased surveillance and encroachment on privacy. These fears are misguided and overblown, with common sense favoring these cards for a host of reasons. With the present degree of mobility throughout the world and the ability to counterfeit documents, biometric identification cards are the only way the nation can be sure who someone actually is, and who may be responsible for criminal acts and terrorism.

The national ID card envisioned would include a photograph and biometric data, either a fingerprint, iris scan, or both. An embedded chip could also contain significant medical data: blood type, allergies, medications, past history, imaging, other tests, in addition to next of kin, emergency contacts and phone numbers, birth date, and Social Security number. Though not its primary reason, the ID card could be invaluable from a medical standpoint. More rapid transfusions could be given after trauma, and allergic reactions and drug interactions could be avoided. Many tests and imaging would not have to be repeated and treatments could be started sooner. The data would be updated at intervals, enhancing medical care and allowing considerable savings for both patients and the health care system.

In terms of national security, the cards would provide an obstacle for terrorists and keep track of immigrants in the country. (As mentioned previously, workers in critical industries would be required to have these cards whether or not they became mandatory for every adult.) The cards would also help keep out illegal immigrants as they would have difficulty obtaining work without them. And crime would be deterred by these cards if used with a national data base. Policemen would immediately know a person's criminal history and whether there were outstanding warrants. Pedophiles and sex offenders would be easier to watch and control when they were released from jail.

(The Taiwanese government has used biometric ID cards to streamline the process of government and make life easier for its citizens.[93] The embedded chips in their cards can be scanned by computers for identifying data, allowing Taiwanese to pay taxes and fees online, as well as apply for driver's licenses, property titles, and other documents.)

The potential for abuse with national ID cards is minor. Protection could be built in as part of any law that authorized their use and provided funding. It would probably take several years to set up the apparatus, bureaucracy, and technology for these cards, falling under the aegis of the Department of Homeland Security. Those in opposition should keep in mind that surveillance and loss of privacy is already a fact of life. In addition to cameras in public places, there are radio-frequency identification (RFID) sensors that monitor cars at bridges and tollbooths, global positioning systems that can locate cell phones, credit cards that can survey how and where men and women spend their money, and various credit rating systems. These have not infringed upon liberties, nor made Americans less free. National ID cards will play no role in people's daily lives unless they engage in suspicious behavior, and will result in no hardships for American citizens. They are a reasonable and practical response to the threats Americans must live with daily and could make the question of illegal immigration moot.

In 2005, Congress passed a law called the Real ID Act, a recommendation of the 9/11 Commission, mandating the creation of a standardized driver's license to be employed in all states by 2013.[94] Even this is being resisted because of the cost and difficulty in implementation, with the states wanting the federal government to pick up a greater portion of the expense. There are also constitutional issues that have been raised by a number of organizations and states. Though applicants have to prove their identity and legal status with government-issued documents, the cards do not require secure biometric identification, and the law should be amended to do this.

## Infrastructure

As with America's unfunded liabilities and national debt, neglecting the maintenance of the nation's infrastructure will leave the job in the lap of succeeding generations. A crumbling infrastructure will damage the economy, and delays in funding will result in expenditures over and beyond what was originally required, as restoration of some elements will no longer be possible. Roads, bridges, tunnels, levees, dams, ports, and so forth, need repair and replacement, and the electric grid and broadband connectivity need to be expanded. And studies have shown that public investment in infrastructure increases productivity.[95] Although a portion of the blame for the neglect of infrastructure falls upon state and local governments, the lion's share rests with Congress, reluctant to take any action that might raise taxes or increase the national debt. President Obama has emphasized the need to upgrade America's infrastructure to aid the economy, but Congress has remained resistant. Part of America's global advantage in the past has been the quality of its infrastructure. At a time when worldwide competition is escalating, it is critical to the nation's future to preserve and augment its infrastructure to keep pace with America's expanding population and economy. Politicians need to think more like businessmen, understanding that investing money in physical infrastructure today will yield greater growth for the economy down the line.

# Universal National Service

National service for Americans has been considered at times in the past in different contexts without receiving much interest from the established political parties and power centers or support among the general population. During the Depression, the federal government devised a number of programs like the Civilian Conservation Corps and Works Progress Administration to provide gainful employment and boost morale, though this was not envisioned to enlist every citizen for a fixed period. Conscription for the military during World War II included the vast majority of able-bodied men, but was only temporary, in a particular time of peril. A number of countries have experimented with service for young people, but joining (except where there is a security need such as in Israel) is for the most part optional.[96]

Currently, there are a number of voluntary programs in the United States under the aegis of AmeriCorps that engage people to participate in different types of service. They seek specific skills that fit with the objectives of individual programs, and all ages and backgrounds can enroll. The website of AmeriCorps notes that its members address certain needs in American communities, including tutoring and mentoring disadvantaged youth, fighting illiteracy, improving health services, building affordable housing, teaching computer skills, cleaning parks and streams, managing or operating after-school programs, helping communities respond to disasters, and building organizational capacity.[97]

AmeriCorps is part of the Corporation for National and Community Service, a federal agency that also manages Senior Corps and Learn and Serve America. Members can obtain a small living allowance and can earn an education award to help pay for college or graduate school, or to repay student loans. Over 1.5 million citizens are involved with these programs in some capacity each year. The Peace Corps is a separate entity started by President John F. Kennedy in 1960, sending Americans to foreign lands to live among and work with their citizens, teaching various skills and assisting on different projects.

Mandatory national service for all Americans for a period of twelve months, fulfilled between ages eighteen and twenty-six, is an ideal worthy of attention. At present, only volunteers in the military serve their country, with the poor and lower-middle-class over-represented. If this new measure were enacted, it would mean everyone would be obligated to spend time in service to America, invoking a sense of shared sacrifice. Feelings of community would grow and patriotism increase. It would also end the tendency toward isolation and self-involvement of many young people. Living in barracks or dormitories could be a leveling experience for corps members, diminishing some of the narcissism and feelings of self-importance common in the upper-middle and wealthy classes. Delaying the quest for financial rewards and mingling with individuals from all cultures, social groups, and educational backgrounds might also make some of the nation's high strivers less materialistic and more tolerant. Part of the program would be educational, with classes on civics and American history required of everyone. Topics related to health might also be offered. The classes could be dispersed throughout the time of service or given in a one- or two-week bloc. In addition, there could be remedial classes for those corps members who were deficient in reading, math, and other basic skills, perhaps helping them to obtain general high school diplomas.

National service could be broken down into specific organizations to which young people could apply to fulfill their obligations. These might include the Teach America Corps, the Health Corps, the Build America Corps, the Conservation Corps, the Auxiliary Police Corps, the Computer Corps, the Peace Corps, and so on, as well as the various branches of the military. Though AmeriCorps now covers many of these areas, there would be a quantum leap with mass involvement under national service, producing a much greater societal impact. Perhaps the new program might also be called AmeriCorps, with the existing organization being absorbed into the newer, larger one.

(In addition to AmeriCorps, there is also the Jobs Corps created by President Lyndon Johnson during the '60s as part of his War on Poverty, to help impoverished young people earn a diploma and learn a trade.[98] In 2006, approximately 60,000 low-income youths joined the Jobs Corps, 75 percent of whom had not graduated from high school. Though 30 percent leave this voluntary program during the first two months, the majority of those remaining are able to obtain a GED, a regular high school diploma, or certification in a trade, the average stay being close to a year. Obviously, those in the Jobs Corps are not doing it to serve their country but to better themselves and improve their prospects. However, in becoming more productive members of society they are also helping America, and participation in the Jobs Corps would be acceptable in lieu of national service.)

Individuals who deferred their service until after college and joined the Teach America Corps could be used as teachers or aides in elementary and high schools, supplementing professionals. They could work with small groups of disadvantaged or challenged students, perhaps even on a one-to-one basis when necessary. To enhance learning and improve student achievement, they could flood the worst-performing schools. Perhaps a number of these "temps" might even be inspired to change careers and teach permanently. Because computers and the Internet are such vital tools in today's world, young people in the Computer Corps who were especially adept could be used to train those who were computer-illiterate or functioning at a low level. This could be done within the school system or out in the community, including older people who were anxious to learn. (Perhaps the computer industry could team up with the government to help those living in poverty acquire low-cost computers and access to the Internet.)

Those joining the Health Corps could function as nurse's aides in hospitals or nursing homes, or as home health aides. Some might choose to work in community health centers educating people about nutrition, proper hygiene, and disease prevention. They might also be trained to give inoculations and gather useful medical information on the prevalence of diseases and risk factors. Some might help with simple duties as receptionists, translators (if they were proficient in another language), or data entry. The Conservation Corps would take men and women who wanted to work outdoors, either in rural or urban areas. They could aid conservation in the national parks and forests, or assist in keeping the cities clean. Those interested in construction might join the Build America Corps and help erect housing for low-income people. The Auxiliary Police Corps would take those who wanted to act as police aides in the cities, freeing regular policemen from routine chores. They could also work in community centers or run athletic leagues for teenagers and different kinds of clubs to keep kids off the streets. The Peace Corps would allow qualified young Americans to serve abroad in various roles.

Because universal national service would be compulsory for all men and women, more of them might choose the military as a way to meet their obligations. Recruitment for the armed services would thus be enhanced, with more educated personnel choosing to enlist. Though service in the military would remain voluntary, there would be a much larger pool of potential enlistees, making it easier to maintain troop strength at appropriate levels.

Though universal national service for all competent, healthy young adults would be the goal, there would have to be exceptions. Individuals with significant physical, mental, or emotional difficulties would be excused as would incarcerated criminals or those with a history of violent crimes. In addition, teachers, or those studying to become teachers, would be excluded if they committed themselves to work in that profession for at least five years. People involved in other critical fields, such as engineering, math, or science would also be able to opt out, again with a minimum commitment of five years of work in those disciplines. Doctors, nurses, and other health professionals could get deferments to complete their studies, with the agreement that they would then practice for at least three years in underserved areas of the country designated by the Health Corps.

Currently, all male citizens and aliens living in the United States are supposed to register with Selective Service when they reach age eighteen in case the draft is ever reinstituted. If national service was enacted, both men and women would have to register.

The undertaking would be a massive enterprise from an administrative standpoint, and would probably require at least several years of preparation. Arrangements would have to be made to house and feed millions of young people, obtain some sort of uniforms and identification cards for them, and provide supervision and instruction. Having the enrollees remain within their geographical regions might make the tasks somewhat easier. There would also be the matter of stipends for participants, salaries for the permanent workers, and daycare for the children of young parents. It would probably be best to start it incrementally, perhaps making it voluntary at first, then mandatory when the kinks were worked out. In America's competitive society, spending time in national service would not put any individual at a disadvantage, since everyone would be participating. National service would forge better citizens and make America stronger, more unified, and more productive.

## Guns and Public Safety

Because social issues in America are so contentious, with no readily apparent answers to bridge the public divide, most should be left in abeyance by the Civic Alliance until pressing economic and national security problems are fully addressed. However, though gun rights are one of the most divisive social questions, current gun laws need to be modified because of the threat to public safety. The recent massacre in Tucson by a crazed gunman who killed six innocent people and critically wounded Representative Gabrielle Giffords is but one of a series of violent episodes that have not generated federal laws to protect the public, including the mass killings at Columbine High School in Colorado and Virginia Tech, multiple murders in the workplace by disgruntled employees, the assassinations of John and Robert Kennedy and Martin Luther King, the shooting of President Reagan and Governor George Wallace, and too many others to mention. These are in addition to violent street crimes and gang wars involving guns. Gun advocates repeat the mantra that "guns don't kill, people do" to try to negate moves to restrict gun ownership. But it is the easy availability of particular types of guns that is responsible for much of the carnage, and measures must be taken to deal with this situation.

While the meaning of the Second Amendment of the Constitution may be open to some debate (whether the people's right to bear arms is within the context of a militia or an individual right), the ability of citizens to own guns has been traditional in America and is not going to change. On the other hand, there is no reason there should not be some commonsense limitations imposed, especially since a large majority of citizens support curbs, according to polls taken over the years. A CBS/New York Times poll from January 15–19, 2011 after the Tucson shootings showed 46 percent desirous of stricter guns control laws, 13 percent less strict, and 38 percent content with the status quo.[99] However, a majority of 63 percent favored a nationwide ban on assault weapons and a similar margin supported a ban on high-capacity magazine clips.

Translating these goals into law is difficult because of the rabid opposition of the National Rifle Association and gun lobby, who have instilled fear in legislators sympathetic to any restrictions related to guns. Representing only a small minority, this organization has had inordinate power, contributing campaign funding and positive and negative advertising for and against those who agree or disagree with them. This explains why Congress did not renew the assault weapons ban, which expired in 2004. Though having guns for hunting and self-protection is understandable, there is no reason for individuals to own assault weapons, sniper rifles, high-capacity magazine clips, rocket launchers, or grenades. The Civic Alliance would introduce and actively support laws with the above limitations while at the same time reaffirming citizens' rights to own guns for recreational use and protection. The Alliance would also institute more stringent checks to prevent felons, terrorists, drug users, and those with mental instability from obtaining weapons. Rigid licensing requirements for gun owners and weapons should be required as well to help law enforcement officers solve crimes where guns are employed. And special attention should be paid to regulating gun dealers who supply the weapons used by Mexican drug gangs, most of which are purchased in the US.

# Realizing the Platform's Planks

To realize any of the objectives of the centrist third party's platform, the partisan gridlock that exists in Washington would have to be transcended and the political system transformed. This would also entail eliminating the fealty that has kept politicians in thrall to the demands of the special interests and ending the culture of corruption that has infected governmental bodies. At some point, the spigot on the financial pipeline leading from the lobbyists and special interests to legislators and government officials would have to be turned off and restrictions on funding enacted. It can be anticipated that the Republicans and Democrats would not accept this agenda without a fight. They might even join forces temporarily to try to maintain their advantage. But their natural enmity would make it difficult for them to remain as partners, and a third party would have a strong lever to pry them apart. With even a small representation in Congress, this new entity would probably hold the balance of power between the two established parties and so could determine which of the two would be dominant. This would give it tremendous bargaining power until it achieved majority status.

In addition to its efforts to end the *quid pro quo* relationship between the special interests and politicians, the centrist third party could be a moderating force in American politics, softening the sharp ideological edges of the left and the right that have made it so difficult to enact important legislation. Conservatives and liberals cannot even agree about how to approach many issues, and measures often do not even reach the starting gate to allow a debate to take place. With a third party offering a middle position on many bills, its members could work with both sides to shape legislation congruent with its beliefs, using the Republicans one time to form a majority and the Democrats another time. Since the number of Republicans and Democrats in the House and Senate is usually fairly even, control of the legislative agenda would remain in the hands of the third party as the swing bloc in Congress.

As previously noted, the defining characteristic of this new party will be its pragmatism and willingness to work with any group to get things done. It will not be wedded to ideology or set beliefs about how the government should be run and society structured. There will be no dogma about the right or wrong way to do things, no insistence that government control of an action is good or bad, or privatization of functions is good or bad. Government will be seen as neutral; useful in solving some problems and detrimental in others. Any proposal about policy or appropriations will be on the table and will get a hearing and evaluation to determine its practicality.

Ted Halstead and Michael Lind have asserted:

> The two national parties, along with the liberal and conservative ideologies they invoke, have failed . . . to provide an agenda that reflects the moral outlook and economic interests of most Americans, or responds to our changing conditions with innovative policy reforms. As a result of this deficit of intellectual and political leadership, we live in a time of profound confusion . . . What America needs at this historic moment is a compelling national vision to guide us into a post-industrial future, along with a coherent program for how to get there. Instead of providing such a vision or program, our reigning political duopoly has only fueled a false sense of national division, while sending a large portion of the electorate into temporary hiding.[100]

The Civic Alliance, or whatever the new third party of the center is called, can furnish the necessary vision and leadership now lacking. If America's citizens can be aroused from their somnolent state to become concerned about the nation's future, the Civic Alliance Party can be the force that brings about change in a dysfunctional system. The party will be able to do this only in partnership with the American people. It will require citizens understanding the problems the country faces, their willingness to participate in finding solutions, and their acceptance of the fact that pain and sacrifice may be required. A permanent third party of the center, such as the Civic Alliance, can act as a catalyst to bring about the required reactions in the political cauldron, altering the chemistry of governmental bodies, allowing the representatives of the people to use rational discourse and common sense in seeking answers to the nation's quandaries. The election of a Democratic or Republican president and Congress in 2012 and beyond will not change the culture of partisanship and corruption that undermines effective government. A new element, the Civic Alliance, needs to be injected into the mix.

# References

[1] Marcus Aurelius, *Meditations*, transl. George Lang, Walter J. Black Publisher, Roslyn, NY, 1945 (written in the second century B.C.E. in Greek), 40.

[2] Larry J. Sabato and Glenn R. Simpson, *Dirty Little Secrets*, Times Books, Random House, NY, 1996, 3.

[3] Ibid., ix.

[4] John P. Avlon, *Independent Nation*, Three Rivers Press, NY, 2004, 20–21.

[5] Adam Liptak, "Justices, 5–4, Reject Corporate Spending Limit," *New York Times*, January 21, 2010.

[6] David D. Kirkpatrick, "Congress Finds Ways to Avoid Lobbyist Limits, *New York Times*, February 11, 2007, A1.

[7] David D. Kirkpatrick, "House Lifts Veil on Practice of Bundling Campaign Gifts," *New York Times*, May 25, 2007, A17.

[8] Wilson Carey McWilliams, "The Search for a Public Philosophy," essay in *The Politics of Ideas*, State University of New York Press, Albany, NY, 2001, 23. Cites an article by Scott Turow in the *New York Times*, October 12, 1997.

[9] Micah L. Sifry, *Spoiling for a Fight*, Routledge, NY, 2002, 281.

[10] Jim Rutenberg and David D. Kirkpatrick, "A New Channel for Soft Money Appears in Race," *New York Times*, November 12, 2007, A1.

[11] "Independent Redistricting," Common Cause, www.commoncause.org/site/pp.asp?C=dkLNK1MQIwG&b=998747.

[12] Brad Setser and Nouriel Roubini, "Our Money, Our Debt, Our Problem," *Foreign Affairs*, July/August 2005, 195.

[13] Steven R. Weisman, "In Major Shift, U.S. Is imposing Major Tariffs On China," *New York Times*, March 31, 2007, A1.

[14] Steven R. Weisman, "U.S. Toughens Its Position on China Trade," *New York Times*, April 10, 2007, A1.

[15] Sherle R. Schwenniger, "America's 'Suez Moment'," *The Real State of the Union*, Ted Halstead, ed., Basic Books, NY, 2004, 47.

[16] Steven R. Weisman, "Fed Chief Warns That Entitlement Growth Could Harm Economy," *New York Times*, January 19, 2007, C1.

[17] Dan Mitchell, "What's Online; Walker, Fiscal Ranger," *New York Times*, March 10, 2007, B5.

[18] Avlon, 19–20. Cites Gallup CNN/USA Today Poll, January 2003 and CBS News Poll, February 2002.

[19] Associated Press, "AP-CNBC Poll: Cut Services to balance the budget," www.foxnews.com/us/2010/11/30-ap-cnbc-poll-cut-services-balance-budget-141965886/.

[20] Reuters, "Most Americans say tax rich to balance budget: poll," Yahoo News, http://news.yahoo.com/s/nm/us_usa_taxes_poll/print.

[21] Department of Education, "The Federal Budget 2011," www.whitehouse.gov/omb/factsheet_department_education/.

[22] Department of Health and Human Services, "The Federal Budget 2011," www.whitehouse.gov/omb/factsheet_department_health/.

[23] Department of Defense, "The Federal Budget 2011," www.whitehouse.gov/omb/factsheet_department_defense/.

[24] Gordon S. Black and Benjamin D. Black, The Politics of American Discontent, John Wiley and Sons, NY, 1994, 59–61.

[25] "The Much-Needed Return of Pay-Go," Editorial, New York Times, March 22, 2007, A24.

[26] John T. Bennett, "Gates announces $78B in defense spending cuts," Military Times, January 6, 2011, www.militarytimes.com/news/2011/01/military-defense-gates-announces-budget-cuts-010611w/.

[27] "The Moment of Truth," December 1, 2010, www.fiscalcommission.gov/news/moment-truth-report-national-commission-fiscal-responsible-and-reform.

[28] Peter Nicholas and Lisa Mascaro, "Panel weighs deep federal budget cuts to trim deficit," Los Angeles Times, November 11, 2010, http://articles.latimes.com/print/2010/nov11/nation/la-na-deficit-commission-20101111.

[29] Phillip J. Longman, "Aging Productively," The Real State of the Union, Ted Halstead, ed., Basic Books, NY, 2004, 145.

[30] Concord Coalition advertisement, January 7, 2007.

[31] Ted Halstead, Preface, The Real State of the Union, Ted Halstead, ed., Basic Books, NY, x.

[32] Norman F. Ornstein and Thomas E. Mann, "When Congress Checks Out," Foreign Affairs, November/December 2006, 67.

[33] James Glanz, "U.S. Agency Finds New Waste and Fraud in Iraqi Rebuilding Projects," New York Times, February 1, 2007, A8.

[34] Scott Shane and Ron Nixon, "In Washington, Contractors Take On Biggest Role Ever," New York Times, February 4, 2007, 1.

[35] Shane and Nixon.

[36] Larry Greenemeier, "IRS Plan To Outsource Tax Collection Raises Security Concerns," Information Week, January 13, 2007, www.informationweek.com/story/showarticle.jhtml?articleID=175804101.

[37] "Here's an Easy One," New York Times, Week in Review editorial, January 15, 2011, 9.

[38] David Leonhardt, "For Federal Programs, a Taste of Market Discipline," New York Times, February 8, 2011, B1.

[39] "Affordable Health Care For America," House Committees on Ways and Means, Energy and Commerce, and Education, March 18, 2010, http://docs.house.gov/energycommerce/summary.pdf.

[40] Jethro K. Lieberman, "Article 2 of the Constitution," The Evolving Constitution, Random House, NY, 1992, 613.

[41] Ibid., 176–177.

[42] Demetrios James Caraley, "Complications of American Democracy: Elections Are Not Enough," Political Science Quarterly, 2005; Vol. 120, No. 3, 383.

[43] Alexander Keyssar, "Shoring Up the Right to Vote for President: A Modest Proposal," The Meaning of Democracy, The Academy of Political Science, 2005, 63–72.

[44] Caraley.

[45] Ibid.

[46] Keyssar, 72.

[47] "National Popular Vote," April 2007, Nationalpopularvote.com/index.php.

[48] Hendrik Hertzberg, "A Swish for N.P.V.", The New Yorker, October 13, 2010, www.newyorker.com/online/blogs/hendrickhertzberg/2010/10/a-swish-fro-npv.html?.

[49] Linda Greenhouse, "New Focus on the Effects of Life Tenure," New York Times, September 10, 2007, A20.

[50] Clive Crook, "Rags to Rags, Riches to Riches," The Atlantic, June 2007, 24.

[51] Maya MacGuineas, "Radical Tax Reform," The Real State of the Union, Ted Halstead, ed., Basic Books, NY, 2004, 51–62.

[52] Lieberman, "The 16th Amendment to the Constitution," 619.

[53] MacGuineas.

[54] "A Dearth of Taxes," New York Times, editorial, October 22, 2007, A20.

[55] MacGuineas.

[56] "Automatic Increases, Contribution and Benefit Base," Social Security Online, downloaded March 5, 2011, http://www.socialsecurity.gov/OACT/COLA/cbb.html.

[57] Richard Kogan and Aviva Aron-Dine, "Claim That Tax Cuts Pay For Themselves Is Too Good To Be True," Center on Budget and Policy Priorities, April 17, 2006, www.cbpp.org/3-8-06tax.htm.

[58] Ibid.

[59] Robert H. Frank, "In the Real World of Work and Wages, Trickle-Down Theories Don't Hold Up," New York Times, April 12, 2007, C3.

[60] Jenny Anderson, "Managers Use Hedge Funds as Big I.R.A." New York Times, April 17, 2007, A1.

[61] Andrew Ross Sorkin, "Dealbook: Of Private Equity, Politics and Income Taxes," New York Times, March 11, 2007, 8.

[62] Robert H. Frank, "Economic View: Why Not Shift the Burden to Big Spenders," New York Times, October 7, 2007, 5.

[63] "Who Pays the Federal Estate Tax?," Citizens for Tax Justice, April 2006, www.ctj.org.

[64] Bloomberg News, "Buffett Says No Estate Tax Would Be a Gift to the Rich," New York Times, November 15, 2007, C8.

[65] "Tax facts," Center on Budget and Policy Priorities, 4/17/06, www.cbpp.org/.

[66] Citizens for Tax Justice, April 2006.

[67] David Cay Johnston, "I.R.S. to Cut Tax Auditors," New York Times, July 23, 2007, 16.

[68] Alan S. Blinder, "Offshoring: The Next Industrial Revolution," Foreign Affairs, March/April 2006, 127.

[69] Donna Smith, "U.S. poverty rate hits 15-year high," Reuters, September 16, 2010, www.reuters.com/assets/print?aid=USN1617702920100916.

[70] Stephen Labaton, "Congress Passes Increase in the Minimum Wage," New York Times, May 24, 2007, A12.

[71] Steven Greenhouse, "A Unified Voice Argues the Case for U.S. Manufacturing," New York Times, April 26, 2007, C2.

[72] Robert Guy Matthews, "US steel industry files anti-dumping suit against China," Wall Street Journal, April 9, 2009.

[73] James C. McKinley, Jr., "Tougher Tactics Deter Migrants at U.S. Border," New York Times, February 21, 2007, A1.

[74] Stewart Powell, "A border fence that never was," Houston Chronicle, front page, January 23, 2011, www.chron.com/disp/story.mpl/front/7394138.html.

[75] Tamar Jacoby, "Immigration Nation," Foreign Affairs, November/December 2006, 61.

[76] "Progress on Immigration," New York Times, April 22, 2007, editorial, Week in Review, 11.

[77] Robert Pear and Jim Rutenberg, "Senators in Bipartisan Deal on Immigration Bill," New York Times, May 18, 2007, A1.

[78] "The Utah Compact," New York Times, December 4, 2010, editorial, Week in Review, 7.

[79] "Public vs. Private Schools," New York Times, editorial, July 19, 2006, A20.

[80] Alan Finder, "Report Critical of Training of Teachers," New York Times, September 19, 2006, A19.

[81] "Who We're Looking For," Teach for America, www.teachforamerica.org/admissions/who-were-looking-for, downloaded 1/23/2010.

[82] Matthew Miller, "A New Deal for Teachers," The Real State of the Union, Ted Halstead, ed., Basic Books, NY, 2007, 117.

[83] James P. Pinkerton, "A Grand Compromise," The Real State of the Union, Ted Halstead, ed., Basic Books, NY, 2004, 112.

[84] David M. Herszenhorn, "Expert Panel Proposes Far-Reaching Redesign of the American Education System," New York Times, December 15, 2007, A33.

[85] Jennifer Washburn, "The Tuition Crunch," The Real State of the Union, Ted Halstead, ed., Basic Books, NY, 2004, 123.

[86] Madeline May Kunin, "A Math Lesson on College Loans," New York Times, June 13, 2007, A21.

[87] Sam Dillon, "Panel Considers Revamping College Aid and Accrediting," New York Times, April 12, 2006, A14.

[88] Mary Beth Marklein, "Panel calls for 'urgent reform' of higher education," USA Today, August 11, 2006, A1.

[89] Nicholas Kolakowski, "U.S. Scientists See H1-B Visas as Major Issue Against progress, Says Survey," IT Management and Project Management News, July 12, 2007, http://www.eweek.com/index2.php?option=content&task=view&id=54791&pop=1&hide_ads=1&page=0&hide_js=1&catid=32.

[90] Robert H. Frank, "A Way to Cut Fuel Consumption That Everyone Likes, Except the Politicians," New York Times, February 16, 2006, C3.

[91] Clifford Kraus, "Exxon and Shell Report Record Profits for 2006," New York Times, February 2, 2007, C3.

[92] Thom Shanker and Jim Rutenberg, "President Wants to Increase Size of Armed Forces," New York Times, December 20, 2006, A1.

[93] Ken Belson, "Taiwan's Model for Electronics in Government," New York Times, June 26, 2006, C7.

[94] Eric Lipton, "Federal Requirement for Tamper-Proof Licenses Will Raise Fees for Drivers by 2013," New York Times, March 2, 2007, A14.

[95] Jonathan Rauch, "Taking Stock," The Real State of the Union, Ted Halstead, ed., Basic Books, NY, 2004, 73–74.

[96] "National Service," http://en.wikipedia.org/wiki/National_Service, downloaded January 30, 2011.

[97] AmeriCorps, "What is AmeriCorps,?" www.americorps.org/about/ac/index.asp, downloaded January 27, 2011.

[98] Erik Eckholm, "Job Corps Plans Makeover for a Changed Economy," New York Times, February 20, 2007, A12.

[99] "CBS/New York Times Poll, January 15–19, 2011," www.pollingreport.com/guns.htm.

[100] Ted Halstead and Michael Lind, The Radical Center, Anchor Books, NY, 2002, 11–12.

CHAPTER 8

# Conclusion

Justice is the end of government. It is the end of civil
society. It ever has been and ever will be pursued until it
is obtained, or until liberty be lost in the pursuit.
　　　　　—James Madison, *The Federalist Papers*[1]

America currently resembles a giant ocean liner adrift at sea, its
crew divided into two opposing camps. They bicker and fight with
each other about what course to follow to bring the vessel safely
into port, while the current carries the ship further away from its
destination and into stormy waters. Meanwhile, the passengers
gamble and gambol, party and play, unaware that the ocean liner's
position grows more precarious each day, their own pleasure taking
precedence over the state of the ship on which they travel. Since
the present sailors are unable to work together to keep the vessel
on course, another complement of seamen must be found to bring
the journey to a successful conclusion. But how is this to be done?
The passengers don't seem to be paying attention to the problem.

America needs a fresh crew to guide her through the troubled
waters in which she is now drifting. America needs leaders who are
not in thrall to the special interests, willing to make the necessary
hard choices and tell citizens the truth about the way things are;
leaders who are not bound by ideological rigidity, but are innovative
and constructive and willing to compromise on the issues critical to
the nation's future; leaders willing to address the problems others
deem too politically difficult to resolve and so have left them for
succeeding generations; leaders who are open, honest, practical,
and competent, willing to tread through the partisan minefields surrounding contentious issues; leaders who are willing to lead and are

uninterested in the perks of power, whose ambition lies in restoring America's ideals and hopes rather than in personal advancement or party ascendancy; leaders with the commitment, wisdom, and selflessness of the Founding Fathers, who will provide direction for the nation and set goals Americans can be proud of and strive to achieve. Unfortunately, the leaders needed are unlikely to emerge from the established political parties whose vision is obstructed and thought processes ossified.

The Republican Party has been kidnapped by religious and economic conservatives who hew to an absolutist view of how the country and the world should be, with no use for the moderates who once held sway. The party of Abraham Lincoln, Teddy Roosevelt, Dwight Eisenhower, and Earl Warren is now dominated by adherents of the Austrian school of economics and the ayatollahs of the right-wing churches whose code of beliefs and behavior potential candidates must accept if they wish to have a chance in the party's primaries. On the other hand, the Democratic Party is controlled by a coalition of liberal activists, minority groups, unions, and trial lawyers who have their own perception of the world that does not countenance competing views. The party of Thomas Jefferson, Andrew Jackson, and Franklin Roosevelt now caters to self-appointed bombastic spokesmen and high-volume leftists as it tries to formulate policy.

Politicians from either of these parties have not shown themselves to be capable of leading America in a global interconnected world, as the vast majority lack flexibility, pragmatism, and creative ideas. However, leadership can arise from a new source, the Civic Alliance, a centrist third party free of ideological constraints and independent of the special interests and lobbyists whose objectives are often in conflict with the concerns of American citizens. But before choosing new leaders, America must decide what kind of nation it wants to be. Some of its citizens are living in unprecedented affluence, with opportunities to enjoy activities available only to kings in the past. Should Americans' main purpose continue to be the pursuit of wealth and pleasure, or do citizens want to work to build a more compassionate nation that meets the needs of its less fortunate brethren, a more secure nation that is not dependent on foreign funds to run its government and foreign oil to run its cars, a wiser nation that does not engage in adventures abroad without compelling reasons, a stronger nation not divided by regional, religious or racial enmity, and united in purpose?

From Colonial times, the United States has been a nation of immigrants, ardent about its freedom and optimistic about its future. Each generation has always chosen to labor and sacrifice for the next, to improve the lives of their children and their children's children. But today's citizens have reversed this pattern, anticipating that their own lives will be better than their children's, or perhaps simply not paying attention about what is to come. For many, narcissism and a thirst for "the good life" have replaced altruism and generosity, sloth and self-indulgence subverting the work ethic. There has been a willingness to shift society's burdens onto the shoulders of succeeding generations to minimize current responsibilities. The new mantra is "live well today and forget about the bill that will be due tomorrow." That is why America's trade deficits, budget deficits, and national debt are ballooning, personal savings rates have plummeted, gas-guzzling SUVs are popular, and there is unwillingness to act to rein in unfunded liabilities. Citizens have been stealing the American dream from their children.

But is this really what Americans want, or have they been led astray by leaders who have not explained matters truthfully to them? Are citizens really willing to ignore the nation's future and disregard the way their children and grandchildren will live because of their profligacy? Have they forgotten why their parents, grandparents, and great-grandparents came to America? Perhaps they are just emulating the politicians and corporate titans who milk the system without considering the needs of their constituents or the stockholders who put them into their positions of power. More reason to seek new leadership and support a new, clean third party of the center dedicated to restoring America's hopes and dreams, bringing people together and setting new goals.

However, given the obstacles, can a new third party be viable, or is it a fantasy that can never be realized? That is in the hands of the American people. While Tea Party advocates are active on the extreme edge of the right, the main barrier to developing a robust, permanent third party of the center is the inertia and lethargy of the nation's moderates and independents. To help overcome the national drift, it is essential that they participate, showing a willingness to confront the nation's problems, looking for answers rather than procrastination or avoidance. Ingrained habits are hard to break, and citizens have been voting for Republicans and Democrats for well over two centuries, their candidates still making promises that will not be kept. A third party of the center would be the best way for America to meet the challenges ahead, for the two established parties are not going to change their inherent cultures of corruption and partisanship.

This new third party must have a foundation of truth and transparency if it is to open America's eyes. There can be no spin and no evasion of painful reality. Because of the lies, misstatements, and misrepresentations that have characterized the nation's political discourse, most Americans do not trust government, politicians, or the political parties, and are unaware of the depth and complexity of the existing problems. This distrust must be overcome if the country is to move forward again. The new party's stark honesty will be in sharp distinction to the obfuscation of the Republicans and Democrats and should appeal to the mass of moderates and centrists once they become accustomed to straight talk from politicians, which has often been pledged but rarely delivered.

Although this third party will originate from the dissatisfaction and disillusionment of the center rather than from fringe elements, it is still a radical concept for citizens to have a real alternative to the nation's two parties when voting. Moderates are generally resistant to abrupt change, wanting transformation to occur incrementally, and indeed, the process of shifting power may require a number of years. However, time is not on America's side. The sooner that change occurs, the more likely significant damage to the economy and society can be averted. Americans must not be afraid to institute whatever reforms are necessary to bring the nation back from the brink. As President Franklin Roosevelt said during his first inaugural address in 1933, "The only thing we have to fear is fear itself . . . which paralyzes needed efforts to convert retreat into advance."[2]

The United States has always shown resiliency in its ability to recover from major crises, evident by its renewal after the Revolutionary War, the War of 1812, the Civil War, the Great Depression, and World War II. It has survived assassinations of leaders like Lincoln and Kennedy, the Cuban missile crisis, the battles over civil rights, and the divisions of the Vietnam years. Today, America is again in a period of great crisis, though obscured from her citizens by the deceit and distortions of the political parties whose missteps were responsible for the problems in the first place. If the nation is to recover and flourish this time, it must be with new leadership at the helm, from a new political party of the center that has not been involved in any of the nation's recent misadventures, with no connections to the corrupting special interests, and lacking any partisan underpinnings.

This new centrist party will also be a party of the middle class and of those who aspire to middle-class status, devoted to protecting their interests. America cannot prosper if only its affluent citizens are thriving. The nation's strength has been and will be its large middle class, the engine of America's economy and the backbone of its workforce. America's entrepreneurs arise from this group, along with its corporate and government managers and professionals. While the policies of this new party will help the impoverished, it is the middle classes who will benefit most along with the nation itself. However, this fledgling third party will also solicit support from wealthy Americans. In determining whether or not to back this party, these individuals will have to choose between their own short-term self-interest and doing what is fair and best for the nation. Monetary support from this group of citizens would be helpful, but even more so their energy and drive.

The challenges ahead are not just about establishing this new party, disseminating its ideas, and positioning it to play a major role in the nation's important decisions. There are also challenges for America's citizens, to change attitudes and goals. Acquisitiveness and self-centeredness must be dampened with a rediscovery of the sense of community that was woven into the fabric of early America. As late as World War II, citizens were willing to put their lives on the line and surrender material comforts for objectives they perceived as worthwhile for the nation. Sacrifice was accepted and expected from every social class. Then, the spirit guiding America seemed to disappear. The horror of 9/11 came and went, an opportunity for citizens to change direction that was missed. Perhaps this was a consequence of egotistical political, corporate, and cultural icons who flaunted their opulent life styles, private jets, gas-guzzling cars, and luxury homes, who sought schemes and shelters to avoid paying taxes they could readily afford, and were seen as role models by their fellow citizens. Now America needs to look for new role models, men and women who put the nation's interests first. The United States must restore its belief in itself and have its citizens working together to lift the nation and achieve worthwhile goals. Americans have always reveled in their "Yankee ingenuity" and can-do mentality, convinced there was no task beyond their abilities if they put their minds to getting it done. They must get it done now.

Though it may be relatively easy to have a centrist third party candidate vying for the presidency in the near future, it is even more important to build permanency and perseverance into this party, so that in the years ahead it can run its candidates for office at all levels of government and become a major and continuing political force. A president alone, without a cooperative Congress, will not be able to bring about the necessary metamorphosis in ethics and values the country requires.

Formation of a new party should generate interest and excitement in the legions of people who have been apathetic or cynical about politics and government. The party will have a natural constituency in the moderate Republicans who have been marginalized by the Tea Party and the conservative faction of their party, centrist Democrats alienated by the views of their party's left wing, and the large body of independent voters who have no party affiliation. It will be a party that stresses integrity, competency, transparency, and pragmatism. With the aid of the Internet, social networks, and a small core of dedicated believers, this third party will be able to organize and disseminate its program quickly. The movement can be a wave rolling across America, drowning politics as usual and bringing reform and revitalization to the surface. It can be an antidote to the poisoned partisanship of the Tea Party. Whether it is called the Civic Alliance or any other name, this party can upset the current political equilibrium and bring about the necessary changes to resurrect America's damaged democracy.

## References

[1] James Madison, *The Federalist Papers*, No. 51, New American Library, New York, NY, 1961, (originally published 1787–1788), 324.
[2] Franklin Roosevelt, "First Inaugural Address," 1933, http://historymatters.gmu.edu/d/5057/.

# Index

501(c) groups, 26
527 Committees, 44, 78
9/11 attacks, 210, 211

## A

A Pledge to America, 28
ABC, 54
abortion issue, 36
Abramoff scandal, 20
Abramoff, Jack, 21
Abu Ghraib, 226
Adams, John, 68
Adelson, Sheldon, 125
Affordable Care Act, 191, 194
Afghanistan corruption, 220
Afghanistan war, 217–221
Africa, sub-Saharan, 240–241
*Against All Enemies*, 210
Agreed Framework, 215
agricultural subsidies, 278–279
Ahmadinejad, Mahamoud, 216, 240
Ailes, Roger, 54
Al Qaeda, 73, 209–212
al-Assad, Bashar, 238–239
al-Assad, Hafez, 238–239
al-Bashir, Omar, 241
al-Maliki, Nouri, 221
al-Najafi, Osama, 222
al-Sadr, Moqtada, 222
Alcoa, 294
Allawi, Iyad, 222
Alliance for American
        Manufacturing, 294

alternative energy, 304
Alternative Minimum Tax, 173
American Bar Association, 43
American Political Institute, 261
American Recovery and
        Reinvestment Act 2009, 189
American resiliency, 330
American Society of Civil Engineers,
        197–198
*American Theocracy*, 46, 136
Americorps, 313
Amtrak, 198
Angle, Sharon, 87
Arab oil embargo, 185
Argentina, 235
Armey, Dick, 26
arrogance of power, 40–43
Ashcroft, John, 25, 210
attack politics, 43–45
Atwater, Lee, 43
Austrian School of Economics, 35
auto companies, 155–156
Avlon, John, 98
Awakening, Councils, 81, 225

## B

Bailey, Doug, 119
bailouts, 56
bank bailout, 84
*Barron's*, 199
basic research, federal support for,
        303
Bayh, Evan, 130–131

Beck, Glenn, 54
Begich, Mark, 134
Behr, Roy, 70, 99
Bell, Ruth Greenspan, 189
Ben Ali, Zine El Abidine, 241
Bennet, James, 37
Bennet, Michael, 87, 133
Bennett, Bob, 86
Bernanke, Ben, 272
Bibby, John, 100
Biden, Joe, 83
bin Laden, Osama, 218
Bipartisan Deficit Commission, 29
Birthers, 45
Black, Benjamin, 97, 272–273
Black, Cofer, 210
Black, Gordon, 97, 272–273
Blinder, Alan, 148
Bloomberg, Mike, 126, 127, 131–132
Blount, Roy, 30
Blue Dog Democrats, 134
Boehner, John, 17, 26, 276
Bolivia, 235
border security, 295
bottom-up creation, 113–114
BP oil spill, 49
Brazil, 235
Bremer, L. Paul, 224
broadband connectivity, 199
Brown, Michael, 50, 232
Brown, Stuart, 160
Buchanan, Pat, 71
Buck, Ken, 87
budget deficits, 166–172, 272–274
Buffett, Warren, 125, 126, 127, 291
bundling, 124
Bush, George W., 24, 42, 43, 48, 49,
    73–74
    administration, 36, 39, 50–52,
    168
    tax cuts, 28, 87
    vs. Gore, 284–285
Bush, Jeb, 74
Business Software Alliance, 159

**C**
CACI International, 277
CAFÉ Standards, 186, 303
Calderon, Felipe, 236
Cameron, David, 246
Campaign Finance Reform Act 2002,
    124
campaign promises, 28
campaign tactics, 142
Canada, 236
cap and trade, 85, 305
Caraley, Demetrios James, 284
Carper, Tom, 134
carried income, 174
Carter, Jimmy, 48
Castle, Mike, 87, 134
Castro, Fidel, 235
Castro, Raoul, 235
CBS, 54
Center for Evaluative Clinical
    Sciences, 192
Center for Public Integrity, 25
Center for Responsive Politics, 24,
    49
Center for Strategic and
    International Studies, 133
Center on Budget and Policy
    Priorities, 168
centrism, 98
centrist groups, 140–141
CEO compensation, 163–164
Chaffee, Lincoln, 133
Chappaquidick, 41
Chavez, Hugo, 235
Cheney, Dick, 27, 41, 52, 210
Chertoff, Michael, 50, 229, 231
China, 243–244
Chinese economy, 155, 159
CIA, 214–215
citizen responsibility, 255–258
Citizens Against Waste, 170
Citizens United, 26, 267
citzen participation, need for, 329
Civic Alliance, 108–109
    campaign committee, 121–122
    creating the, 109–116

endowment, 124–127
  potential candidates, 127–135
civic education, 258–261
Clapper, James, 213
Clark, Wesley, 77, 132
Clarke, Richard, 210
Cleland, Max, 44
Clinton administration, 36
Clinton, Bill, 30, 72
Clinton, Hillary, 82–83, 118
CNN-USA Today Gallup poll, 77
CNN, 54, 69
Coalition for Evidence-Based Policy,
  279
Coalition Provisional Authority, 224
college and graduate education
  reform, 301–302
Collins, Susan, 133
Colombia, 235–236
*Columbia Journalism Review*, 53
Comey, James, 51
Commission on Presidential
  Debates, 70
*Common Sense*, 16, 207, 252
competence, 105–107
Concord Coalition, 133, 140, 274
Congressional Black Caucus, 21
Congressional Ethics Committee, 21
Constitution
  Article 2, 41, 42, 284
  2nd Amendment, 318
  15th Amendment, 72
  17th Amendment, 68
  19th Amendment, 68
Consumer Products Safety
  Commission, 40
Contract With America, 28, 72
Coons, Chris, 87
corporate corruption, 161
corporate taxes, 174–175
Corporation for National and
  Community Service, 313
Cranston, Alan, 28
creationism, 183
Crist, Charles, 86, 134
cronyism, 50–52

Crook, Clive, 163–164, 288
Cuba, 235
Cunningham, Randy, 20
currency manipulation, 159

**D**

da Silva, Lula, 235
Davis, Tom, 134
Dean, Howard, 118
Defense Contractors Scandal, 20
Deficit Reduction Commission, 168,
  274
DeLay, Tom, 21
Democratic party, 17, 36–37
Department of Homeland Security,
  228
deregulation, 56
Diamond, Larry, 224, 226
differentiating a new party, 101–108
Disch, Lisa Jane, 58, 101
Dixiecrats, 34
Dodd-Frank bill, 56
Dream Act, 196
*Drudge Report*, 117
Duncan, Arne, 181, 298
duopoly of power, 92

**E**

earmarks, 22, 170–172, 276
economic growth, 147
education, 178–182
education reform, 298–302
Edwards, John, 77, 82–83
Egypt, 241
Election 2000, 73–74
Election 2004, 76–78
Election 2006, 79–82
Election 2008, 86–87
Election 2010, 20
elections, 19
Electoral College system–change of,
  284–285
Electoral College, 68–69
electrical grid, 198
energy conservation, 304
energy independency, 303–305

Energy Policy and Conservation
    Act, 186
energy policy 2001, 52
energy policy, 184–190
environment, 189–190
Environmental Protection Agency,
    198
estate tax, 174
Ethics Commission, 279
*Ethics of Spinoza*, 252
European Union, 245–246
evaluation panels, 105–106
excess compensation, 161

**F**

*Facebook*, 116, 119, 143
Falwell, Jerry, 38
farm subsidies, 171
FBI, 211
Federal Clean Air Act, 305
Federal Reserve, 151
*Federalist Papers*, 18, 35, 65, 94, 143,
    326
federalists, 68
fee-for-service payment, 281
FEMA, 50, 231–232
Ferguson, Niall, 178
*Fiasco*, 222
filibuster, 33
financial meltdown, 56–57
FISA, 41, 50
fiscal responsibility, 270–276
Flynn, Stephen, 230
Foggo, Kyle, 214
Foley, Tom, 27
Ford, Henry, 149
*Foreign Affairs*, 160, 189, 212, 234,
    271, 297
foreign oil dependence, 184–185
foreign policy, 232, 306–308
Foster, Vince, 72
Founding Fathers, 34
Fox News, 54
fragmentation of current parties,
    114–115
Friedman, Tom, 182

Frist, Bill, 47
Fuld, Richard, 164
fundraising, 24, 121–127

**G**

Gamesa, 157
Garner, Jay, 224
Gates, Bill, 125, 126, 127
Gates, Robert, 81
Gbagbo, Laurent, 241
Gemayel, Pierre, 238
generational disconnect, 328
Genesis, 146
Gephardt, Dick, 77
Gergen, David, 141
gerrymandering, 38, 90, 270
Giffords, Gabrielle, 317
gifted children's programs, 181
Gillani, Yousaf Raza, 242
Gillibrand, Kirsten, 140
Gingrich, Newt, 27, 72
Glaeser, Edward, 89
Glass-Steagall, 56
global warming, 189–190, 305
globalization, 152–161
Goldsmith, Jack, 42
Gonzales, Alberto, 50–51
Goodyear, 294
Gore, Al, 73–74
Goss, Porter, 214
government contracts, 276
government surveillance, 37, 41
Graham, Lindsey, 42, 133
*Gray Dawn*, 177
Green Party, 75–76
Green, John, 261
Greenspan, Alan, 168
guest workers, 296–297
Guiliani, Rudolph, 82–83, 141
guns and public safety, 317–318

**H**

H-1-B visas, 303
Hadley, Stephen, 210
Hagel, Chuck, 129–130
Hagelin, John, 71

Hakim, Peter, 234
Halstead, Ted, 98, 254, 274–275, 320
Hamas, 238
Hamilton, Alexander, 18, 68, 94
Hannity, Sean, 54
Hansen, James, 190
Hariri, Rafik, 238
Hariri, Saad, 238
Harris, Katherine, 74
Harvard University, 59
Hayden, Michael, 214
Hayek, Friedrich, A., 35
health care, 191–194
    administrative costs, 192
    Health Care Reform Bill 2010,
    30
    overhead, 281
    reform, 84–85, 280–283
    unnecessary, 192, 281
Health Corps, 315, 316
Henry J. Kaiser Family Foundation,
    59
Hershey, Marjorie Randon, 257,
    258–259
Hezbollah, 238
Hickel, Walter, 93
Homeland Security, 228–232
Hoover, Herbert, 48
House Bank Overdraft Scandal, 27
House Judiciary Committee, 51
Huckabee, Mike, 54, 82
human rights, 306
HUMINT, 211, 309
Huntsman, Jon, 134
Hurricane Katrina, 40, 50, 231–232
Hussein, Saddam, 212–213, 223
Hutchinson, Asa, 232

**I**

ideology and partisanship, 31–34
ideology of current parties, 34–37
illegal immigrants, registration for,
    296–297
immigration bills, 2006–2007, 196
immigration reform, 295–298
immigration, 194–197

Impact channel, 119
impartial redistricting, 269–270
income inequality, 161–165, 287–288
incompetence and ineffectiveness,
    48–50
increasing school year, 300
incumbency, 19–20
*Independent Nation*, 98
India, 243
Indian nuclear program, 208
industrial policy, 154–158, 294
infrastructure, 197–200, 312
Institute for Global Ethics, 44
integrity, 102–104
intellectual property, 159
intelligence failures, 208–217
intelligence sub-contractors, 214
intelligent design, 183
International Court, 211
Internet and social networks,
    116–121
Internet fund raising, 118
Internet primaries, 117–118
Iran hostage standoff, 185
Iran nuclear program, 209, 216
Iran, 240
Iraq, war, 221–228
Iraqiya, 222
IRS contractors, 278
ISI, 242
Israel, 237–238
Israeli-Palestinian conflict, 306–307
Ivory Coast, 241

**J**

Jacoby, Tamar, 297
Japan, 244–245
Japan, Inc., 154
Japanese economy, 153–155
Jefferson, Thomas, 68
Jefferson, William, 21
Jeffords, James, 32, 115
Job Corps, 314–315
Jobs and Growth Act 2003, 187
jobs, 293
Jones, Paula Corbin, 72

Jordan, Hamilton, 119
judicial reform, 286–287

**K**

K Street Project, 20
Kaine, Tim, 130
Kaplan, Robert, 210, 232
Karzai, Hamid, 218, 219, 220
Karzai, Walid, 220
Kaus, Mickey, 161
Kayani, Ashfaq Parvez, 242
Keating Five, 27
Keating, Charles, 28
Kennedy, Paul, 207
Kennedy, Ted, 41
Kenya embassy bombing, 209
Kerry, John, 44, 76–78
Keyssar, Alexander, 285
Khamenei, Ali, 240
Khan, A.Q., 208
King Abdullah, 239
King, Angus, 93, 119
Kirchner, Christina, 235
Kirchner, Nestor, 235
Klein, Joe, 45, 99
Koch, Charles, 125
Koch, David, 125
Kohl, Herb, 134
Kopechne, Mary Jo, 41
Korean companies, 153–154
Kyoto Protocol, 190

**L**

Lamont, Ned, 137
Landrieu, Mary, 134
Larry King Live, 69
Latin America, 234–236
Lay, Ken, 24
Lazarus, Edward, 70, 99
leadership PAC's, 26
leadership void, 29–31
Lebanon, 238
Lee, Mike, 86
legacy costs, 155–156
Levey, David, 160
Lewinsky, Monica, 72

Libya, 241
Lieberman, Jethro, 65
Lieberman, Joe, 93, 134, 137
Limbaugh, Rush, 55
Lind, Michael, 98, 254, 320
lobbyists, 18, 20–28
*Los Angeles Times*, 214
Loy, James, 232
Lugar, Richard, 133

**M**

Machiavelli, Niccolo, 97, 146, 207
Maddow, Rachel, 54
Madison, James, 18, 31, 35, 65, 68,
    143, 326
Maisel, Sandy, 100
Mann, Thomas, 277
manufacturing, 147, 152–158,
    293–294
Marcus Aurelius, 266
Marshall Plan, 152
Massachusetts Health Care Reform,
    194
materialism, 328
Matthews, Chris, 54
McCain-Feingold, 267
McCain, John, 24, 28, 38, 42, 45, 73,
    83–84
McCaskill, Claire, 134
McConnell, Mitch, 17, 26
McKinnon, Mark, 141
McWilliams, Wilson Carey, 268
medical marijuana, 37
Medicare Board, 282–283
Medicare Prescription Drug Act, 24,
    29, 193
*Meditations*, 266
Medvedev, Dimitry, 236
Mehlman, Ken, 116
Merkel, Angela, 246
metrics of productivity, 279
Mexico, 236
Middle East, 237–240
military, improved incentives for
    personnel, 309
Millennium plot, 211

Minerals Management Service, 49
minimum wage, 165–166, 293–294
Miqati, Najib, 238
Mission Accomplished speech, 77
Mitchell, George, 238
MITI, 154
monitoring ports, 230
Montgomery, Bruce, 53
Morales, Evo, 235
Mousavi, Hossein, 240
Moveon.org, 44
Mozillo, Angelo, 164
MSNBC, 54
Mubarak, Hosni, 241
Mugabe, Robert, 241
Murdock, Rudolph, 54
Musharraf, Pervez, 242
*Myspace*, 119

**N**

Nader, Ralph, 75–76, 78–79
Nader's Raiders, 75
NAFTA, 70, 196
naming the party, 108–109
Napolitano, Janet, 229
National Academy of Sciences, 186
National Accreditation Foundation,
     302
National Association of
     Manufacturers, 294
national debt, 166–172, 272–274
National Highway Traffic Safety
     Administration, 186
national ID card, 230–231, 310–312
     for illegal immigrants, 296
     medical data, 310
     opposition to, 311
     photo, fingerprints, 310
     for workers, biometric, 308–309
National Intelligence Estimate, 76
National Popular Vote Initiative, 285
National Rifle Association, 23, 218
national security, 308–310
national standards of proficiency,
     298
Natural Law Party, 71

NBC, 54
NBC/Wall Street Journal poll, 16
need for new leaders, 252–255, 326
need for political parties, 66–67
negative campaigning, 142
Nelson, Ben, 134
New England Republicans, 136–137
New Medicare, 281–283
New Third Party, 94
*New York Times*, 55, 175
*Newsweek*, 99
Ney, Bob, 21
Nicaragua, 235
Nigeria, 241
Nixon, Richard, 40
No Child Left Behind, 180, 181, 298
No Labels, 140–141
Nord, Nancy, 40
North Korea nuclear program, 209,
     215
Northern Africa, 241
Nuclear Nonproliferation, 208–217
Nuclear Threat Initiative, 133
Nunn, Sam, 132–133
Nye, Joseph, 208

**O**

O'Donnell, Christine, 38, 87
O'Neal, Stanley, 164
O'Reilly, Bill, 54
Oath of Ethical Conduct, 102–104,
     139
Obama administration, 49, 53
Obama, Barack, 24, 44–45, 82–84,
     118
Obamacare, 85
off-shoring, 148
Office of Congressional Ethics, 21
Office of National Intelligence,
     213–214
Okinawa bases, 245
Omar, Mullah, 218
Oracle, 25
Oregon Death with Dignity law, 37
Ornstein, Norman, 277
Ortega, Daniel, 235

Osama bin Laden, 40
Ouattara, Alassane, 241
oversight , lack of, 39–40
oversight, 279–280

## P

Paine, Tom, 16, 207, 252
Pakistan nuclear program, 208
Pakistan, 241–243
Palin, Sarah, 54, 83
pandering, 47–48
Panetta, Leon, 215
partisanship, 38
party as organization, 66
party in government, 66
party in the electorate, 66
*Party Politics in America*, 257
party's adverse effects, 67
Pashtuns, 218, 220
Paul, Rand, 86
Paul, Ron, 118
pay-go rule, 277
Peace Corps, 314
Pelosi, Nancy, 17, 26, 137
Pension Benefit Guaranty
   Corporation, 176
pension reform, 175–176
Perot, Ross, 69–71, 99
Peterson, Pete, 127, 167, 168, 169,
   177
Petreaus, David, 81, 225
PHARMA, 25
Phillips, Kevin, 46, 136
Pillar, Paul, 212, 223
Pinkerton, James, 300
Pioneers, 24
PMA Lobbying Scandal, 20
political
   consultants, 45–46
   corruption, 20, 27–28
   education, 258–261
   independents, 59
*Political Parties and Democracy's
   Citizens*, 256
political parties in the 1990's, 69–73

political parties, deficiencies,
   326–327
political parties, structure of, 89–91
*Political Science Quarterly*, 32, 44,
   53, 139, 285
*Politico*, 117
politics and the media, 54–55
*Politics Lost*, 45
polls, 16, 17, 19
   about citizens' knowledge of
   political issues, 2007, 258
   on deficit, 272
   on guns, Jan 2001, 318
   political fund raising, 267
   trust in government, 267
pork, 22, 170–172, 230–231, 276
poverty, 165–166
Powell, Colin, 128–129, 210
pragmatism, 104–105
Presidential election 1996, 19
Presidential election 2000, 19
Presidential election 2008, 19
Prestowitz, Clyde, 154
preventative medicine, 283
primary system and partisanship,
   38–39
Prince, Charles, 164
private contractors, 277–278
product recalls, 40
*Proverbs*, 1
Public Citizen, 75
public sector workers, 150–151
push polls, 45
Putin, Vladimir, 236

## Q

Qadaffi, Muammar, 241

## R

Race To The Top, 181, 298
radical middle, 99
Rafshoon, Gerald, 119
Rangel, Charles, 21
Rangers, 24
Reagan, Ronald, 59

Real ID Act, 311–312
Realizing the Platform's Planks,
    319–321
recession, the, 147–151
recruitment, for Civic Alliance,
    135–141
redistricting, commissions, 269–270
reducing government inefficiency,
    276–279
reducing government waste,
    276–279
reform of campaign financing,
    266–269
reform of lobbying, 267, 269
reform of political ethics, 266–269
Reform Party, 70–71
Reid, Harry, 17, 26, 87
religion and politics, 46–47
Republican party, 17, 35–36
Republican-Democrats, 68
research, 183
Reynolds, Thomas, 79
Rice, Condoleezza, 210
Ricks, Thomas, 222
Ridge, Tom, 229
Right to Privacy, 37
right wing third party, 141
RINOS, 34, 136
*Rising Above the Gathering Storm*, 182
Robertson, Pat, 38
robocalls, 45
Rockefeller Republicans, 31
Rogers, Harold, 231
Romney, Mitt, 39, 82
Roosevelt, Franklin, 329–330
Rosenstone, Steven, 70, 99
Rostenkowski, Dan, 21
Roubini, Nouriel, 271
Rousseau, Jean Jacques, 255
Roussoff, Dilma, 235
Rove, Karl, 43, 73
Rubio, Marco, 86
Rumsfeld, Donald, 81, 223–224, 226
*Running on Empty*, 168
Russia, 236–237

**S**

Saboto, Larry, 266
sacrifice, need for, 330–331
Salazar, Ken, 49
Saleh, Ali Abdullah, 239–240
Sanders, Bernie, 93
Sandler, Herbert, 125
Sandler, Marion, 125
Santos, Juan Manuel, 236
Sarkozy, Nicholas, 246
Saudi Arabia, 239
Savidge, Martin, 55
Scaife, Richard Mellon, 125
Scarborough, Joe, 141
Schiavo, Terry, 36, 47–48
Schneck, Stephen, 256, 257
school funding, 300
Schroeder, Gerhard, 246
Schumer, Charles, 174
Schwenninger, Sherle, 160, 271
science and technology, 182–184
science and technology, enhancing,
    302–303
scientists, financial incentives for,
    302
scientists, recognition for, 302
Senate hold, 54
Senate Office of Public Records, 25
Setser, Brad, 271
Shaheen, Jeanne, 134
Shinseki, Eric, 223
Shogan, Robert, 258
Sifry, Micah, 100, 268
signing statements, 43
Simpson, Glenn, 266
Snowe, Olympia, 133
social ethics and values, 261–264
Social Security privatization, 177
Social Security, 176–178, 274–275
Somalia, 241
Soros, George, 125
South Korea, 245
Southern Sudan, 241
special interests, 18, 20–28
Special Tribunal for Lebanon, 238

Spector, Arlen, 32, 115
Spinoza, Baruch, 252
starving the beast, 36
state budget deficits, 172
*State of Denial*, 210
states' financial problems, 88–89
stimulus package, 84, 149–150
Stuxnet worm, 216
Sudan, 241
suffrage, 68
Supreme Court, 42
surge, the, 81, 225
survey on student cheating, 263
Swiftboat Veterans, 44, 78
Syria, 238–239

**T**

Talabani, Jalal, 222
Taliban, 217–221
Tanzania embassy bombing, 209
Tauzin, Billy, 24
tax laws, 289–292
tax policy, 168, 172–175
tax reform, 287–292
Tea Party, 16, 17, 19, 38, 86–87, 136
Teach America Corps, 314–315
teacher competency, 181, 299
teaching corps, 299
Telecommunications Act 1996, 199
Telesur, 235
Tenet, George, 210
Texas Transportation Institute, 198
*The Age of Turbulence*, 168
The American Recovery and
        Reinvestment Act 2009, 189
*The Atlantic*, 37, 58, 163–164, 288
*The End of Equality*, 161
*The Evolving Constitution*, 65
*The Fate of the Union*, 258
*The Politics of Ideas*, 261
*The Prince*, 97, 146, 207
*The Radical Center*, 254
*The Real State of the Union*, 274
*The Rise and Fall of the Great
        Powers*, 207
*The Social Contract*, 255

*The Terror Presidency*, 42
*The World is Flat*, 182
third party
        formation of, 331–332
        need for, 1, 3, 16, 37–60, 252–
        255, 328–332
        obstacles, 91–93
        successes, 93, 94
        transparency, 329
*Third Parties in America*, 92–93, 99
third parties, previous, 69, 71
Thompson, Fred, 82
Tibet, 243–244
Tier One coverage, 281–282
Tier Two coverage, 282
toll roads, 199
top-down creation, 111–113
Tora Bora, 218
Toshiba, 157
trade deficits, 152, 271–272
*Trading Places*, 154
Trafficant, James, 21
transparency, 52–54, 107–108
Transportation Security
        Administration, 228
Tunisia, 241
*Twitter*, 116, 119, 143
two-party system, 65, 67–69

**U**

Udall, Mark, 134
unemployment, 147–151
United Steelworkers, 294
United We Stand America, 70
Unity '08, 119–120
Universal National Service, 313–317
unnecessary projects, 278
Uribe, Alviro, 236
USA Today/Gallup poll, April, 2007,
        on immigration, 297
USS Cole bombing, 209
Utah Compact 2010, 297

**V**

Venezuela, 235
Ventura, Jesse, 71, 93

Villaraigosa, Antonio, 140
von Mises, Ludwig, 35
Voters, 19

# W

wages, 293
Wahhabi, 239
Walker, David, 272
Walker, Scott, 88
*Wall Street Journal*, 55, 156
Wall Street, 56
Walsh, Mary Williams, 175
Ward, Adam, 89
Warner, John, 42
Warner, Mark, 130
*Warrior Politics*, 232–233
*Washington Post*, 55, 59, 222
Washington, George, 65, 68
Washington's farewell address, 65
Waters, Maxine, 21
wealth accumulation, 287–288
weapons systems, 309
Webb, Jim, 134, 137
Weicker, Lowell, 93

Westinghouse, 157
Whitewater, 72
Wikileaks, 234
Wolfowitz, Paul, 210
Woodward, Bob, 210
World Trade Center bombing 1993,
209
World Trade Organization, 158, 159
World War II, re-building after, 152
Wright, Jim, 21

# X

Xinjiang, 243–244

# Y

Yemen, 239–240
Yergin, Daniel, 184
*YouTube*, 119

# Z

Zaedari, Asif Ali, 242
Zimbabwe, 241
Zinni, Anthony, 223

Made in the USA
Lexington, KY
30 August 2013